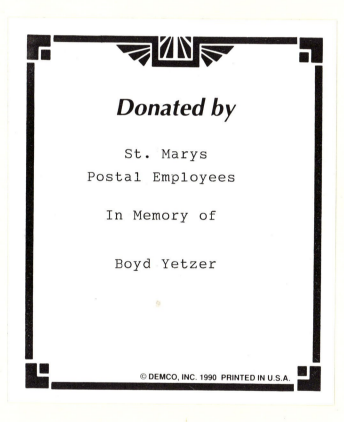

Donated by

St. Marys
Postal Employees

In Memory of

Boyd Yetzer

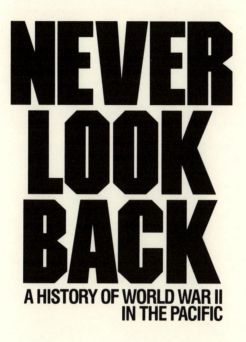

NEVER LOOK BACK

A HISTORY OF WORLD WAR II IN THE PACIFIC

William A. Renzi and Mark D. Roehrs

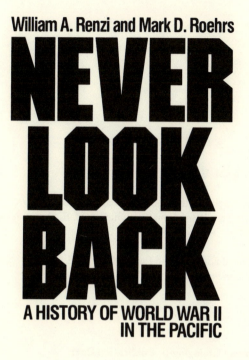

NEVER LOOK BACK

A HISTORY OF WORLD WAR II IN THE PACIFIC

M.E. Sharpe, Inc.
Armonk, New York
London, England

91-1380

Library of Congress Cataloging-in-Publication Data

Renzi, William A., 1941–
    Never look back : a history of World War II in the Pacific / by
William A. Renzi and Mark D. Roehrs.
        p. cm.
    Includes bibliographical references and index.
    ISBN 0-87332-808-6
    1. World War, 1939–1945—Campaigns—Pacific Area. I. Roehrs, Mark D., 1965– .
II. Title.
    D767.9.R46   1991
    940.54′26—dc20   90-25884
                                                                          CIP

Printed in the United States of America

                        ⊗

MV   10   9   8   7   6   5   4   3   2   1

For Judy and David
and
In memory of Uncle Bill

Across the sea, corpses float on the water,
Across the mountain, bodies litter the fields;
I shall die in the service of my emperor,
I will never look back.

—popular Japanese war song (circa 1941)

Contents

Maps and Photographs

Photographs *(continued)*

Preface

This book exists for several reasons. First, the authors have devoted years to the study of the Second World War, one having had his interest in the topic begun by the late Gordon W. Prange, for whom he was graduate assistant for five years. In the last decade, moreover, a spate of fresh primary and secondary source materials has become available. As our bibliography attests, we have made liberal use of these riches, together with, of course, the best of the old, or standard, works on the topic that are likely to remain classics.

We have concentrated on the Japanese-American episodes of the conflict in "The Great Pacific War" (which is what the war is called in Japan) for the simple reason that they were decisive. British participation, as well as Australian and New Zealander efforts in the struggle and the China-Burma-India theater, are all dealt with, but not to the same degree. We do not mean to negate or disparage the action in these other theaters, but since the conflict was primarily a Japanese-American one, this central perspective is maintained in order to retain a balanced narrative.

The reader will remember, of course, that Japan lies across the International Date Line. Like almost all other authors, we have retained zone times (also known as "local," "real," or "actual" times) in the narrative. Thus, December 7, 1941, was December 8 in Japan, and Pearl Harbor Day, a national holiday by imperial proclamation, was celebrated on December 8 in Japan during the war years. We have not used a standard system of transliteration for Oriental names, for the simple reason that many of the actors are already well known and being doctrinaire in the matter might well be confusing; in most instances, we have employed the usual or most common transliteration for the family names involved.

We have tried to give both the Japanese and American points of view toward the conflict, in both its origins and actual conduct. The American side is relatively well known to many English-language readers; the Japanese side, perhaps less so. We have tried to keep a relatively even balance, but if we tend occasionally to explain Japanese motives and values a bit more than American ones, it is in the simple belief that they will be of greater interest to the reader.

Acknowledgments

The authors are in the debt of a fair number of people who aided them in the course of their research. Among these are Professors David Healy and David Buck, who read all or parts of this manuscript. We have profited greatly from their suggestions and criticisms. Gail Jacobsen, our department's chief secretary and an author in her own right, provided many favors, including financial assistance for the photographic work. Michael Weber, our chief editor, not only worked with us very constructively but also did a good deal of line editing himself (he won't get a chance to edit this line out). M. E. Sharpe's project editor was Alexandra Koppen; the manuscript was copyedited by Bessie Blum. The United States Army, Navy, and Air Force, and the National Archives provided many of the photographs used in the text, and Patrick Steele and Jeanine Pagliaro drew the maps. Lastly, many veterans on both sides of the Pacific shared their memories with us, and we owe them a debt greater than can be stated. If their individual efforts have not been acknowledged, it is only because our debt is so great. For any errors we alone are responsible.

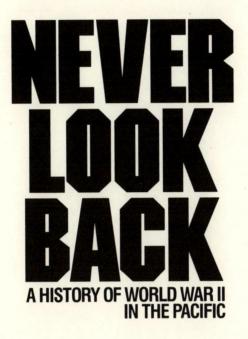

NEVER LOOK BACK

A HISTORY OF WORLD WAR II IN THE PACIFIC

1.   Prelude to Conflict

Japan Comes of Age
Japanese-American Relations after 1900
Japan's Growing Military Commitment in China
The Drift toward War with the United States

The year 1868 was as dramatic and important in Japanese history as the year 1941. In 1868 the boy emperor, Meiji, guided by a small group of warlord-noblemen, or *genro,* established the Japanese capital in Tokyo and began the modernization of Japan. The motives that impelled the Japanese to begin industrialization are diverse. The traditional explanation on the American side of the Pacific has been that U.S. Commodore Matthew Perry's three trips to Japan in the 1850s somehow forced an end to Japanese isolation. Doubtless Perry had some influence on the Japanese decision to terminate isolation. But the major force that motivated the Japanese was the arrival of the Russian empire on its Pacific seaboard and the subsequent founding of the port of Vladivostok—its name may be literally translated as "rule over the East"—on the Sea of Japan, which had heretofore been a virtual Japanese lake. Japan has always viewed Russia as its greatest enemy. Further, any influence America might have had was doubtless terminated by the U.S. Civil War, which seemed to Japan to demonstrate American weakness and incompetence.

In less than fifty years Meiji's *genro* and their followers industrialized the country. They copied the best of each European nation's contribution to modern society. The Japanese Navy was built on the British model; their army was modeled on that of imperial Germany. From America very little was copied, for the simple reason that the recent Civil War made it seem unwise to do so. But the Japan that they modernized had been a feudal military dictatorship. Meiji demolished isolation and brought the Japanese into the twentieth century. Unlike the case of industrialization in the Western world, however, the Japanese central government brought modern technology to a population that had just been liberated from several centuries of unbridled military despotism. And Japan terminated isolation and entered the world arena in the late nineteenth-century heyday of Western imperialism, when all of the great powers were engaged in conquering Africa and Asia. The Japanese joined the imperialist bandwagon, but they did so rather late in the game. In a certain sense, it might be argued that World War II in the Pacific was, at least in the first instance, nothing more than the logical extension of nineteenth-century imperialism, albeit long after the rest of the world had begun to abandon imperialism as being overly aggressive, immoral, and unprofitable.

Japan's most important colony was to be Korea. The Japanese engaged the Chinese in a rivalry for control of that strategic peninsula. China refused to yield, and the Japanese attacked Chinese forces in Korea in July 1894, declaring war four days later. The Chinese armies retreated; by the end of the year China's government indicated a willingness to negotiate. Negotiations ensued and in the peace treaty of March 1895, China gave Japan the right to exploit Korea and ceded outright several other territories, Formosa included. Three of the European powers, France, Germany, and especially Russia, were determined to exploit or at least preserve the Korean peninsula for themselves. In 1895 these three powers informed the Japanese that Korea could not become a literal Japanese conquest. "The Triple Intervention," as the Japanese named it, constituted a body blow to Japanese prestige. Here was undeniable proof for the first time that the other great powers would not acknowledge Japan as an equal, at least not in the realm of colonial ambitions. The resultant shock was great in Japan and only encouraged further Japanese conquests.

The Japanese live on four home islands roughly the size of the state of Idaho. They have absolutely no natural resources, except for meager coal deposits and some "white coal," or hydroelectric power. From the Japanese standpoint in 1900, therefore, they were merely implementing their own version of what Americans termed Manifest Destiny. But the Japanese (not totally unlike the Americans) did so without regard for the cultural integrity of the peoples they were to conquer. Lip service was given to preserving local customs and language, but such preservation remained notional. The Asian mainland—particularly Korea and Manchuria—beckoned as an area rich in resources. Japan's attention focused first on Korea, where Russia became its chief rival for domination of that timber rich country.

The Japanese were prepared to fight the Russians if necessary, especially after 1902, when a Japanese-British naval alliance was signed that would have benefited the Japanese had Russia acquired even one ally in the forthcoming war. The alliance also enhanced Japanese prestige and provided for mutual assistance if either Britain or Japan were attacked by two or more powers in the Pacific. The Russians nonetheless refused to yield on the Korean question.

By January 1904 the Japanese had decided on war. On February 9, the Japanese Fleet, under Admiral Heihachiro Togo, attacked the Russian Far Eastern Fleet at Port Arthur on the Yellow Sea. After crippling the fleet, Japan declared war a day later. With the Russian Navy no longer a threat, troops poured across Korea and entered Manchuria, China's industrialized northern heart, on May 1. Port Arthur was also besieged and eventually fell to the Japanese. The Russians hastened to field an army in Siberia, 6,000 miles distant from European Russia. The tsar's forces were subsequently defeated in three major engagements, the largest of which took place in Mukden, Manchuria, in March of 1905, but retreated with their armies intact. The most celebrated battle of the war, however, occurred at sea.

Tsar Nicholas II ordered the Russian Baltic Sea Fleet to the Pacific, an 18,000-mile voyage. The Russians evidently did not expect victory, since each warship was equipped with a Japanese flag to hoist in the event of defeat. (Perhaps the Russians were not sure the Japanese would appreciate a white flag, even if it were hoisted as a token of surrender.) The ensuing battle of Tsushima, on May 27, 1905, was a resounding Japanese victory. American President Theodore Roosevelt offered to act as a mediator between the warring nations. The war ended in September 1905 with the signing of the Treaty of Portsmouth (New Hampshire). Japan gained recognition of its right to incorporate Korea into its empire, a lease on the Liaotung peninsula, and possession of the southern half of Sakhalin Island. The treaty riveted Japanese attention on the United States, as well it might have.

Japanese-American relations had been unsatisfactory ever since the American acquisition of Hawaii and the Philippines in 1900. The U.S. "Open Door" proclamation of 1900 had been made in part to discourage Japan from aggression against China, toward which America had shown a measure of good will for several decades. The 1900 acquisitions made the United States a Pacific power in every sense of the word, and for the better part of two decades—since the 1880s—Japanese newspapers had spoken of Japan's "frontier" in the Hawaiian Islands. Worse, in the first decade of this century, the state of California, urged on by native jingoists including the Oakland-born novelist Jack London, all but declared war on Japan. In part the jingoists focused on the "yellow peril," which the Japanese were sometimes made to exemplify particularly (perhaps because Japanese immigrants were a bit wealthier than the Chinese and sometimes purchased farmland). In the aftermath of the San Francisco earthquake of 1906, for example, the Japanese residents of that city were nearly banished to Los Angeles. President Roosevelt later had to intervene to persuade the San Francisco school board not to force Japanese schoolchildren to attend a specifically segregated school with their Chinese classmates, even though the number of Japanese schoolchildren affected was small. In 1908 the so-called Gentleman's Agreement restricted Japanese blue-collar immigration to the United States, which mollified some of the more ardent anti-Japanese in this country, who evidently believed that a "racial mongrelization" would eventually manifest itself in the form of intermarriages between Japanese and Americans, unions then prohibited by law. During his last year in office, Roosevelt became so concerned over anti-Japanese sentiment, particularly on the West Coast, that he sent an American battleship fleet on a world cruise with a stop in Tokyo included to calm jingoist bluster. Their Tokyo reception was stage-managed beautifully but did nothing to relieve Japanese-American tensions.

"We were near war with Japan in 1913," wrote Secretary of the Navy Josephus Daniels with pardonable exaggeration. Anti-Japanese sentiment persisted on the West Coast and even in Hawaii, the most tolerant of American possessions, to such an extent that on America's western seaboard Japanese were forbidden to buy or lease land in some neighborhoods, and in more than a few they were not welcomed even as visitors.

The Japanese contended that since America had acquired a Pacific empire by annexing Hawaii and conquering the Philippines, Japan had a perfect right to pursue similar ambitions. A few American jingoists actually called for war, being particularly concerned to protect the great powers' freedom to trade in China. A conflict might have erupted in the second decade of the century, especially after 1912 when the emperor Meiji died and was succeeded by his son Taisho, who was mentally defective, and/or an alcoholic. Taisho was less effective in counseling restraint on Japanese jingoists. But the outbreak of World War I in August 1914 gave the Japanese other priorities.

Japanese diplomats have always enjoyed a reputation for objective factual reporting. This era was not an exception. The Japanese cabinet met several times that August and, based partially on information available from their European embassies, determined that the Allies would win the war, after a conflict that would last approximately three years. They were determined to take advantage of the European war to achieve further gains in Asia, reasoning that the great powers would now be preoccupied. Hence, they delivered an ultimatum to Germany and entered the war against it on August 23, 1914.

The Japanese had no intention of actively participating in the European theater of conflict. They began by besieging Tsingtao, the only German naval base in China, which fell on November 7, 1914. They then gained their first experience of amphibious operations by seizing German colonies north of the equator, including the Marshall, Mariana, Palau, and Caroline islands. The Japanese moved against neutral China via diplomacy. Their interest in China was natural because of its size, the fact that the Chinese revolution of 1911 left China politically fragmented and unstable, and because recent Japanese immigration into northern China had placed nearly 140,000 Japanese in that area. And the Japanese had designs on Manchuria's western neighbor, Mongolia, which must have seemed huge and underpopulated by Japanese standards.

In January 1915 the Japanese ambassador in Peking delivered an ultimatum to the Chinese government, subsequently known as the Twenty-One Demands. The ultimatum was typed on paper literally watermarked with armaments. The document demanded extensive commercial concessions, some of which the Chinese were forced to grant, for China could no longer play off one great power against another to maintain its sovereignty. After the armistice of 1918 ending World War I, the Japanese were determined that the forthcoming peace treaty would ratify their possession of former German colonies. They easily obtained the German islands north of the equator at the 1919 peace conference of Versailles, but they were unable to obtain a coveted racial equality clause specifically requested by Emperor Taisho. The Japanese blamed this largely on President Woodrow Wilson. A spate of jingoism ensued in Japan, evidently encouraged by the government.

Japan entered a period of relative drift, in part because of the declining mental health of Taisho. The emperor became increasingly unstable, his condition was at the least worsened by his heavy drinking. In 1921, after the emperor, among other oddities, rolled up a scroll and employed it to scrutinize members of the Diet, his son, Hirohito, assumed power as regent. New political parties of the left appeared, while the collapse of the postwar economic boom in 1921 began a decade-long inflationary period.

A naval arms race among the great powers followed the end of the war. The competition was tempered at the Washington Naval Conference of 1921–22. The conference agreed on a 5:5:3 ratio for capital ships (excluding aircraft carriers; they were covered by a different ratio), which meant that if each power built to treaty strength, the Japanese Navy would be three-fifths the size of the American and British navies. Erection of new fortifications in the Pacific were forbidden, with exceptions made for the U.S. base of Pearl Harbor on Oahu, Hawaii, and for many Japanese areas. From the Japanese standpoint, insult was added to injury when a few years later the Japanese discovered that the American delegation had learned via cryptography that Japan would accept such a ratio only as a last resort.

The conference had scarcely concluded when the United States enacted the Immigration Act of 1924, which forbade further Japanese immigration. The Japanese had also resented, with less reason, American intervention in the Russian civil war; American leaders considered the intervention necessary to counteract Japanese influence in Siberia stemming from the dispatch of Japanese troops to eastern Russia. Japan gained little from its own intervention, but the last Japanese troops left Soviet soil only in 1925.

With the demise of Taisho, who had lived in seclusion, on Christmas Day of 1926, Emperor Hirohito's reign officially began. From the first the new emperor, who had chosen the motto *Showa*—enlightened peace—as his posthumous "throne name," disliked the plans his military were obviously hatching.

As a cure-all for Japan's problems, a Japanese "expedition" to occupy and "bring order" to Chinese Manchuria, which was admittedly in disarray, was openly bruited about Tokyo in the late 1920s. There is no doubt that barbarism and banditry were the order of the day in Manchuria. But in actual fact the Japanese coveted Manchuria for its extensive iron ore, coal, and oil resources. Such resources would free Japan from its dependence on foreign nations, particularly the

United States, for raw materials, and would ensure its status as a great power.

Some Japanese, admittedly a minority, viewed bringing order to China's northern provinces as a duty, since the government in Peking obviously could not do so. Emperor Hirohito reigned, but he did not rule and hence had no voice in the actual formulation of policy; he could only watch the drift toward conquest and war, as helpless as any civilian. If the emperor objected to any particular military stratagem, the army, via the time-honored doctrine of *gekokujo,* could simply declare that the emperor was being ill-advised and that true obedience dictated the course the military had chosen. And some Japanese viewed the emperor's position as so lofty that they considered mundane affairs of state to be beneath him. In any event, it would be easy to fabricate an excuse for military action in Manchuria, since Japanese troops had long exercised the right to guard Manchuria's rail lines.

On the night of September 18, 1931, the plot against Manchuria unfolded. An explosive charge was planted under a rail line near Mukden; it duly exploded, although it merely scattered some of the roadbed's ballast. Nonetheless, that same evening the Japanese Army occupied Mukden and seized the Chinese arsenal in that city. A subsequent investigation of the incident by the League of Nations disclosed that a train had passed safely over the line only twenty minutes after the explosion and revealed the homemade nature of the entire episode. Japan withdrew from the League, however, when the findings were made public.

The Mukden incident marked the ascendancy of the Japanese military in national politics and in the cabinet itself. When coupled with several army-inspired assassinations of political figures opposed to war, it brought about the end of political parties and began the military domination of the government. The army or navy could bring down any cabinet by ordering its service ministers (Ministry of War and Navy) to resign. This right, inherent in the Japanese governmental structure by common accord, was henceforward greatly abused. The extent of the military's power on the course of Japanese policy may be inferred by the fact that it could enjoy the luxury of internecine warfare among its own factions after 1931.

Japan had conquered Manchuria but she did not effectively rule it, for bandits plundered the countryside by night. And Japan's rule cost its economy as much in iron ore and oil as it obtained from Manchuria.

Small wonder that two factions emerged among staff officers in Tokyo, both calling for further expansion to find Japan a suitable area for exploitation and possible colonization. A large majority of the adherents of both groups were majors and colonels, although it was generals who determined membership and ideology. The *Kodo* faction held that the Soviet Union was Japan's primary enemy, and that after Manchuria had been pacified, Japanese expansion should take place at the expense of the USSR. The opposing *Tosei* group also desired that gains in Manchuria be consolidated, but believed that Japan's destinies lay to the south. Specifically, the *Tosei* believed that the Philippines, Hong Kong, the Malay Peninsula, Thailand, Burma, and particularly the Dutch East Indies constituted Japan's version of Manifest Destiny. In the early 1930s officers of both schools first used the term "Eldorado of the South" to describe the latter areas. Some officers actually subscribed to both schools of thought, and debate between them at first seemed routine. By early 1936, however, the *Kodo* felt they had lost ground. They attempted to redress the balance by staging an insurrection in the heart of Tokyo. In the early morning hours of February 26, 1936, just after a severe snowstorm had blanketed the city, troops commanded by *Kodo* officers seized control of a portion of the capital adjacent to several of the foreign embassies. They hoisted helium-filled balloons with streamers proclaiming the virtues of their cause and assassinated some high-level officials, including several of cabinet rank.

Hirohito determined that he would not remain a spectator. He ordered the *Kodo* to surrender and reportedly ordered his own palace guard units to mobilize fully. Order was restored late in the evening of February 29, and the emperor ordered harsh treatment, including the institution of courts martial, for the officers involved. The army, however divided, closed ranks and looked after its own. They circumvented the emperor's orders without his knowledge. But the back of the *Kodo* had been forever broken. As many of the foreign ambassadors in Tokyo reported, future Japanese overseas expansion was now more likely to be southward. And in 1936 Japan ceased abiding by the terms of the Washington Naval Treaty of 1922. By invading Manchuria, Japan seemed to many foreigners to be imitating the expansionism advocated by the European fascist dictators. Americans, who always held an idealized view of China, were particularly incensed, in part because they viewed the Pacific as an area for American commercial expansion.

Early in 1937 Hirohito resolved to stem further military adventures. He ignored tradition by appointing a nobleman, Prince Fumimaro Konoye, as premier. Konoye was in every way an unusual choice. One of the emperor's few personal friends, he was a reputed socialist and virtually a professional pacifist. A youthful bout with tuberculosis left him with a streak of laziness and indifference that was to prove frustrating. Konoye took office with the intention of making the military his servants. When he could not realize this ambition, he lapsed into indifference without giving up the seals of office. The greatest irony of his several premierships would be his approval of *Operation Hawaii,* the surprise attack of December 7, 1941.

Konoye was scarcely in office when a crisis in China suddenly erupted, sparked by the Marco Polo bridge incident. On July 7, 1937, in a demilitarized zone near Peking, a Japanese soldier disappeared during night maneuvers in the treaty port of Tientsin. The Japanese demanded Chinese help in finding the missing soldier, implying that he had been kidnapped. Local fighting between Chinese and Japanese ensued, and each side believed it was the aggrieved party. (The soldier reportedly turned up several weeks later as a deserter.) After a series of high-level conferences in Tokyo, the Japanese military responded to this incident with force. The military assured the government that the conquest of additional Chinese provinces would take no more than six weeks. Konoye reluctantly agreed, believing that Japanese national pride was involved.

When the desired results were quickly achieved, the emperor forgave Konoye, but not his military. In consequence he refused to declare war against China, hoping that the Western world would perceive that he had not desired a major conflict. His signals were misread. World opinion presumed that the lacking declaration of hostilities was a manifestation of Japanese duplicity, and embarrassed Japanese diplomats were forced to refer to hostilities in China as the "China Incident," as if using a nonplural noun would somehow terminate the conflict. American opinion was particularly aroused. Again Japan seemed to be following the fascist pattern of Hitler and Mussolini against a helpless China. Sentiment on the West Coast was particularly strong, and more than one Sunday school class contributed funds to help the Chinese government.

Konoye further obliged the military in November 1937 by proclaiming the Greater East Asia Co-Prosperity Sphere, more commonly known in Japan itself as *Dai Nippon,* meaning literally (and much more simply) "greater Japan." As originally worded and conceived by Konoye, this was a proclamation of Asia for the Asians and an end to white colonialism. But the common Japanese expression *Dai Nippon* conveyed the military's (not Konoye's) true intent. The Chinese government responded by ordering a full mobilization, and a full-scale war in China began. In Japan many household commodities and foodstuffs became scarce as the war weakened the economy. For the Japanese the war in the Pacific began in 1937, reputedly as a result of Chinese aggression.

Japanese behavior in China became atrocious. Chinese soldiers attempting to surrender were frequently executed on sight. Civilians were openly massacred, the slaughter following the fall of Nanking in December 1937 being only the most notorious example. About 250,000 civilians and POWs were put to death on that single occasion alone. Konoye attempted to arrest the conflict with diplomatic initiatives, but his efforts failed. Worse, in early December 1937, Japanese planes flying from an aircraft carrier deliberately sunk the American gunboat *Panay* in the Yangtze River. American President Franklin Roosevelt was outraged. He gave a speech calling on America's friends to "quarantine aggression," the reference in part being to Japanese involvement in China.

Roosevelt's secondary response was to write to American industrialists and request that they begin curtailing trade with the Japanese. This he could plausibly do because American manufacturers knew they could easily market the same materials to customers in Europe. American companies, including Standard Oil, complied with the president's request, although at first the Japanese did not know of the president's role in the matter. When his role was appreciated, the Japanese grew fearful lest a complete trade embargo leave them stranded in their home islands with no raw materials.

In consequence Konoye submitted his resignation to the emperor in January 1939. At the emperor's personal request, Konoye returned to the government in July 1940. In a glaringly contradictory statement, Konoye promised to resolve the war in China while at the same time advocating further enlargement of the military. Worse, Konoye's choice as foreign minister, Yosuke Matsuoka, was a strident militarist. Although evidently desirous of peace with all nations, Matsuoka was greatly impressed by Nazi Germany. He became a firm advocate of a direct military alliance between Japan and Germany. He found allies among many army staff officers in Tokyo who deluged Konoye with letters and phone calls advocating such an alignment. When Konoye objected that such an alliance would be resented in the United States and would brand Japan as a fascist aggressor, Matsuoka, who had been educated in Oregon, replied that he knew American public opinion better than anyone else in the cabinet and that America would not be alienated. The foreign minister voiced this opinion so vehemently and with such unction that his cabinet colleagues began to doubt his mental stability. On one occasion, a close friend asked Konoye if Matsuoka was insane; Konoye replied that this was unfortunately not the case, as insanity would at least furnish a precedent for removing him from office. (When Matsuoka died in 1946, he was clearly psychotic.) But Konoye could not remove him, for Matsuoka had many army allies in Tokyo.

In the end Matsuoka had his way. A military alliance with Germany, and Italy as well, was signed in Berlin in September 1940. Of ten years' duration, the alliance pledged the signatories to aid one another if attacked by a power not yet involved in warfare in the Orient or Europe. Years later, in reviewing prewar events, Hirohito specified the signature of the alliance as the most important cause of war with America. He may have been wrong, but from this point forward the American press openly viewed Japan as a fascist state. On more than one occasion it even assumed that Hitler was dictating Japanese policy! No assumption could have been more mistaken, but the idea was not implausible in the more naive era before satellite communications and jet transportation.

President Roosevelt's response to the alliance was simple but dramatic. Having already abrogated America's trade treaty with Japan, the president began specifically (and rather stiffly) to limit the licensing of those firms that would be allowed to trade with the Japanese. In effect, Roosevelt began undisguised, direct control of the materials being shipped to Japan from the United States. Matsuoka's frantic explanations to the Japanese cabinet did nothing to alleviate the situation. Sensing the nearness of war, Matsuoka traveled in March of 1941 to Berlin and then Moscow. With Hitler's consent, Matsuoka negotiated a neutrality pact with Soviet leader Joseph Stalin. Signed April 13, 1941, the pact was a pledge of mutual neutrality, in which the Soviet Union recognized Japan's conquest of Manchuria in return for a Japanese promise to respect Soviet sovereignty over Mongolia. The agreement was valid for five years. When Matsuoka entrained in Moscow for Vladivostok, Stalin made a surprise appearance on the platform and openly proclaimed: "Japan can now expand southward."

In a last attempt to preserve peace, the emperor ordered that the Japanese embassy in Washington ask the U.S. State Department under what conditions normal trade could be restored. The task was almost hopeless. Roosevelt had committed his prestige to opposing further Japanese expansion. And Cordell Hull, his secretary of state, was notoriously anti-Japanese. Ambassador Kichisaburo Nomura nonetheless complied, opening trade negotiations in Washington in early March 1941. The talks proceeded slowly. Hull bluntly told the U.S. cabinet that he did not believe the Japanese were sincere and that he thought they were negotiating merely to gain time. Nomura dutifully did as Tokyo ordered, even though Hull's racial views might have proved offensive to him. Nomura lived in the same building as Hull, the Wardman Park Hotel, and they frequently met on Sundays in the informal surroundings of Hull's quarters.

In entering into trade talks with the Japanese, the United States enjoyed one advantage unknown to the Tokyo government. In September 1940 American cryptographers had penetrated Japan's most complex *diplomatic* cipher system, named simply the "purple" cipher by the American cryptographic team. *Operation Magic,* as the American decrypting effort was entitled, was the most secret matter in Washington at the time. Worked jointly by the American army and navy, the fruits of *Magic* yielded to the American leadership every telegram exchanged between the foreign ministry in Tokyo and all Japanese embassies abroad. Only twelve American leaders were cleared to read the resultant intercepted traffic. These included President Roosevelt, Secretary of State Hull, and several military leaders, none of whom held overseas commands. But *Magic* could not give specific warnings of the Pearl Harbor attack for two reasons. The Japanese diplomats in Washington were not told of the operation because, first, they had no need to know, and second, had they been told, they might have inadvertently revealed the plan to the Americans.

The flow of decrypted traffic gave the American leadership a false sense of security. Reading the other fellow's mail is a time-honored intelligence technique, but the Americans were new at the game. Very careful scrutiny, analysis, and experience are necessary. Various messages beyond the routine were intercepted. But as will be seen, no warning specific enough was detected to warrant transmitting it verbatim to the commanders at Pearl *at the time.*

In July 1940 the Japanese had occupied the northern portion of French Indochina, the area technically being under the control of the collaborationist French Vichy government. Washington was not pleased, but the Japanese could argue that they needed the area as a strategic base for directing further hostilities in China. In July 1941 the Japanese decided on further actions, but this time the United States reacted sharply. First, Konoye resigned and then reconstructed his government in a single day, dropping the troublesome Matsuoka as foreign minister and replacing him with the relatively easy-going Admiral Teijiro Toyoda. Virtually the first act of the new government was to order the occupation of the southern half of Indochina, making it perfectly clear that Japan intended to use that former French colony as a springboard for further conquest in southeast Asia.

President Roosevelt reacted with urgent fury. He began implementing a series of executive decisions that resulted in the suspension of all trade with Japan. All Japanese assets in the United States were frozen on July 26, 1941. Britain and the Netherlands followed suit, thereby depriving the Japanese of any other major trading partners. This move created both panic and confusion in Tokyo. The Japanese government held that its actions were legal under the existing precepts of international law—which, perhaps, they were. But the Japanese Navy had carefully calculated that it had only a two-year supply of diesel fuel accumulated, and this was by peacetime consumption standards. No one knew how much fuel oil might be burned in wartime operations.

The American blow was a stunning one, and the Japanese press universally echoed one theme: the American eagle had bared its claws and shown its aggressive intent towards the Japanese people. The Japanese maintained that they were merely fulfilling their version of Manifest Destiny, as the Americans had done a century before. The American government thought otherwise. It may well be that the United States failed to appreciate fully the seriousness of Japan's economic situation. The United States could afford to be relatively complacent about its own natural resources. America was nearly self-sufficient, and the 120 million Americans enjoyed a gross national product five times that of Japan proper.

Washington had issued several war alerts to its various Pacific commands before freezing Japan's assets. Thus, the commanders at Pearl Harbor would later state that the situation had seemed more tense in July than at the beginning of December, and perhaps, superficially, it was. There was no one point in time when a majority of the Japanese cabinet agreed that war was inevitable, but July marked a turning point in their collective thought patterns. War with America was now viewed as much more likely, the only question being: if it could not be avoided, at what date should hostilities commence?

Secretary of State Hull openly told the American military that the Japanese were continuing trade negotiations only to gain time and that he would like to wash his hands of the entire affair. Everyone in Washington cleared to receive *Magic* knew that war was almost a certainty. Obviously, it would come at the convenience of the Japanese. The most important question remaining for the Americans was: would the Japanese leave their flank open if they moved to conquer the Eldorado of the South by leaving the Philippines untouched, or would the Japanese seize those islands as well, bringing instant war with America? No one in Washington knew the answer, but they did know that the Japanese had never left their flank open at the beginning of a conflict in the past.

By early September 1941, the emperor determined that a decision for war or peace must be made soon. He was prompted by nothing more basic than the calendar, since high summer was approaching south of the equator, the ideal time for conquest of the Dutch East Indies. Furthermore, north of the equator, particularly in Burma, an invasion in midwinter would pose no real obstacles and would avoid the monsoon rains that dominate the summer months there. The Japanese Navy added that if war must occur, the sooner it came the better, since the navy was running on reserve fuel supplies obtained before the trade embargo.

Premier Konoye grew frantic. He reiterated a longstanding proposal for a summit meeting with President Roosevelt, possibly in Alaska. This Roosevelt rejected. He did not doubt that Konoye himself sincerely desired to avoid conflict, but he feared that any promises Konoye made would be repudiated by the Japanese military as soon as Konoye returned to Tokyo. Ambassador Joseph Grew, America's representative in Tokyo, argued otherwise, pleading the case for Konoye's credibility with the Japanese military, but Roosevelt remained unconvinced.

The emperor was moved to action. Earlier he had called for a series of special Liaison Conferences to include the more important cabinet members as well as the Chiefs of Staff of the Japanese Army and Navy. The emperor strongly liked attending Liaison Conferences, because there was little protocol for them and the participants would more readily voice their individual opinions. One such conference met on September 3, 1941. The emperor remained silent and listened as his service chiefs outlined the need for war. Another conference was held on September 6, and the emperor had the meeting prefaced with a statement to the effect that there was too much emphasis on armed conflict rather than on diplomacy as a means for settling grievances. Unknown to the conferees, Hirohito had brought with him the emperor Meiji's famous poem:

If all men are brothers,
Why are the winds and waves of the world so troubled,
Why cannot all men live in peace?

The emperor broke tradition and read the poem to the assembled military personnel, some of whom had never before heard his voice. At the end of the conference, nonetheless, all present agreed that if there was not "reasonable hope" that America would restore trade with Japan, war was inevitable.

Since the Japanese were unwilling even to consider withdrawing from China or Indochina, which was bound to be America's minimum price for the restoration of trade, the situation remained deadlocked. For them, the situation was not unlike that faced by a later generation of Americans in Vietnam: they were engaged on the Asian mainland in a war they could not win, but Japanese imperial prestige was engaged and they could not withdraw. Further conquest suggested itself as the only plausible alternative to economic stagnation.

Konoye's next move was to summon Ambassador Grew for a confidential off-the-record meeting whose only other participant was, evidently, Konoye's mistress. The Japanese premier reiterated his desire for a summit meeting with Roosevelt, insisting he would bring enough military leaders with him to insure than any decisions rendered could not be rescinded upon his return to Tokyo. It was evidently after Konoye determined that a summit meeting was ruled out that he decided to submit his resignation to the throne. On October 16 Konoye returned the seals of office to the emperor, pleading that far from terminating the China incident he had brought Japan to the verge of war and could not control the military leaders. In the course of a twenty-minute conversation with the monarch, Konoye, amid other suggestions, recommended his Minister of the Army Hideki Tojo as his successor, on the grounds that Tojo was a respected army leader who was relatively moderate and not automatically in favor of war.

When Tojo's name was subsequently suggested by others, the emperor made him premier. The American press headlined that the military had taken over the government. In actual fact, Tojo, for all of his fire-eating bluster, was a moderate compared to many other ranking army officers. And Tojo's selection of Shigenori Togo as foreign minister was also a hopeful sign in that Togo was genuinely committed to further negotiation with America and got along well with Ambassador Grew. Through his private secretary, Koichi Kido, the emperor communicated his only command to the new cabinet: "Go back to blank paper." In effect, Hirohito had rescinded the decisions of the imperial Liaison Conferences and had instructed his ministers to restart negotiations with America, beginning at square one.

From Washington's standpoint, however, Tojo's first really significant act concerned embassy personnel in the American capital. Ambassador Nomura, like all educated Japanese, read English with dispatch and had a fair oral grasp of the language as well. Hull's particular Tennessee backwoods accent, however, was often incomprehensible to the ambassador, and was reportedly worsened by ill-fitting dentures. Only on the rarest of occasions were translators employed. Further, Nomura deeply regretted the lack of progress in negotiations and had several times unsuccessfully offered his resignation. When Togo learned that Nomura's physician believed him to be nearing a mental and physical breakdown, a second envoy was dispatched.

Saburo Kurusu had signed the Tripartite Alliance with Germany and Italy in 1940 but resigned the next day from the diplomatic service in protest. He was a retired admiral and, like most naval officers, was opposed to the pact. Thereafter, Kurusu had repaired to Japan and lived in seclusion with his American wife. Since English was his household language, Foreign Minister Togo had sent him packing in early October. Via a Pan Am clipper from Hong Kong, Hawaii, and San Francisco, he eventually reached Washington. Hull viewed his coming with distaste. Kurusu may have known idiomatic English, but his marriage to a white woman was viewed with disdain by Hull. The secretary of state was also offended by the fact that Kurusu had signed the Tripartite Pact and was apparently unaware of his subsequent resignation.

Hull, while well meaning, was also ignorant of another crucial fact. The translators who worked *Operation Magic* labored at a very difficult task. Diplomatic Japanese is susceptible of numerous translations, and precise shades of meaning were sometimes lost on the *Magic* personnel. Whenever they were faced with two or more possible translations for any particular sentence, for their own professional protection they inevitably chose the more belligerent version, evidently assuming that the cryptographers in the Japanese embassy less than a mile away on Massachusetts Avenue would do the same. They were often wrong. When Hull noted that Nomura and Kurusu often seemed to voice less belligerent language than their instructions apparently ordered, he assumed that they were following a policy of deliberate duplicity. Thus, Hull fell victim to inaccurate translations that were noted only in the late 1960s.

Basically Hull, like Roosevelt, was wedded to a policy of deterrence, hoping that maintaining the U.S. Pacific Fleet at Pearl Harbor and enlarging the Army Air Corps in the Philippines would suffice to deter Japanese aggression. But America was fighting an undeclared naval war with Nazi Germany in the Atlantic, and the Pacific Fleet had been weakened. The policy proved unavailing. True, a deterrent works only when it is creditable. But even stationing every major American warship in Pearl Harbor, assuming that the United States possessed the tankers to refuel them during possible subsequent operations in the Pacific, would almost certainly have had no substantial impact. Admiral Yamamoto, who conceived of the Pearl Harbor attack, was a gambler by nature and instinct; moving the entire fleet back to San Diego would have prevented a surprise attack against it that fateful Sunday morning, but it ran contrary to the policy of deterrence, and would have dismayed America's possessions and allies in the Pacific, from Hawaii to Guam to Australia and New Zealand.

The *Magic* personnel were electrified on November 22 when they intercepted a message to the ambassadors in Washington from Togo indicating that the situation had so ripened that the deadline for any further negotiations would be November 29. (Tokyo had several times set deadlines, then revised them.) The telegram concluded, "It is absolutely certain that this deadline cannot be changed, *because after No-vember 29 things are automatically going to happen"* (emphasis added). Here was as clear an indication as would ever be had that a war plan was afoot and by inference that, as was the Japanese tradition, hostilities would not be proceeded by a declaration of war. Colonel Rufus Bratton of the U.S. Army Signal Corps read the intercept in his office and was instantly alarmed. When this information was added to the details of Japanese naval troop movements shared with the United States by British intelligence, Bratton concluded that the Japanese were preparing for the commencement of hostilities against America and her possessions. He galvanized the military into action. An army and navy alert order was sent out. Bratton opined that the Japanese might launch surprise attacks against American bases in the Pacific the following weekend, November 29–30. When those days passed quietly, Bratton personally lost credibility, but no one doubted that the situation was still critical.

Meanwhile Hull was moved to action by the Japanese deadline. On November 26 he finally articulated the conditions under which the United States would consent to reopening trade. In essence, Hull seemed to state that the Japanese must withdraw from all of China, Indochina, and Manchuria and recognize the Chiang Kai-shek govern-ment in China. The Japanese assumed that Hull included Manchuria—or Manchuquo as the Japanese had renamed it—when he employed the noun *China;* Hull, however, meant to indicate only China proper, or those portions of the Chinese countryside south of Manchuquo. The Japanese did not know Hull's true meaning until the 1960s, although it scarcely mattered in the long run.

The Japanese cabinet had concluded that withdrawal from any part of continental Asia was unacceptable as a prerequisite for the resump-tion of trade. News of Hull's November 26 statement was first known in Tokyo during a cabinet meeting late on the 27th, Japanese time. The cabinet was stunned. The ministers promptly labeled the document an ultimatum. It was not: an ultimatum is a specific set of demands with an exact time limit that threatens action if not accepted. Obviously, Hull delivered no such document to the Japanese. But it is possible that even he did not realize how critical the problem of raw materials was for the Japanese, and how prophetic had been Ambassador Grew's warning that if the trade issue could not be settled peaceably, war might come "with daring and dramatic suddenness."

On December 2 fleet intelligence at Pearl Harbor learned that all Japanese naval radio ship call designations had been changed, the second such change within a month; this was the first time in anyone's memory that two such changes had been made in such rapid succession. Admiral Husband Kimmel, naval commander at Pearl, asked his fleet intelligence staff about the location of Japan's aircraft carriers. When Captain Edwin Layton's reply did not fully satisfy Kimmel, he inquired, perhaps lightheartedly, "Do you mean to say they could be rounding Diamond Head [a point on Oahu] and you wouldn't know about it?" Layton, replying on the basis of the best information available to him, stated: "I would hope they could be sighted before that."

In the next few days Roosevelt was so sure that war was imminent that he informed the Australian and New Zealand governments that if British territory was attacked, America would join in the fight even if it had not been the victim of aggression itself, a pledge he fortunately never had to honor. *Magic* disclosed that Japanese troop transports were still headed south, evidently for Thailand or Malaya, with heavy naval escort. Japanese embassies abroad, including those in London and Washington, received orders to begin destroying codes and classified materials, and this last information was passed on to the naval authorities at Pearl. Secretary of War Henry Stimson decided to remain in Washington that coming weekend, rather than retreat to his Long Island estate, since, as he confided to his diary, the "atmosphere indicated that something was going to happen." Roosevelt was concerned enough that early on the evening of Saturday, December 6, he dispatched via Ambassador Grew a personal telegram to the emperor. The president asked that negotiations begin again, requesting that the emperor act to preserve peace "for the sake of humanity."

Saturday, December 6, might have been a routine day for the officers who worked *Operation Magic,* but it was not. That morning the Tokyo-Washington telegraph circuit suddenly came to life when a message flashed from Togo to his ambassadors in Washington, advising them to stand by "for reception of a very long message in fourteen parts." Why send a message on a Saturday afternoon when the embassy would normally not contact the American government until Monday morning? Bratton and his naval opposite, Lt. Commander Alvin Kramer, were intrigued, and Bratton ordered the full staff of translators to be called back, most having left at noon. The incoming message was sent via both international telegraph agencies, RCA and

Macay. The first thirteen parts of the message did not arrive in order, but as soon as the "purple" machine had decrypted them, they were discovered to be in English, needing no translation. This too was a first.

By 8:30 PM the Americans had typed up the first thirteen parts and readied them for distribution to all *Magic* recipients. Tokyo was holding the fourteenth part until morning. The document was a recapitulation of recent Japanese-American trade relations and was evidently going to reach a negative conclusion in its still missing final section. Kramer decided to make the rounds with it, incomplete though it was. He stopped first at the White House, dropping off a copy for the president. When Roosevelt read it, he remarked simply to his chief aide, Harry Hopkins, "This means war." Hopkins agreed, observing that America might strike the first blow. Roosevelt rejected this suggestion, stating: "No, we can't do that. We are a democracy and a peaceful people. But we have a good record." The other *Magic* recipients had less dramatic reactions, though all were disturbed. General George Marshall, army chief of staff, had retired early and was not awakened.

The next morning the fourteenth part arrived, stating simply that further negotiations were useless. It was followed by a message ordering Nomura and Kurusu to present the document to Hull at precisely 1:00 PM Washington time that same day. A further message ordered the embassy to destroy all remaining codes, ciphers, and confidential documents. Still later, Togo personally telegraphed his two ambassadors, congratulating them on their efforts to preserve peace and, in effect, relieving them of any responsibility for the fact that they had not succeeded.

Secretary of the Navy Frank Knox was among the first to learn of these new messages. One of his staff suggested that he call Admiral Kimmel on Oahu and advise him that hostilities were about to commence. The 1:00 PM deadline would be 7:30 AM in Hawaii, or just after dawn. Stark reached for the phone but then thought better of the matter. Kimmel was not cleared to receive *Magic*. Worse, anyone could be a silent third partner to their conversation over a line protected only by a simple scrambler device. Stark attempted to call the White House instead, but could not reach the president, who was talking on the phone himself, after which he was closeted with his personal physician for sinus treatment.

Colonel Bratton meanwhile attempted to contact General Marshall, who still knew nothing of the fourteen-part message and subsequent documents. But Marshall, a habitual early riser, had left his quarters at Ft. Myer near Washington to participate in his one recreation, horseback riding, and could not be reached. When he finally returned to his quarters, he learned that Bratton urgently desired to speak with him, so he showered and reached his office in Washington about 11:29 AM. About twenty minutes passed while Marshall read the accumulated messages. The general, the most authoritative military figure in the capital, perceived that the fourteen-part message might well be, in effect, a substitute for a declaration of war. On a yellow legal pad, Marshall swiftly composed a telegram for all army navy commanders in the Pacific. It read:

> *First Priority Secret. The Japanese are presenting at 1 PM Eastern Standard Time today what amounts to an ultimatum. Also they are under orders to destroy their code machine immediately. Just what significance the hour set may have we do not know, but be on the alert accordingly. Inform naval authorities of this communication. Marshall.*

Within about forty minutes the message was well on its way to its intended recipients in Panama, San Francisco, and the Philippines. But the army message center could not raise the army authorities at Ft. Shafter on Oahu because of atmospheric conditions. A more powerful naval transmitter nearby was available, but rather than admit failure to the navy and risk further possible delay if that means failed as well, the army message center sent the encrypted message as a telegram to General Walter Short, the army commander in Hawaii. The wire was not sent at the urgent rate, and until received and decrypted at Ft. Shafter, those who processed it had no hint of the critical nature of its content. Western Union handled the wire and nonetheless sent it with a fair amount of dispatch. Relayed to San Francisco, it reached Honolulu several minutes before the attack but was delivered to Ft. Shafter by an American boy of Japanese ancestry only after the attack was underway. Both Admiral Kimmel and General Short reacted with predictable anger when the delayed message finally reached them, but it actually was unlikely, as will be seen, that prompt delivery would have alerted them to the Japanese attack.

Suggestions for Further Reading

A good introduction to Japanese culture and folkways is provided by former ambassador Edwin Reischauer in *The Japanese* (Cambridge, MA: Harvard University Press, 1981). The standard work on the place of the military in Japanese society remains Ruth Benedict, *The Chrysanthemum and the Sword* (Boston: Little, Brown, 1946). Tessa Morris-Suzuki, in *Showa: An Inside History of Hirohito's Japan* (New York: Schocken Books, 1985), follows the lives of three Japanese coming of age in prewar Japan. One of the most useful general texts detailing the prewar history of Japan is Kikiso Hane's *Modern Japan: A Historical Survey* (Boulder, CO: Westview Press, 1986). One of the best surveys of Japanese-American relations prior to the conflict is Charles E. Neu, *The Troubled Encounter: The United States and Japan* (Malibar, FL: Krieger, 1981); Robert Butow's *Tojo and the Coming of the War* (Stanford, CA: Stanford University Press, 1961) is still standard on the subject. Herbert Feis, *The Road to Pearl Harbor* (Princeton, NJ: Princeton University Press, 1950), is a good *factual* account of the events culminating in the attack of December 7, 1941. Jonathan G. Utley, *Going to War with Japan, 1937–1941* (Knoxville: University of Tennessee Press, 1985), gives very useful insights into the mechanics of diplomacy and military policy formulation during the last years of peace, especially the U.S. executive decision that unintentionally escalated to the point of freezing all Japanese assets in America in July of 1941. Ambassador Grew's views are given in his *Two Years in Japan* (New York: Simon & Schuster, 1944) and in *Turbulent Era*, 2 vols. (Boston: Houghton Mifflin, 1952). A good essay on Matsuoka, by Barbara Teters, "Matsuoka Yosuke: The Diplomacy of Bluff and Gesture," is in *Diplomats in Crisis: United States–Chinese–Japanese Relations, 1919–1941*, ed. by Richard D. Burns and Edward Bennett (Santa Barbara, CA: ABC-Clio Press, 1974), pp. 275–96. Diplomacy in the mid-1930s and the role of the Japanese Navy are covered in Stephen E. Pelz, *Race to Pearl Harbor: The Failure of the Second London Naval Conference and the Onset of World War Two* (Cambridge, MA: Harvard University Press, 1974). A more general survey of the origins of the war is provided by Akira Iriye, *The Origins of the Second World War in Asia and the Pacific* (London: Longman, 1987). Paul Haggie, *Britannia at Bay: The Defense of the British Empire against Japan, 1931–1941* (New York: Oxford, 1981) is well researched from recently released British primary sources, as is Peter Lowe, *Great Britain and the Origins of the Pacific War* (Oxford: Clarendon Press, 1977). Specific studies of Japanese-American trade relations, from opposite political viewpoints, are found in Michael A. Barnhart, *Japan Prepares for Total War: The Search for Economic Security, 1919–1941* (Ithaca, NY: Cornell University Press, 1987), and James R. Herzberg, *A Broken Bond: American Economic Policies toward Japan, 1931–1941* (New York: Garland, 1988). The standard Japanese work on the origins of the conflict, translated into English, is *Japan's Road to the Pacific War*, 5 vols., ed. by James Morley (New York: Columbia University Press, 1976-85). For the Japanese theory and way of war, Tsunetomo Yamamoto's *Hagakure: The Book of the Samurai* (New York: Kodansha, nd) is invaluable, but see also S. R. Turnbull, *The Samurai: A Military History* (New York: Macmillan, 1977). Lee Chong-tung, *Counterinsurgency in Manchuria: The*

Japanese Experience, 1931–1940 (Santa Monica, CA: The Rand Corporation, 1967) gives a unique view of the problems the Japanese military faced in Manchuria. Finally, the first volume of S. E. Morison's history of U.S. naval operations during the war, *The Rising Sun in the Pacific* (Boston: Little, Brown, 1947), remains a reliable, if brief, sketch of the origins of the conflict.

2. Planning *Operation Hawaii*

Operation Hawaii, as the attack on the United States Pacific Fleet in Pearl Harbor was first code-named, was the conception and responsibility of one man: Admiral Isoroku Yamamoto, commander in chief of the Japanese combined fleet since August 1939. Paradoxically, Yamamoto had lived in the United States, admired American culture, and believed that Japan probably could not win a protracted conflict with the United States. Born in 1884, Yamamoto was a graduate of Japan's naval academy, Eta Jima. As a promising young naval officer, he had participated in the Battle of Tsushima in 1905, losing two fingers when one of the guns on his own ship exploded. In the 1920s he attended Harvard for two years and also served an equal amount of time as Japan's naval attaché in Washington. He was an early and ardent advocate of naval air power and greatly admired General William "Billy" Mitchell, although there is no evidence they ever met.

Yamamoto came to respect greatly American industrial potential and spoke English fluently. He also became an ardent poker player while he lived in Washington. Yamamoto became the master of the calculated risk; indeed, some American officers who rather consistently lost to him at cards were convinced that he cheated, so good was he at bluffing. Once, soon after the war had erupted, a fellow officer asked him what he intended to do after Japan won: after a thoughtful moment, he replied, perhaps only half jokingly, "Ideally, I would like to retire to Singapore and open a gambling casino, to repay the emperor the cost of the conflict."

A true leader in every sense of the word, Yamamoto seemed to inspire absolute confidence in those under his command. He represented Japan at several international naval conferences in the 1930s and then became naval viceminister. He repeatedly cautioned against war with America, warning that the United States was not a decadent nation and that any enemy who wished to vanquish her would have to be able literally to occupy Washington and dictate peace terms in the White House. He opposed naval cooperation with the army and with Nazi Germany so vehemently that fellow officers felt his life was in danger. Some contend that a reward had actually been offered for his assassination; fellow officers sometimes deemed it prudent, reportedly, not to accept a ride in his automobile. Hence his posting to sea duty as commander in chief of the combined fleet in August of 1939; it would be almost impossible for any assassin, at least any member of the army, to reach him. Not long after Yamamoto assumed this post, the emperor summoned him and inquired about the possibility of winning a war with America. Yamamoto candidly replied: "For the first six months of a conflict I will run wild like a boar, and for the first two years we will prevail; but after that, I am not at all sure of events."

Since 1919 America had maintained a Pacific fleet at Pearl Harbor; the fleet's alternate base was at San Diego. Roosevelt ordered the fleet to remain at Pearl to act as a deterrent to Japanese aggression on the western rim of the Pacific Ocean. Japanese naval planners had long talked of a surprise attack against the American fleet at Pearl, but there were no specific plans. The difficulties involved were formidable: Pearl Harbor lay 3,500 miles from Japan, and the Japanese did not view themselves as possessing a true deep-water navy. Prior to 1941 every naval battle in Japanese history had been fought within 200 miles of one of the home islands. The fuel capacity of Japanese ships, as compared to those of the same type in the American navy, was slight. An attack against Pearl would necessitate steaming 3,500 miles undetected to the world's strongest naval base, a seeming impossibility.

Yamamoto, however, was never a man to be daunted by obstacles. He told the naval general staff in Tokyo that their battleships—particularly the forthcoming leviathans *Yamato* and *Musashi,* 70,000 tons each—were "about as useful as the Great Wall of China." The naval general staff disagreed; it did not share Yamamoto's enthusiasm for the aircraft carrier and aerial torpedo. The staff believed they had no cause for concern. As commander in chief of the combined fleet, Yamamoto was only their servant; the naval general staff was the fountainhead of all naval planning. Any innovative ideas Yamamoto might breed would theoretically be safely contained on the bridge of his own flagship at sea. They reckoned, however, without the force of Yamamoto's personality.

In the late spring of 1940, after observing a demonstration of Japan's new aerial oxygen-driven torpedo (a variant of the submarine "long-lance" torpedo), which left no tell-tale stream of bubbles in the water after being dropped, Yamamoto wondered aloud to his then chief of staff, Vice Admiral Shigeru Fukudome, whether a torpedo attack against U.S. ships in Pearl was now possible. Fukudome believed the thought had merely flickered through Yamamoto's mind randomly. Certainly the suggestion appeared impractical. Any aerial torpedo would dive upon being dropped to a depth of at least seventy-five feet before leveling off to its preset running depth. The deepest portion of Pearl Harbor, battleship row, was only forty-two feet deep. For the moment Yamamoto shelved the idea.

His interest revived suddenly early in November of 1940 when the British Mediterranean fleet executed a surprise dusk attack against the Italian fleet at Taranto. The British utilized twenty-one old Swordfish biplanes flying from the deck of aircraft carrier *Illustrious* in the attack. Three Italian battleships were sunk with aerial torpedoes, while only two British aircraft were lost. The British had used torpedoes that had run at a very shallow depth from the moment of release from their aircraft. Yamamoto was intrigued. If the British could overcome the difficulties involved, so could the Japanese Navy. In December of 1940 he set portions of his staff to planning a surprise attack against the Americans at Pearl Harbor.

Yamamoto ultimately chose Minoru Genda, the air commander of the carrier *Kaga*, Japan's leading naval ace and a veteran of the China conflict, to write the plan that would be used against the Americans. Genda warmed to the idea. He quickly produced a rough sketch of how such an attack should be carried out. The plan had some flaws but was basically quite sound. Next Yamamoto turned the plan over to another acquaintance famous for his thoroughness and good judgment. The real burden of editing thus fell to Captain Kameto Kuroshima, a man who favored long working hours and would live like a hermit in his cabin until any particular project was completed. Other hands as well worked to refine Genda's original concepts. Genda had no mere hit-and-run air raid in mind. He called for massing six carriers for a decisive air blow against the American Navy at Pearl Harbor. Battleships and cruisers had no essential role in the attack and were in fact added to the Pearl Harbor task force largely to placate the naval general staff in Tokyo.

The problem now became gaining approval in Tokyo for so bold a plan. Yamamoto told his staff that Japan could not attempt to conquer the Eldorado of the South without securing her left flank. Since the Philippines would have to be conquered, American intervention was assured. Yamamoto decided that only his attack plan to neutralize or sink outright the U.S. fleet in Hawaiian waters would allow Japan the time needed to consolidate its empire. The war would have to begin with a massive blow against the U.S. Pacific Fleet. Note that the Japanese placed their emphasis on the attack against the American Pacific Fleet and not against its shore installations on Oahu.

At no time did anyone realize in advance that an attack against the U.S. Pacific Fleet's oil supplies at Pearl, which were then still stored above ground in conventional "tank farms," would force the fleet to withdraw to San Diego, albeit intact. Nor did the Japanese fully realize how efficient the naval establishment ashore was. Each ship the Japanese produced was a unique creation; each captain was told not to lose his ship, for he would never receive another. They failed even to target the far vaster machine shops, repair facilities, and so on which allowed the U.S. Navy to rebuild as rapidly as it did. For all of his knowledge of America, Yamamoto failed to appreciate its true naval strength.

Certainly he had a more immediate concern: gaining approval in Tokyo for his daring Pearl Harbor plan. Here he decided on a drastic move. In July of 1941 he wrote a letter concerning *Operation Hawaii* to Admiral Osami Nagano, chief of the naval general staff, discussing the wisdom of the operation. The document was entrusted to Kuroshima, who was authorized to state that if Tokyo would not approve *Operation Hawaii,* Yamamoto and his entire staff would resign and undertake civilian pursuits. The naval general staff caved in and very reluctantly agreed to the operation, which they code-named *Operation Z,* after the famous Z flag Admiral Togo had flown as his personal banner during the victorious battle in the Straits of Tsushima in 1905.

They gave Yamamoto his way in recognition of his forceful personality, the soundness of many of his basic strategic concepts, and the confidence in him that the emperor had often voiced. Hirohito treasured Yamamoto's opinions almost as much as he did Konoye's. He often remarked to Kido that Yamamoto and Konoye were the only two leaders who would speak to him with complete honesty and candor. Nonetheless, the naval general staff had the gravest reservations about

Operation Z; if it failed Japan would lose the war on the first day. At least one member of that body planned to commit suicide if that should happen.

By nature a gambler, Yamamoto probably enjoyed making his superiors in Tokyo uneasy. He knew the risks involved in *Operation Hawaii* but never voiced the misgivings heard in Tokyo. Instead he strove to ensure the attack's success in all but one respect. He had been willing to tell the naval general staff that he was better informed than they, particularly when it came to air power, but he was not willing to tell the same officers that he was their social equal. He let them choose the commander of the Pearl Harbor attack force, and their choice was not a fortuitous one. Vice Admiral Chuichi Nagumo was selected to command the task force of six carriers and assorted support vessels.

Nagumo was fifty-four years old at the time of his selection. He was a torpedo expert but of the submarine rather than the aerial variety. While not unaggressive, he had little faith in or understanding of naval air power. Hence, he viewed his assignment with trepidation. His colleagues in Tokyo made a somewhat more fortunate choice when they named Rear Admiral Ryunosuke Kusaka as his chief of staff. Kusaka had previously skippered two different carriers. He had no more faith in Yamamoto's plan than Nagumo had, but he gave Yamamoto more credit than did Nagumo; if Yamamoto desired *Operation Hawaii,* Kusaka reasoned that his faith in the plan had to be justified. Kusaka's one constant phrase of advice to his superior was "Don't worry," a phrase for which he became justly famous well before his six carriers reached Hawaiian waters.

The Pearl Harbor task force was officially designated the First Air Fleet. Partially on Genda's advice, one Commander Mitsuo Fuchida, a seemingly fearless and somewhat daredevil aviator, was selected to lead the 350-odd carrier-borne aircraft into their target. The plan called for launching only half the aircraft at one time, because no one had ever launched so large an aerial armada before and theoretically there was risk of confusion, midair collision, and the like. There would be two assault waves, thirty minutes apart. Technically, Fuchida would command only the first wave. That wave would be comprised of forty torpedo bombers, each bearing one long-lance torpedo, horizontal bombers, dive bombers, and the new Zero-type fighters for defense. The second wave would be similarly comprised, except that torpedo bombers would not be included, since they required too great an approach time to their targets once the element of surprise was lost. But whether surprise was achieved or not, Yamamoto meant the attack to go forward. He warned the pilots that they might have to fight their way into the area, a fact that should scotch the stories that the First Air Fleet had orders to abort the mission if it was detected before launch.

The undersea phase of the attack, which scarcely materialized, was intended to reinforce the air attack. The Japanese dispatched fifteen *I*-class submarines to Hawaiian waters, where they arrived some days before the attack. Five of these craft carried midget, two-man subs on their decks that were to be launched prior to the air attack so that they might penetrate the harbor itself once the air attack had begun. Since radio reception is uncertain in an area as close to the equator as Hawaii, and because the subs could transmit or receive only when on the surface, recalling them would have been difficult.

Nor would the attack have been canceled if the American fleet had moved to sea that fateful weekend. Contingency plans had been made for locating the American ships wherever they might be, and the Japanese fervently hoped that the U.S. Pacific Fleet would not be anchored in Pearl, but at the Lahaina anchorage, off the island of Maui. Lahaina's far deeper waters would have insured that any ship the Japanese Navy sunk there could not have been raised and salvaged.

Japan had only one extraordinary source of intelligence concerning Hawaii and the security of America's Pacific Fleet. This was Takeo Yoshikawa. A former officer in the Japanese Navy, Yoshikawa was officially removed from navy service because of poor health and intelligence work was offered him. He arrived in Honolulu at the end of March 1941. At the Japanese consulate he used the name Tadashi Morimura. There is no evidence that he had been told of the Pearl Harbor attack. Nor, contrary to later claims, did he engage in romantic escapades of the spy thriller genre. He kept largely to himself, and most of his intelligence to Tokyo consisted simply of reporting things like what ships were in the harbor at any particular moment. He never used a camera in his work and aroused no suspicions, at least none outside the Japanese consulate.

Yoshikawa was quietly repatriated with the rest of the Japanese diplomatic personnel posted to the United States when war came. Only after the cessation of hostilities did his true role become known. He did provide the Japanese with invaluable reliable information, even if he probably never broke American law. The Japanese indirectly obtained confirmation through him that the fleet was inevitably in port on weekends, was not protected by antitorpedo nets, and that barrage balloons had not been raised in the harbor. He was, in short, a small but vital cog in the Japanese machinery that enabled them to surprise the Americans on the morning of December 7, 1941.

The American Army and Navy leadership on Oahu were unaware of Japan's specific aggressive intent toward the fleet in their care. In part this was because many in Hawaii, and in Washington, deemed it suicide for Japan to initiate hostilities against a power with five times Japan's gross national product. Misunderstanding also played a crucial role in America's estimate of Japanese intentions. If the Japanese leadership thought the average American soft, dedicated to a materialistic life, and unwilling to fight on the other side of the Pacific, many American military leaders believed the Japanese were inferior warriors and particularly unsuited as aviators. More than one American star or flag-grade officer was heard to observe that because of shoddy training, lack of first-rate aircraft, and the Mongolian fold in the ear (which was thought to impair severely the sense of balance), the Japanese aviator was simply not to be taken all that seriously. And, of course, the same arguments that dismayed the naval general staff in Tokyo lent comfort to Hawaii's defenders: Japan had never launched a surprise naval attack so far from home, and so on. Finally, the actual physical climate and the lush tropical vegetation that characterized the Hawaiian islands almost automatically lulled one into a false sense of security. The "Tahiti Syndrome," as some later called it, was no dream. One has to visit or live on the islands to appreciate fully the extent to which nature itself contributed to the Japanese success.

When the fleet lay at anchorage, as it did that Sunday morning, the U.S. Army on Oahu was basically responsible for protecting it. Lt. General Walter Short had commanded the army on the Hawaiian island chain since February of 1941. Short, having taken his officer's oath in 1902, was due for retirement. He would have preferred to live out his final days in khaki stationed in his native Texas, but at George Marshall's specific request, he was posted to Hawaii instead. Short's task was not easy, in that Oahu was traditionally a naval preserve. But he did discourage interservice rivalry and had a fair amount of both men and material to work with in executing his tasks. He ultimately commanded the Hawaiian Air Force, the Army Air Corps contingent on Hawaii. (Officially, the Air Corps became the Army Air Forces in March 1941.) He was also responsible for the only fixed or shore radar that might warn of approaching ships or planes.

So far, so good. But Short, although he unquestionably did his best, simply did not understand the nature of his ultimate task. He revealed later that he believed the danger of a Japanese air raid against Pearl was greatest when the fleet was *not* in port, betraying a misunderstanding not only of his mission but also of just which targets on Oahu the enemy might find most tempting. On at least one occasion he told his pilots that when war came they might find themselves shouldering rifles, a remark that could scarcely have encouraged Air Corps morale. And, perhaps above all, he was preoccupied by the possibility of sabotage.

It is true that over 140,000 Americans of Japanese ancestry lived on Oahu alone, although most were native-born U.S. citizens. Having been impressed with Nazi "fifth column" actions in Europe, Short was convinced that antisabotage measures were his prime task. Unknown to anyone in Washington, he instituted no less then three degrees of military alerts. Alert number one was against sabotage only; alert number two was against sabotage and an air raid; only alert number three was a true alert in that it contemplated dealing with anything the Japanese might attempt, including invasion.

Short did not reveal to Washington his retrograde system of alerts, which had no precedent in modern American military history. George Marshall later accepted blame for not having caught a phrase Short used in detailing the response to one of the war warnings he had received from Washington—Short notified Marshall that he had gone on alert one status. Marshall erred, but the primary blame must fall on Short's shoulders. Short was encouraged in his preoccupation with sabotage by the Honolulu office of the FBI, which was naturally concerned with such matters but overstressed sabotage in its liaison work with Short. Far worse, in the belief that segments of the local population might try to destroy his aircraft, he ordered them parked together in the center of his air fields instead of dispersed around the apron of the fields, a standard precaution against enemy air raid. He also naively assumed that the navy was routinely conducting air patrols to detect enemy air planes; this was not the case. And he did not give sufficient attention to his radar stations. To be sure, the radar at Short's disposal was not the sophisticated device it is today. It had a range of perhaps 150 miles, and there was no way to determine the altitude of a contact.

But Short held it in far more contempt than did the army commanders in Panama or on the West Coast (although not those in Manila), as will be seen.

Short had his faults, but still greater unpreparedness was demonstrated by the navy. Admiral Husband Kimmel was as dedicated an Annapolis man as that institution has ever produced. A graduate of the class of 1904, he had been thirteenth in his class. On February 1, 1941, he assumed the post of commander in chief, U.S. Fleet, which was a misnomer, and also his actual working title, Commander in Chief, Pacific Fleet (CINCPAC). Here Kimmel for the first time in his career may have been over his head. He routinely worked longer hours than any officer probably should, projected an arrogant image, and would not abide criticism even in the most muted form. He demonstrated little grasp of the potential of naval air power and, like many naval leaders of the day, he believed that come the day of reckoning with Japan, he would lead his fleet across the Pacific to the vicinity of the Philippines, where his fleet would engage the Japanese in a classic battleship against battleship encounter that would decide the mastery of the Pacific.

He was an aggressive-minded leader who did not tolerate his word being questioned. Kimmel was greatly concerned by the undeclared naval war in the Atlantic, since his warships and tankers were being taken through the Panama Canal for convoy escort duty against Hitler's submarines. On one occasion he went directly to the White House to arrest further weakening of his fleet. But, as he himself privately admitted to his defense attorney during a subsequent investigation of the Pearl Harbor tragedy, he simply did not believe that the Japanese were capable of attacking his fleet while it was anchored at Pearl. He obviously knew nothing of Yamamoto. Like many leaders, Kimmel believed that the best defense was a good offense, a strategy that could not be expected to protect his fleet when the Japanese would obviously have the luxury of striking the first blow. And, finally, his selection of key subordinates was poor.

In only one case, however, is this significant for the situation at Pearl as the Japanese found it that Sunday morning. Rear Admiral Claude Bloch, Kimmel's third in command, also held the title of commander of the fourteenth naval district. This gave him direct responsibility for coordinating the navy's air and sea patrols with the Army Air Corps in scouting the skies for Japanese intruders. Bloch took this task very lightly. He was in his last post before retirement; evidently he therefore viewed his position as something of a sinecure. The most damning testimony concerning his role in the tragedy came from his own mouth when, during the various investigations following the Japanese attack, he proved himself a master of the nonresponsive reply and outright evasion. His liaison work with the army was particularly sloppy, and Kimmel should have removed him. Hindsight is always twenty-twenty, but in Bloch's case, more than one army officer had been disturbed by his careless performance well before the Japanese attack.

Meanwhile, unknown to anyone at Pearl, Admiral Nagumo's First Air Fleet had begun quietly gathering in November at Hitokappu Bay, north of the home island of Hokkaido, in the Kurile Islands. His task force comprised thirty-three ships. Nagumo would fly his flag from carrier *Akagi,* roughly 40,000 tons, but built from a converted battle cruiser hull. The same was true of her sister carrier, *Kaga.* Two newer but smaller carriers, *Soryu* and *Hiryu,* dating from 1937, were also assigned to the operation, as were two brand new flat tops, *Zuikaku* and *Shokaku,* which would sail to attack Pearl on what was to be, in effect, their maiden voyages. These last two carriers displaced roughly 30,000 tons each.

Two battleships, three cruisers, eleven destroyers, three submarines, and several tankers rounded out Nagumo's flotilla. At 6:00 AM on November 26, 1941, the task force sailed for Pearl Harbor. They stood out to sea undetected. Indeed, they could not have asked for more perfect weather for their purpose of sailing undetected. Nagumo and his officers and crews saw neither sun, moon, nor stars until the morning they launched their attack, which did make navigation difficult. The weather also made their refueling periods more difficult, although no one was lost overboard while refueling, as some contend. They took a course to Pearl following a northern route, which offered the least possible chance of detection. The identical route had been followed by several passenger liners belonging to the Japanese government, and the area was generally vacant sea, devoid of any maritime traffic. They did not have permission to attack when they sailed, however. But on December 2 they received the message, *"Yama Niitaka nobore"*—*climb Mount Niitaka,* giving them authorization to attack their prey. Obviously, by that date the Japanese government was absolutely convinced

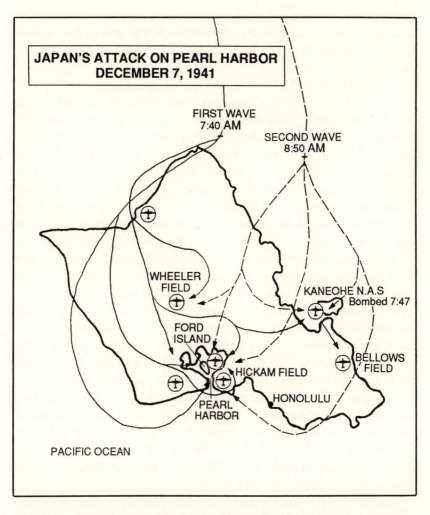

JAPAN'S ATTACK ON PEARL HARBOR
DECEMBER 7, 1941

FIRST WAVE
7:40 AM

SECOND WAVE
8:50 AM

WHEELER
FIELD

KANEOHE N.A.S
Bombed 7:47

FORD
ISLAND

BELLOWS
FIELD

HICKAM FIELD

HONOLULU

PEARL
HARBOR

PACIFIC OCEAN

that war was a necessity. Nagumo's fleet sailed in a complete communication blackout, in seas heavy with swells.

On December 7 they reached launch position, which was supposed to be 200 miles north of Pearl but was in actual fact 180 miles north, a small error indicative of their excellent navigation given the weather. At 5:30 AM Nagumo launched two high-altitude scout planes, one to overfly Pearl itself, the other to fly over the Lahaina anchorage. These were tracked by the army signal corps radar station at Opana Point, which covered the island's northern approaches. The radar information center at Ft. Shafter assumed they were friendlies. No one could guess

their altitude, and the radar set itself operated only from 4:00 to 7:00
AM. Hawaii was then almost exclusively a playground of the wealthy,
no small number of whom had private planes that could and did produce blips that morning.

A little before 6:00 AM Nagumo turned his carriers into the wind
and began the launch of his first assault wave. The pitch of the carriers
was fifteen degrees that morning. Normally, with a pitch of over five
degrees, the launching would have been canceled; at a fifteen-degree
pitch, the carriers rode up and down on each successive swell, necessi-
tating each pilot to begin his launch run as the carrier rode downward
in order to clear the end of the carrier deck as it pitched upward.
Worse, waves crashed over the carriers' decks. This was dangerous, and
had water shorted out the circuits of the forward flight elevators, Nagumo
could have launched no more aircraft. Of the 180-odd aircraft comprising
the first wave, only one was lost in launch. The second wave, launched
soon after the first, had no casualties. Nagumo now had 351 aircraft
speeding toward Pearl, about ninety minutes due south.

It was almost, but not quite, a routine morning at Pearl Harbor. The
Japanese *I*-class subs and their five midget sister craft had arrived in
Hawaiian waters some days before. As the aviators had feared, the
submariners were overzealous, for at 6:45 AM destroyer *Ward* had
opened fire on one of the Japanese midgets, which had jumped the gun
by attempting to enter the harbor's mouth. *Ward* promptly notified the
fourteenth naval district, but her report met initial skepticism, since
earlier supposed sightings had proven false. The report reached Bloch
and then Kimmel. Kimmel admitted he was not certain what the report
meant but agreed to come to his office to await its verification. By the
time he arrived there, war had erupted.

Similarly, the Opana Point radar station picked up both incoming
waves of Japanese aircraft, but again Japanese luck held. The radar
contact, reported just after 7:00 AM to the radar information center at
Ft. Shafter, was written off as routine because a flight of B–17s was
due in that morning from the West Coast, and, like the Japanese, they
had orders to approach Oahu from the north. Indeed, whenever aircraft
were due in from California, the military would pay one of Honolulu's
two radio stations to remain on the air all night so that the incoming
planes could home in on its signal. The Japanese did not know this in
advance, but in their aircraft Fuchida and his men received last-minute
weather reports from the American station and were able to make

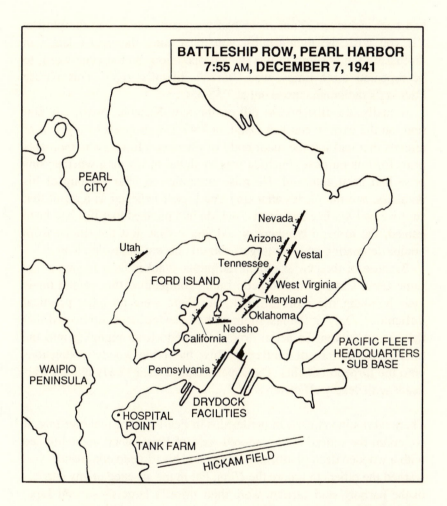

BATTLESHIP ROW, PEARL HARBOR
7:55 AM, DECEMBER 7, 1941

PEARL CITY

Nevada

Arizona

Utah

Vestal

Tennessee

FORD ISLAND

West Virginia

Maryland

Oklahoma

Neosho

California

PACIFIC FLEET
HEADQUARTERS
•SUB BASE

WAIPIO
PENINSULA

Pennsylvania

DRYDOCK
FACILITIES

•HOSPITAL
POINT

TANK FARM

HICKAM FIELD

minor course corrections by using the station's signal. Still, Fuchida grew apprehensive as he approached his target, since the cloud cover began to thicken. If he overflew his target, the sound of his planes' engines would certainly alert Pearl's defenders. Then, suddenly—even dramatically—the clouds parted and the island of Oahu was evident. In minutes, traditional American isolation from "foreign entanglement" would be history.

Japanese do not think in fortune cookie English any more than Americans do. However, Yamamoto himself had selected the code word with which Fuchida was to signal Nagumo's ships that surprise had been achieved. Yamamoto had frequently employed the phrase, "If you wish the tiger's cubs, you must enter the tiger's lair," in discussing the wisdom of the Hawaii operation. So the code word, to be repeated three times, was *"tora"*—literally, *tiger*. This phrase Fuchida's radioman tapped out at 7:53 AM.

Actually, the first bombs fell on the new Kaneohe Naval Air Station, on the eastern coast of Oahu, at 7:47 AM, dropped by a group of aircraft that had left the main body of Fuchida's force some moments prior for this purpose. Fuchida was to signal to his men whether surprise had been achieved. He miscommunicated with a group of his bombers, and the planes attacking Pearl itself believed as a result that surprise had *not* been attained. Fuchida had planned that if it had been gained, the torpedo bombers would attack first, lest the smoke from bombs detonating on other targets should obscure Battleship Row.

Because of the confusion, all the pilots attacked their targets at the same time; some of the torpedo pilots complained that smoke made their bombing run more difficult, but there were no other practical difficulties. Only at the last moment had the Japanese discovered that they could prevent an aerial dropped torpedo from plunging into the mud at the bottom of Battleship Row by fixing wooden extensions onto the torpedo tail fins. The Japanese used their newly altered warheads with deadly efficiency.

There were nine American battleships in Pearl Harbor that morning, if we count the retired *Utah,* moored west of Ford Island and equipped with a wooden deck platform. Fuchida and his torpedo commander had warned the others to ignore the *Utah,* but in the absence of any carriers in the harbor—and carriers were their priority targets—several Japanese pilots attacked her. There were eight serviceable battleships in port that morning, counting *Pennsylvania,* the flagship of the fleet, which was in drydock. Three of the seven battleships on Battleship Row were anchored alone, while *Tennessee* with *West Virginia,* and *Maryland* with *Oklahoma* were anchored in tandem. The inside ships in the pairs were invulnerable to torpedo attack and sustained the slightest damage. Since an aerial attack of this magnitude against heavily armored naval vessels was such a novel experience, the Japanese were forced to use innovative techniques. Because they did not possess a bomb capable of penetrating a battleship's gun turret, the Japanese placed fins on armor-piercing shells from battleship *Nagato* and dropped them from their high-level bombers. These shells were responsible for the destruction of the battleship *Arizona.*

On December 6 *Arizona* had reportedly received too large a supply of powder; rather than return the excess, it had been temporarily stored outside the forward magazine in passageway areas. Whatever the truth to this report, when an armor-piercing shell penetrated the *Arizona's* number-two forward turret, it produced an explosion that detonated the forward magazine, lifting the ship out of the water and breaking her in two. The explosion was awesome. The ship was surmounted by a huge fireball, flecked with bits of debris and exploding shells from her magazine. It actually put *out* fires on the adjacent repair ship *Vestal,* littering her deck with bodies and debris. Windows in downtown Honolulu were reportedly shattered by the blast. The *Arizona,* broken in two, settled into the mud of Battleship Row, fracturing the water mains that supplied Ford Island. A clock later found during salvage operations aboard the ship has its hands fused to its face at 8:06 AM, very probably the exact moment of the ship's destruction. Over a thousand men died in that single moment. Her captain, on the bridge, was cremated instantly; a rescue party later found only a puddle of melted gold where he had been standing: it was his Annapolis class ring, all that remained except ashes.

As torpedoes tore into the vitals of the ships on Battleship Row, diesel oil poured into the harbor, for in American battleships the ship's fuel was stored between the inner and outer hulls, inviting a fire if any battleship took even one torpedo. The oil made swimming almost impossible for survivors. Its eventual ignition produced awesome billows of jet black smoke. Patches of burning oil drifted down to the harbor's mouth and literally out to sea with the tide. Many survivors to this day remember the burning oil as the most threatening spectacle they have ever witnessed.

Several ships' captains gave the signal "all ships sortie," although it was eventually canceled by Kimmel, who suspected, correctly, that Japanese submarines might be lurking outside the harbor's mouth. The largest ship to leave the harbor was the cruiser *St. Louis.* Very early on in the attack, the radio signal "air raid Pearl Harbor this is no drill" had been flashed out from two separate sources at almost the same moment (later it was amended to "air raid Pearl Harbor, this is not drill") but it was the announcement as first worded that forever woke most Americans from their long isolationist somnolence. Nonetheless

Honolulu's two radio stations continued for a time with their standard Sunday morning fare, although early on they did request all service personnel to return to their posts.

Kimmel arrived in his office during the attack but could only watch helplessly as great ships, albeit outdated dreadnoughts, died before him. In addition, the Japanese strafed the airfields and bombed planes, which were conveniently bunched together in the center of the fields. By 8:35 AM, the first wave had finished its work and began winging its way back toward Nagumo's carriers. A lull of about twenty minutes ensued, during which Fuchida remained over the harbor.

By 9:00 AM the second wave, commanded by Lt. Commander Shigekazu Shimazaki, arrived. As Pearl came into view, the sight that greeted his fliers must have riveted their attention. The pride of the American Pacific fleet lay burning in the harbor: battleships *Maryland* and *Tennessee* damaged, *Arizona* destroyed, *Oklahoma* capsized, *California* and *West Virginia* resting on the bottom of the harbor, their superstructures still burning. *Nevada* was the only survivor capable of getting underway after the first attack, and she made a run for the mouth of the harbor.

Nevada had steam up on her gauges when the attack had commenced because the captain had wished to test her newly reconditioned boilers. She had taken a few hits from contact bombs, but retained sufficient watertight integrity to allow her to attempt to clear the harbor and enter the open seas, where she could maneuver freely. *Nevada* became the primary target of the second wave's attack. Fuchida and other Japanese pilots had realized that if they could sink just one such ship in the harbor's narrow mouth, they would bottle up the entire harbor for months. F. W. Scanland, captain of the *Nevada,* realized that as well, and opted to beach his ship after she took several more direct hits rather than risk closing Pearl indefinitely.

By this time American antiaircraft batteries were putting up a spirited defense. Admiral Kimmel, who had placed great emphasis on rote training, had not realized that frequent handling of the delayed fuses in antiaircraft shells would damage them. Moreover, storing the ammunition at the ready, where it was subject to physical shock and the elements, caused it to deteriorate as well. Consequently, Kimmel's training programs paid off in a rapid rate of fire but ineffective marksmanship. The army had not practiced such tactics and scored a much higher rate of accuracy; in contrast, many of the naval shells actually plummeted to earth in downtown Honolulu, several miles away, where they exploded and caused substantial damage.

The final target of the Japanese attack was the flagship *Pennsylvania,* which received several hits from contact bombs before its drydock was flooded in an attempt to control fires. Unfortunately the water that rushed in from the harbor became covered by a heavy layer of diesel fuel from the ship's own fractured fuel tanks. This oil ignited and caused the magazines of the destroyers *Cassin* and *Downes,* sharing the drydock forward of the flagship, to explode. The intensity of the resulting fires actually buckled the armor plates of the *Pennsylvania.*

By 10:00 AM the attack had terminated, though few at Pearl realized it. The Japanese had lost only 29 of their 351 planes. Nagumo had been told he might expect to lose about one-third of his planes and ships, so he was all the more elated at this stunning victory. When Fuchida arrived back aboard the carrier *Akagi,* he urged that a third wave be immediately readied. Nagumo, however, was already planning to retire and return to Japan. Air commander Genda, who had not taken part in the attack, argued together with Fuchida that one should press one's advantage to the utmost.

Fuchida also reported that he had seen a plane with carrier markings land at Pearl during the attack. This was correct. Carrier *Enterprise* was closing on Pearl; she was only 200 miles distant when the attack began. Genda volunteered to lead half the aircraft aloft to search for American carriers, while Fuchida would return to Pearl to bomb American shore installations and what remained of the American fleet. There was ample daylight left to accomplish all of these tasks and still retire safely with a total victory in hand, while most of the pilots stated they were not fatigued and were ready for the job. Nagumo argued that a great victory had already been won, and that he did not feel authorized to leave Japan's strike force in jeopardy any longer than absolutely necessary. Furthermore, he averred that its supply of oil was low, and that American submarines might find them. And, admittedly, another attack would be no surprise. That was the end of the conversation; the First Air Fleet, its location still undetected by the Americans, turned westward and steamed out of Hawaiian waters, its job only half done.

The military on Oahu had not located Nagumo's fleet, a failure that was perhaps, in a sense, greater than having been caught by surprise. Achieving surprise is always, to a degree, a measure of luck. But in searching to the south, using *Enterprise's* planes to assist, the military authorities gave the Japanese both a tactical and strategic victory. And the American Navy was still capable of action, since Kimmel possessed numerous cruisers, destroyers, and submarines with which the attack could be carried to the enemy fleet.

But navy and army personnel at Pearl did not realize that the Japanese were retiring. Indeed, they began preparing for the worst. Many expected not only renewed air attacks but an actual invasion. Having underestimated the Japanese for so many years, the pendulum now swung the other way and the Japanese Navy was suddenly given credit for much more offensive potential than it possessed. Many trained, seasoned observers later swore (under oath) that enemy air attacks continued until dusk. General Short mobilized the local militia and retired to the Aliamanu Crater, where he prepared to repulse the expected invasion. Families of naval officers boarded buses and moved "inland." Since there was very little actual inland, the drivers were instructed to continue driving until they received new orders. Soldiers were posted at defensive positions along the coastline and awaited the first waves of Japanese troops. Rumors also spread that the Japanese had poisoned the local drinking water supply. Thus, no few residents of Oahu resorted to bottled liquids, some of the alcoholic variety. One of the local residents, evidently noted for his sobriety, reported that he had spotted a dog on Ewa Beach barking, obviously in code to an offshore Japanese submarine. The report was actually checked out, although it is very doubtful that it was really taken seriously.

Less humorous was the naked vengeance some pilots exacted on the Japanese population of Hawaii. The local fishing fleet, almost all without radios, were deliberately tagged as "unidentified" vessels. American planes shot them out of the water, some several days after the attack. When survivors complained to the authorities, they were informed that Japanese aircraft planes were responsible. Many innocent people in uniform and out also lost their lives during the next few nights as they were unable to respond with the proper code word or phrase when suddenly challenged by trigger-happy sentries.

The Japanese had succeeded in neutralizing the American fleet. They had also killed nearly 4,000 Americans, if we count those who later died of infection and related causes. Of 231 U.S. Army planes on Pearl, 166 were reportedly repairable or untouched; of 250 naval aircraft, only 54 remained. But the American carriers, not in port that morning, were untouched, as were the shore installations, tank farms included. As for the battleships, they were in reality World War I–type dreadnoughts, which, when raised (all but two, excluding the *Utah,* saw action again), were to prove valuable in bombarding islands prior to an amphibious landing but played no other substantial role in the conflict. And of course the very fact of a surprise attack, begun before Japan's ambassadors in Washington could deliver notice of termination of economic negotiations, united the American people against Japan as nothing else could have done. For all of these reasons, Yamamoto considered the attack to be but 50 percent successful. Some commentators have contended that the Pearl attack was virtual suicide for the Japanese in the long run, but without it, they felt Japan could not safely embark on the conquest of the Eldorado of the South. Hence, whatever the long-range consequences, it was a short-term victory in every sense, undertaken, in the end, regardless of the risks or international morality involved.

Kimmel, Bloch, and Short, in that order, must bear responsibility for being caught unawares. Apologists claim that Washington withheld vital information from them. Some point to the "winds execute" phrase (so-called by later congressional investigating committees)— "East Wind Rain"—as evidence that Washington deliberately denied Kimmel and Short vital information. Much ink has been spilled concerning this relatively minor matter. Briefly, several weeks before, anticipating that normal communications with embassies abroad might be ruptured, Tokyo had arranged to signal imminent danger of war with America by including the phrase "East Wind Rain" in commercial weather forecasts to alert the Washington embassy that war was near. No evidence can be found that the Japanese ever used this "winds execute" phrase. And why should they have? Normal communication remained intact through the attack. And even had they employed it, the phrase merely signalled imminent *danger* of war. Similarly unimportant was the fact that the *Magic* staff decrypted several intercepts from the spy Yoshikawa in Honolulu detailing the position of Kimmel's warships and indicating the direction from which torpedo planes might best attack them.

After the event it is easy to pick out the relevant clues from a mass of raw "noise." Kimmel and Short knew nothing of the "winds execute" plan and they were not notified of Yoshikawa's telegrams. It seems scarcely likely that these clues would have made any difference.

If an intruding enemy submarine, and a midget one at that, almost certainly operating from mother craft, does not suffice to indicate that hostilities are imminent, it seems doubtful that knowledge of Yoshikawa's telegrams would have altered events. All diplomatic legations gather information of this sort, although it should have been transmitted to Kimmel and Short as a routine security precaution, since it did directly concern the potential security of the fleet. But in view of the fact that no one thought the Japanese capable of launching an attack at Pearl, Yoshikawa's telegrams are insignificant. Witness that when the Marines at Kaneohe Naval Air Station phoned Kimmel's headquarters and indicated in language as strong and with as much urgency as could be mustered that they were under Japanese attack, they were told to knock off the nonsense and sober up. In the end, the very daring nature of the scheme insured its success: the American commanders at Pearl can only be blamed to a degree for not anticipating what was considered, by the best naval minds of the day, to be impossible, or very nearly so.

Suggestions for Further Reading

The definitive work on the planning of the Pearl Harbor attack is *At Dawn We Slept* by Gordon W. Prange (New York: McGraw-Hill, 1980), from which the authors have taken many details of this narrative. Hiroyuki Agawa's *The Reluctant Admiral: Yamamoto and the Imperial Navy* (New York: Kodansha, 1979) is the best biography of Yamamoto available. Roberta Wohlsetter's *Pearl Harbor: Warning and Decision* (Stanford, CA: Stanford University Press, 1962) gives the American background of the attack. A. A. Hoehling, *The Week before Pearl Harbor* (New York: Norton, 1963) relates something of a personal view of the personalities in the nation's capital relevant to the Pearl Harbor saga. The definitive account of the Pearl Harbor attack itself is *December 7, 1941: The Day the Japanese Attacked Pearl Harbor* by Gordon W. Prange (New York: McGraw-Hill, 1988), but see also: Edwin T. Layton, *And I Was There: Pearl Harbor and Midway—Breaking the Secrets* (New York: Morrow, 1985); Kazuo Sakamaki, *I Attacked Pearl Harbor* (New York: Associated Press, 1949); Andrew Lind, *Hawaii's Japanese: An Experiment in Democracy* (Princeton, NJ: Princeton University Press, 1946); Allen Gwenfread, *Hawaii's War Years* (Honolulu: University of Hawaii Press, 1950); and Correspondents of *Time, Life,* and *Fortune* magazines, *December 7: The First Thirty Hours* (New York: Knopf, 1942). F. C. Jones's, *Japan's New Order: Its Rise and Fall, 1937–45* (London: Oxford University Press, 1954) is an outdated but still useful work. John Stefan's *Hawaii under the Rising Sun: Japan's Plans for Conquest after Pearl Harbor* (Honolulu: University of Hawaii Press, 1984) is an interesting speculative piece.

3. From Pearl Harbor to Java Sea

MacArthur and the Philippines
The War Spreads
The Fall of the Philippines
More Japanese Victories
A New Kind of War

The failure of the American military on Oahu to anticipate the Japanese attack is perhaps understandable. No such excuse can be proffered to explain the negligence of U.S. Army command in the Philippines. General Douglas MacArthur has less excuse than any of the other American commanders on Pearl Harbor day. A graduate of West Point, class of 1903, his first posting was to the Philippines, where he assisted his father, who was the military governor of the islands. MacArthur then had been an observer of the Russo-Japanese war in 1905. He had been received in audience by the emperor Meiji and was conversant with Japanese military strategy and tactics. Perhaps partially due to an overly doting mother (she had lived on post at the Point during his four years as a cadet), he was sadly involved with his own ego, and reliable evidence indicates that he was suicidal by the 1930s. Forced in 1935 to resign as army chief of staff by President Franklin Roosevelt because he was discovered to have a Eurasian mistress, MacArthur resigned his commission as well and became field marshall of the newly forming Philippine Army. The most revealing account of his personality was dispatched to London during the conflict by a British observer at his headquarters. It read in part:

> He is shrewd, selfish, proud, remote, highly-strung and vastly vain. He has imagination, self-confidence, physical courage and charm, but no humor about himself, no regard for truth, and is unaware of these defects. He mistakes his emotions and ambitions for principles. With moral depth he would be a great man: as it is he is a near-miss, which may be worse than a mile.

MacArthur did his best to prepare the Filipinos to meet the Japanese on the beachheads. "War Plan Orange" called for a retreat from Manila and central Luzon to the Bataan Peninsula and the island of Corregidor once the Japanese landed, to await relief from the American Navy. MacArthur discarded the plan as defeatist. In July 1941 he regained his commission in the U.S. Army. He was awakened early on the morning of December 8, local time, and informed of the attack on Pearl Harbor.

He evidently panicked or else demonstrated nothing short of criminal stupidity by misinterpreting Japan's hostile intentions. With his talent for insulating himself from reality, MacArthur had not even heard of radar until the fall of 1941, when Admiral Thomas Hart explained to him the principles and benefits of the new technology. As soon as the attack on Pearl had been verified, Army Air Corps General Lewis Brereton asked his permission for a preemptive strike against Japanese airfields on Formosa. MacArthur denied the request; he even claimed Brereton had not made it, which is untrue and all the more damning, for as supreme commander for the Philippine area, *MacArthur should have then ordered such a strike himself.* As a direct result, nine hours after Pearl Harbor his air force was destroyed on the ground at Clark Field, north of Manila. The bulk of his planes were lost, including eighteen B–17s and fifty-three P–40s.

Not only had the Philippines been warned that Pearl had been attacked, but it had always been assumed that in the event of war, MacArthur's air force would be a primary Japanese target. Evidently, however, a contingency plan did not exist to protect them. The American people already had villains in the persons of Kimmel and Short, who could, to a degree, plead that an attack against Pearl could not have been anticipated. In the case of MacArthur, his most ardent followers to this day cannot excuse his negligence. He was not relieved of command, as were Kimmel and Short, presumably because calling public attention to his errors would have made the entire American command structure in the Pacific seem incompetent.

All of this greatly affected the leadership in Washington. President Roosevelt remained calm, despite telephone calls from congressmen urging that the West Coast be abandoned and that battle lines be established in the Rocky Mountains. The military wished to surround the White House with tanks, but this Roosevelt wisely rejected. On Monday, December 8, Roosevelt addressed the Congress and asked for a declaration of war against Japan only, which was promptly voted. Roosevelt did not mention Germany or Italy, despite the fact that many in Washington evidently believed that the Germans were behind the attack (in fact, Germany had been told nothing of the Pearl attack plan), and some even believed that Germans had piloted some of the attacking aircraft at Pearl as well as the Philippines. Several days before the attack, *Magic* intercepts had indicated that Hitler had promised that Germany would unquestionably declare war against America should Japan do so. Three days later Hitler kept his promise, and Italy similarly followed with a declaration of war. (The United States declared war on Germany and Italy on December 11.) Roosevelt did ask that a state of war be declared to exist with Japan as of the moment of the attack, since the navy had already ordered the initiation of unrestricted submarine warfare against Japan.

In London, Prime Minister Winston Churchill went to bed the evening after Pearl Harbor more relaxed than he had been since the war in Europe had begun. He was now certain of ultimate Anglo-American victory over Nazi Germany as well as Japan. But in a very few hours he began to experience reservations. Evidently one or more members of the American embassy in London indicated that America might devote almost its full military might to crushing Japan first. There had been talk between the Americans and British of a ''Germany-first'' policy as early as January 1941, should the United States find itself at war. Churchill was all the more genuinely alarmed and quickly arranged to visit Washington that coming Christmas for a conference on overall strategy. A full-dress conference ensued, code-named *Arcadia*.

On the evening of December 22, 1941, Churchill arrived in Washington and was billeted on the second floor of the executive mansion itself. Roosevelt and Churchill rather quickly reaffirmed the Germany-first policy, the details of which took several weeks to hammer out. At Roosevelt's suggestion they discussed the appointment of a supreme commander for all Allied forces in the Far East. The president himself suggested General Archibald Wavell, former commander of the British eighth army in Egypt, then in India. When he was informed of his appointment, Wavell dryly remarked, ''I have heard of men having to hold the baby, but this is twins.'' Wavell made haste to inspect his command. Little did he know how short-lived it would be.

Concomitant with the attack on Pearl Harbor, the Japanese struck other Allied territories as well. The U.S. possessions of Midway Atoll, Wake, and Guam Islands were bombarded on December 8, Japanese time. The island of Guam, a U.S. possession since the Spanish-American war, had never fully been absorbed into the American Pacific commonwealth. The military establishment in the United States had chosen not to strengthen Guam's small garrison force nor to equip her with any defensive weapons larger than a .30-caliber machine gun. After a brief struggle in which seventeen Americans and one Japanese soldier lost their lives, Guam fell to Japan on December 12, 1941.

Similarly, the American garrison of 300 marines and civilian volunteers on Wake Island was forced to stage a futile defense against a far superior Japanese force from December 11 to 23. Although the Americans were able to rout the first invasion wave of 560 Japanese Marines on December 11, the garrison fell to a much larger force twelve days later. The defense of Wake Island, however, proved to be the high point of America's initial resistance to the Japanese offensive of December 1941, accounting for the loss of 500 Japanese soldiers, two destroyers, and several landing vessels. These casualties were caused largely by the small air force delivered to Wake by the carrier *Lexington* just prior to the attack on Pearl, along with shore artillery batteries commanded by Major James Devereux. Most of Wake's garrison was executed by the Japanese in October 1943, after being forced to rebuild the runways and buildings destroyed during the preinvasion bombardments.

The British crown colony of Hong Kong, thirty-two square miles in size, was besieged on December 8 by the veteran Japanese Thirty-Eighth Army Division. Retreating to the island portion of that colony, a small force of regulars and volunteers held out as long as the water supply lasted. Lack of water would have meant epidemics, and on Christmas Day they capitulated.

To the south, the British were much more confident, indeed even smug. The fortress of Singapore had been touted as impregnable by assault from the sea. It had been fortified during the 1920s at a cost of millions of pounds sterling. British plans called for the defenders to hold out until the arrival of the American Navy would lift the siege. Lt. General Arthur Percival was in charge of the multinational garrison at Singapore. Eight- to fifteen-inch naval rifles defended the seaward approaches and it was generally assumed that the fortress could hold out against a siege for up to ninety days. No one had foreseen that the American fleet might be resting on the bottom of its anchorage by the end of the first day of the conflict.

At 5:45 AM Hawaiian time (11:45 PM local time) on December 7–8,

Japanese forces commanded by Lt. General Tomoyuki Yamashita landed at Kota Bharu on the eastern coast of the Malay Peninsula. The initial invasion took place two hours before the air raid on Pearl Harbor. Originally the schedules were to coincide, but Yamamoto argued that adherence to this timetable, to which he had initially agreed, would force his Pearl Harbor task force to launch its strike well before dawn, and he requested that the army delay its bombardment and landing by two hours. This was refused. As it turned out, Winston Churchill heard of the air raid on Pearl before news of the Malay invasion reached him.

Complacency was the order of the day in Singapore, despite the fact that its fortifications were seaward only, and useless if the Japanese penetrated the Malay Peninsula and attacked the city from the rear. When Percival telephoned the governor of the colony to inform him of the Japanese invasion, Shenton Thomas replied, "Well, I suppose you'll shove the little men off." There was some reason for optimism. One of Britain's newest battleships, the *Prince of Wales,* accompanied by the battle cruiser *Repulse,* had recently anchored in Singapore harbor. And many in both the navy as well as the army regarded the peninsula as impenetrable. It is 600 miles long, is transected north to south by a mountain range, and has dense jungle and deep rivers.

The Japanese attack plan consisted of securing British air strips in the northern portion of the peninsula and then using them to support the drive through the interior. Eventually, they would drive the British back to the island of Singapore itself, which is separated from the end of the peninsula by the narrow, shallow Straits of Johore. There were to be no carriers used in support of this campaign; thus, securing the British airfields took first priority. After the Japanese had taken the airfield at Kota Bharu, they began shuttling planes to it from bases in southern Indochina. It was during one of these transfers that the *Prince of Wales* and *Repulse* were discovered searching for the supply vessels of the Japanese Army. Percival had ordered Vice Admiral Thomas Phillips to take his ships north and destroy the supply ships of the Japanese invasion force. Phillips had protested on the grounds that he had no air cover. Percival could promise nothing to Phillips; however, a handful of antiquated Brewster Buffalo aircraft did attempt to support his sortie after news of a Japanese attack against them was received.

When the Japanese pilots first encountered the *Prince of Wales,* they were hesitant. They had studied American ship silhouettes, but not those of the Royal Navy. The *Prince of Wales* bore a striking similarity to a Japanese *Kongo*-class battleship. Not until the pilots dropped to 1,500 feet were they sure of the identity of their target. In less than two hours both capital ships had been sunk, at a cost of four Japanese aircraft. More significant than the loss to the Singapore garrison was the fact that a fully operational battleship under full steam and with full freedom of maneuver had been sunk by aircraft, a fact that stunned Yamamoto's critics in the naval ministry.

Percival had over 80,000 men to hold the peninsula and thus slightly outnumbered the Japanese. These he strung out thinly, to stop the three-pronged Japanese advance down the peninsula. Morale was at its nadir in the British divisions, particularly among the Indian troops, who resented being treated as inferiors. Morale took a further blow when it was learned that the government of Thailand, after little resistance, had agreed to surrender to the Japanese. (This was primarily the work of several pro-Japanese in the Thai government.) Malaya was now cut off from Burma. Percival gave uninspired leadership and very little guidance of any sort. Retreating to the island of Singapore itself, he deployed his men around the perimeter of the island to repulse a Japanese landing. On the night of February 8–9, 1942, the Japanese swarmed across the Straits of Johore and were soon ashore, for Percival had left no reserves for a counterattack.

By February 13 the defenders had regrouped just north of the city and were evidently preparing to contest its possession block by block. Japanese aircraft flew at will over the city, and Percival would not order a complete blackout lest British residents of the city be overly offended; he ordered a "brownout" instead, which supposedly shielded the more tempting targets from Japanese bombsights. By the morning of February 15, when the city's last remaining water reservoir had fallen to the Japanese, they had not yet reached the city limit itself. Apprised by his commissioner of public health of the resultant danger of an epidemic, Percival requested a truce.

Yamashita was not sure of Percival's intent in doing so. His own army, which had advanced partly on bicycles, was chronically short of ammunition because of the length of its supply lines and its unexpectedly rapid advance. Also, his troops were using amphetamine sulfate to limit the need for rest, and many were reaching the limit of their physical endurance. In particular, Yamashita feared that the British

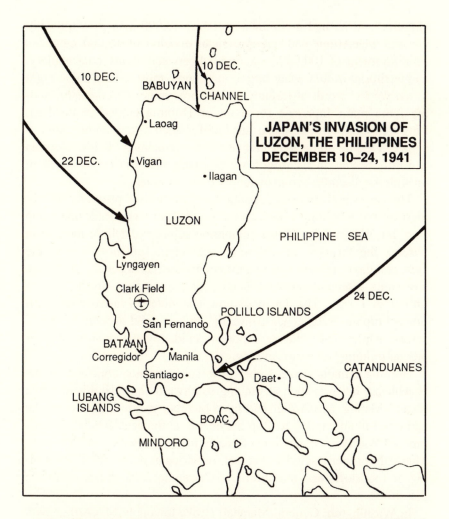

would contest the city piecemeal, which was in fact what Churchill had ordered. Great was Yamashita's relief when he learned that the British would capitulate outright. Fighting ceased at about 8:30 PM on February 15. The emperor proclaimed a special holiday, as he had for Pearl Harbor, but Singapore Day witnessed far greater celebrations. Even schoolchildren were sent on holiday, a very rare event in Japan, and the entire nation celebrated the fall of Britain's vaunted Gibraltar of the Pacific.

The fall of Singapore caused dismay in the Philippines. The Japanese had entrusted the capture of the Philippines to General Masaharu

Homma, and he had a combined total of 43,000 men to work with. General MacArthur had one American division of 15,000 men; his Filipino forces of 100,000 men, divided between scouts, constabulary, and territorial militia, were largely untrained, most having about eight to ten weeks' worth of training. After some minor diversionary landings, the main Japanese force under Homma landed in northern Lingayen Gulf, which MacArthur had foreseen as the landing area of choice. Despite some interference by the remaining B–17s, Homma had little trouble in securing his initial landings or in following them up with the disembarkation of supply train columns.

The very small American Asiatic Fleet, comprised primarily of submarines but including a few cruisers and destroyers, sank one troop ship, but nothing else. Some submarine skippers did little more than observe the Japanese approaching, submerge, and move out of the area, and then surface to radio their enemy contact. Then on Christmas Eve came a second Japanese landing at Lamon Bay, on the eastern littoral of Luzon. The Japanese now encountered varied resistance. Some Filipino units, at least initially, gave a good account of themselves, while others did very poorly; evidently the quality of their prewar training had varied greatly.

Homma's main strike force, however, was not confined to the beachhead, but was soon advancing southward along Highway Three toward Manila. MacArthur had no choice but to admit tacitly that he had erred in attempting to stop the enemy at the beachheads. He now ordered War Plan Orange into effect. Evidently only then was the prior MacArthur order rescinded that had forbidden as defeatist the stockpiling of foodstuffs and munitions on Corregidor. The result would be disastrous.

In Washington, General Marshall strove to supply MacArthur with every sort of reinforcement, but his efforts were largely in vain. The Washington naval establishment, understandably shaken by the Pearl Harbor attack, were convinced that supplies could not be gotten further than Australia. Some freelance merchant marine "captains" refused at any price to move into Philippine waters, which had been mined and declared blockaded by the Japanese. And given the Europe-first decision, any reinforcements sent would only have been destroyed or surrendered to the Japanese. This MacArthur, perhaps understandably, would never understand, much less forgive.

On January 6, 1942, the last retreating American troops reached the

Bataan Peninsula, where they were now besieged. The total number on that rocky peninsula included 15,000 Americans and about 65,000 Filipino troops, with enough food for about a month. Also, there were over 25,000 civilians who had retreated with the armies, and they too had to be fed. At this juncture the Japanese made one of their few errors. Homma had taken from his command the battle-seasoned Forty-Eighth Division, which was now detailed for the conquest of Java. Its replacements were over-aged garrison troops from Formosa with little battle experience. And Homma failed to recognize that the Allied forces were determined to fight, despite the severe shortage of foodstuffs. By early February Homma realized he faced a far greater task than was at first apparent; he withdrew to consolidate, and until April 3 the Bataan front was relatively quiet.

Meanwhile, on February 23, 1942, Roosevelt had ordered MacArthur to leave the Philippines for Australia. On March 12, MacArthur, accompanied by his wife and son, left Corregidor in a PT boat. On March 17 he reached the vicinity of Port Darwin in Australia, during a Japanese raid on the harbor's facilities. Command on Bataan and Corregidor had been left to Major General Jonathan Wainwright. On the evening of May 5 Wainwright, pushed back to the tunnels in Corregidor, began surrender negotiations. His troops were hungry and sick. By May 9 all American units in the Philippines had surrendered, although some individual groups on islands south of Luzon disobeyed orders and fought on as guerrilla units. The first of the Bataan death marches had meanwhile begun on April 11. About 600 Americans and many more Filipinos perished by deliberate Japanese cruelty. But others following the same route were relatively well treated; evidently much depended on the personality of the officers commanding each individual march.

Japan next advanced into British Borneo to seize its oil fields. Then a three-pronged attack was mounted against the Dutch East Indies. The great prize was the central island of Java. Here the Japanese were aided by the native population, who had been much oppressed under Dutch rule. Small paratroop units were even used by the Japanese. On the night of February 28, the first Japanese landed on Java itself. This led to the Battle of the Java Sea. The Dutch had built a small but modern battle fleet in the late 1930s. After Hitler overran Holland, the Dutch fleet was posted to the East Indies. On the evening of January

27, Rear Admiral K.W. Doorman sought out the Japanese in order to interdict their troop transports bound for Java. In three separate engagements, he lost his ships. Two Dutch cruisers and two British destroyers were sunk. In a later action, one American and one Austrian cruiser were also lost. On March 8 all of Java capitulated to the Japanese.

Burma, bordering on British India, suffered a similar fate. It had first been attacked as early as December 11, when two key airfields in the southernmost portion of the country were seized. Having lived under British rule for scarcely two generations (the entire country had not been occupied by the British until 1885), the Burmese openly aided the Japanese. The seizure of Burma would threaten India, which was already ripe for revolt against British rule, deal a crippling blow to British pride in their *Raj,* and cut the Burma Road, leaving China completely isolated. Lt. General Shojiro Iida jumped off from the northern Malay Peninsula on January 20. The only British hope was the monsoon rains, which would begin in late May. Iida quickly drove northward, as Burmese freely volunteered information on the location of British or Indian troops and supplied other intelligence as well. Some Burmese refused to side with either the British or the Japanese, however, and fought for Burmese independence against both their old and new masters! On March 8 Iida occupied the capital, Rangoon, which the British had abandoned. Using the captured port as a supply base, Iida now received reinforcements and opened an offensive on March 19 to seize the remainder of the nation.

He was now opposed by a new enemy, a Chinese army under American Lt. General Joseph Stilwell. Sent to be Chiang Kai-shek's chief of staff, Stilwell had entered the fray hoping to delay the Japanese until the monsoon rains rendered Burma impassible. This he could not do, however. By May 20 the British had completed the longest retreat in their military history. The monsoon rains came on schedule, too late to save Burma.

The Japanese had meanwhile moved to codify and round out their new empire. Northern New Guinea, the Gilbert Islands, and the Solomon Island group were added to the lists of conquests. By May 1942 the Great East Asia Co-Prosperity Sphere, which Konoye had reluctantly proclaimed, was a reality.

The Emperor Hirohito awoke one morning to read a report from Kido informing him that he had just acquired over 400 million new subjects. "The fruits of victory are falling into our mouths perhaps too quickly," he promptly observed. The Japanese had done the seemingly impossible. Inhabitants of the conquered regions would soon label the area the "Co-Poverty Sphere," but no one could doubt that Japan had gained her Eldorado of the South with dispatch. The American holdout on Bataan and Corregidor notwithstanding, the Japanese had exceeded their timetables for conquest of the Eldorado of the South by about 20 percent.

All this dismayed the American Navy; it also disturbed Yamamoto, for the emperor proceeded to proclaim that the conflict was at an end, while his chief Pearl Harbor targets, the American aircraft carriers, still roamed the Pacific. In mid-March 1942 General Wavell lost his position as Allied Commander, Far East. MacArthur, now headquartered in Australia, assumed direct American responsibility for the Southwest Pacific area, which initially included the Solomon Islands. Most of the remainder of the Pacific fell under the command of Admiral Chester Nimitz, who had succeeded Kimmel at Pearl. But there were to be many exceptions to the demarcated zones of command. Admiral Ernest King, who had succeeded Stark as chief of naval operations in Washington, never permitted a fleet carrier to be placed under MacArthur's command, for example. King also proved to be very distrustful of the British and never revealed America's Pacific strategy to them; he also contested the Europe-first decision at every turn, often in a highly abrasive fashion.

The war in the Pacific was fought in a manner the world had never before witnessed. The advent of new weapons of war led to new strategies and tactics as well. For the first time, control of the skies as well as the battlefields would weigh heavily in the outcome of the struggles. Some farsighted commanders had foreseen this and had adapted their thinking to accommodate this new reality. The most notable of these was Admiral Isoroku Yamamoto, who insisted that the future of the Japanese Imperial Navy lay not in its ability to engage in surface combat but rather in its potential to launch devastating long-range aerial attacks.

Back in 1921 Brigadier General William (Billy) Mitchell had tried to prove to the American joint chiefs and the world that an aircraft with contact bombs could sink a man-of-war at sea. Using the decommissioned German battleship *Ostfriesland* along with some aged

American ships, Mitchell and his airmen demonstrated how properly administered aerial bombs could negate the superiority of large naval guns. Since the ships were anchored during the demonstration, some of the witnesses argued that if the ships were mobile, they could easily defend themselves. Mitchell found few supporters among the naval planners, who still adhered firmly to the battleship theories promulgated by Alfred T. Mahan. The prevailing thought among the American naval planners remained the same: the American Navy, at the sign of imminent war, would sortie out from either Norfolk or San Diego and engage the enemy in a major surface action. This remained the predominant strategy up to the beginning of the Pacific War in 1941.

Some other nations were more impressed than the Americans, though. The Japanese, and especially Admiral Yamamoto, were most impressed by Mitchell's demonstration, and took the lesson to heart. When in the mid-1920s the Japanese were forced by naval treaties to refit two of their large battle cruisers or dismantle them, they chose to turn them into their first two modern, full-size aircraft carriers, *Akagi* and *Kaga*.

The United States too initiated a carrier force as early as 1922, when an old collier had her superstructure removed and a wooden deck was laid down in its place. The result was the United States' first aircraft carrier, *USS Langley* (Carrier Vehicle–1). Five years later, the carriers *Lexington* (CV–2) and *Saratoga* (CV–3) were built on the reconverted hulls of two battle cruisers and were far and away better equipped for duty than *Langley* had ever been. For the U.S. Navy, however, the aircraft carrier continued to represent an advanced reconnaissance vehicle until the mid-1930s. Then, in 1934 the first U.S. carrier that was laid down as such, *Ranger* (CV–4), was commissioned and stationed at Norfolk. Improvements in aircraft and weaponry led the navy to reexamine its focus on the role of carriers. Their potential as offensive weapons in the American arsenal was researched and naval aviators became increasingly important to America's defense strategy.

Meanwhile, the Japanese had realized the potential striking power of an advanced air force during the Manchurian and subsequent Chinese campaigns. Superior aircraft and close support tactics had given them a decided advantage over their industrially backward foe. At sea as well, the Japanese had advanced. By 1941 they boasted one of the most modern and capable striking forces in existence, utilizing their carriers off the China coast to lend close tactical support to the army.

In Japan as in America, though, some doubt still remained about the practical limitations of carrier-based warfare. Japan's most famous naval hero, Admiral Togo, had defeated the Russians in two major surface battles without the benefit of any aerial support. Many senior naval officers failed to see the need for a change in their thinking. Old habits (and viewpoints) die hard, and young naval officers in Japan were consistently forced to confront the old time battleship strategists in the naval ministry when considering the empire's future.

The real break came in 1941, when the navy found itself confronted with the limits on its fuel supply brought about by the U.S. embargo. This forced decisions on how to progress pursuant to American strength in the Pacific. It is a testament both to the influence of Admiral Yamamoto and to the desperate situation in which Japan found itself that the leaders decided to support the strike on the fleet at Pearl Harbor. Never in the nation's past had the Imperial Navy operated over 200 miles from any of the home islands or possessions. And never before had it chosen so formidable a goal as the American base at Pearl Harbor, the most closely guarded naval base in the world.

The Pearl Harbor attack had relied on the Japanese Strike Fleet's long-range attack capabilities and the element of surprise. If successful, the Japanese had hoped to destroy the American battleship and carrier forces at their anchorage and then to dominate the Pacific Ocean. The attack on Pearl Harbor was not a true test of the aircraft carriers' capacity for air-to-surface combat.

In 1941 the American Navy boasted seven active-duty carriers, of which three were stationed in the Pacific. Each carrier contained approximately seventy aircraft comprised of fighter, bomber, and torpedo planes. Before 1940, naval aviators had been required to qualify in all three types of aircraft, so that they could alternate between them if necessary. This was made possible by the relatively small number of aviators, who chose to remain in the service rather than opting for the more lucrative civilian jobs available to trained pilots. An increased emphasis on the need for trained flyers, however, drove the navy to offer better pay and opportunity for advancement to their aviators and stimulated an increase in recruitment as well. This in turn led to a greater flexibility on the part of the navy, which could now afford to allow their pilots to specialize in only one aircraft. Consequently, the length of training decreased. By December 1941 the United States had a very impressive group of aviators manning their carrier forces.

Japan's inability to deal a death blow to this carrier force at Pearl Harbor would hurt it more than anyone could have known at the time.

Suggestions for Further Reading

Thomas David, *The Battle of the Java Sea* (New York: Stein and Day, 1969) is a useful study of this neglected battle, but see also F.C. Van Osten, *The Battle of Java Sea* (Annapolis, MD: Naval Institute Press, 1976). Much of the technical detail on aviator training and carrier operations has been drawn from John Lundstrom's seminal, if little known, study, *The First Team: Pacific Naval Air Combat from Pearl Harbor to Midway* (Annapolis, MD: Naval Institute Press, 1984). The best biography of MacArthur is D. Clayton James, *The Years of MacArthur,* vols. 1 & 2 (New York: Houghton Mifflin, 1972–75). For MacArthur's negative personality traits, see Joseph C. Goulden, *Korea: The Untold Story of the War* (New York: McGraw-Hill, 1982), esp. pp. xxii-xxiii.

4.   Coral Sea and Midway

The Doolittle Raid
The Battle of the Coral Sea
    and Its Consequences
Midway

In the weeks after Pearl Harbor, the American Pacific Fleet carriers engaged in harassment operations against the Japanese. This kept up navy morale to a degree and did minor damage to the enemy, but it may have only served to demonstrate to Yamamoto that the sooner the American carriers were destroyed, the better. In late January of 1942 the United States had only two operative carriers in the Pacific—*Enterprise* and *Lexington*. *Saratoga* was in drydock in Puget Sound from a submarine torpedo hit on January 11, 1942. The last two operative U.S. fleet carriers—*Yorktown* and the newly completed *Hornet*—were transferred from the Atlantic quickly enough.

Then President Roosevelt, in conjunction with Admiral King and General Henry Arnold of the Army Air Corps, conceived the idea of bombing Tokyo, using planes flying from an aircraft carrier. This was a grave risk; it would entail the use of two of the four operative carriers, since one would be needed to supply air cover for the attack carrier. The plan seemed hopelessly risky until an officer on King's staff opined that the Army Air Corp's longer-range B–25s, twin-engine bombers, might launch the attack from the deck of an American carrier, which then could be further out at sea than otherwise would be possible. The 500 feet of runway afforded by a fleet carrier might well be sufficient to launch such aircraft, but their flight elevators would never suffice to stow them on the hangar deck below. With the explicit backing of President Roosevelt, pilots were selected, and training began.

Sixteen B–25s would comprise the assault team, the planes being lashed down to the decks of carrier *Hornet* at Alameda Naval Air Station in San Francisco Bay. The bombers were to be led by Lt. Colonel James Doolittle. *Hornet* rendezvoused with Halsey aboard *Enterprise* north of Pearl on April 13, 1942. After launch, Doolittle's fliers would bomb Tokyo and several smaller targets. Each would approach its target at a different altitude, from a different direction (relatively), and no two bombers would, theoretically, drop their loads at exactly the same moment, so that the Japanese would have maximum difficulty in pinpointing their exact time and point of launch. They were then to transit the Sea of Japan and land behind Chiang Kai-shek's lines in northern China, adding their aircraft to Chennault's forces. Launch was to take place 400 miles from the Japanese coastline.

The Japanese may well have detected Halsey's task force without his knowledge, but it made no difference—they did not know he carried twin-engine bombers, which had a longer effective range than any existing single engine carrier bombers in either navy. But when Halsey visually sited a contact (two Japanese fishing boats, with radio masts) on April 18, at a distance of approximately 650 miles from the Japanese coastline, he felt he had no choice but to launch his aircraft prematurely. All were successfully airborne. Halsey did not, however, signal Washington or Chiang Kai-shek's regime in Chungking that his planes were airborne, as per his specific orders. In the end, it probably mattered little. A Doolittle description of the raid is worth quoting in full:

> We approached our objectives just over the housetops, but bombed at 1,500 feet. The target for one plane was a portion of the navy yard south of Tokyo, in reaching which we passed over what apparently was a flying school, as there were a number of planes in the air. One salvo made a direct hit on a new cruiser or battleship under construction. They left it in flames.
>
> After releasing our bombs we dived again to the treetops and went to the coast at that altitude to avoid antiaircraft fire. Along the coastline we observed several squadrons of destroyers and cruisers and battleships. About 25 or 30 miles to sea, the rear gunners reported seeing columns of smoke rising thousands of feet into the air.
>
> One of our bombardiers strewed bombs along a quarter of a mile of aircraft factory near Nagoya. Another illuminated a tank farm. However, flying at such low altitudes made it very difficult to observe the result following the impact of the bombs. We could see the strike, but our field of vision was greatly restricted by the speed of the plane and the low altitude at which we were flying. Even so, one of our party observed a ball game in progress. The players and spectators did not start their run for cover until just as the field passed out of sight.
>
> Pilots, bombardiers, and all members of the crew performed their duties with great calmness and remarkable precision. It appeared to us that practically every bomb reached the target for which it was in-

tended. We would like to have tarried and watched the later develop-
ments of fire and explosion, but even so we were fortunate to receive a
fairly detailed report from the excited Japanese broadcasts. It took them
several hours to calm down to [sic] deception and accusation.

During the attack, one of the bombers passed so close to an American-
made Japanese passenger plane that the pilot could recognize the nationality of the B–25's crew. The plane was carrying Premier Tojo,
who was evidently on his way to inspect an army flying school. The
potential import of this brush with death was not lost on Tojo, who
may well have been affected by the incident for the rest of his term in
office. The navy had assured him it would be safe to go aloft that day,
an error for which he never forgave the naval general staff.

Lacking enough fuel to reach Chiang Kai-shek's lines, one plane
turned toward Vladivostok, where its crew was interned by the Russians, although they were later allowed to escape via Iran and India.
The remainder of the crews evidently bailed out, most over Chinese
soil. Of eighty air crew who participated in the raid, seventy-one eventually returned home. Three were killed, and eight were captured and
brought to Tokyo and tried. In the grim words of Yamamoto's chief of
staff, Vice Admiral Matome Ugaki, the captured airmen were "made
to tell the truth" (very likely they were tortured) and revealed that they
had flown from carrier *Hornet*. Three were executed by the Japanese
on the grounds that they had bombed schools. Yamamoto was morti-
fied by the raid, but no one could now doubt that the American carriers
indeed constituted a threat to the Japanese home islands themselves.
The Japanese Army was similarly embarrassed. In China it took repri-
sals on villages that had received Doolittle's flyers, executing some
250,000 civilians in reprisal.

Meanwhile, the Japanese First Air Fleet had returned to Japan, then
turned southward. Four of its carriers assisted in the conquest of the
Bismarck Islands and a portion of the Solomon Islands. Port Darwin,
Australia, was then raided on February 19, 1942. Afterward, Nagumo
sailed into the Indian Ocean and attacked two ports, Trincomalee and
Colombo, on the island of Ceylon. Two British cruisers, *Dorsetshire*
and *Cornwall,* the light carrier *Hermes,* and the destroyer *Vampire* fell
prey to Nagumo's aviators. Nagumo, however, lost forty skilled pilots
in the Indian Ocean operations. His carriers then headed for home,

with the exception of *Zuikaku* and *Shokaku,* which were detached for duty in the upcoming Coral Sea campaign.

The Japanese Navy and Army had been split over strategy. The army, while not unaggressive, favored a holding action and consolidation of gains already made. Also, on the grounds that Hitler might defeat the Russians, they wished to adopt a "wait and see" attitude toward the Soviet Union. Yamamoto believed he could not afford this attitude, reasoning that the American carriers might take the initiative against Japan. His staff had planned for a major operation against the tiny atoll of Midway, part of the Hawaiian chain but 1,200 miles west of Pearl. He envisioned a major engagement that would capture the atoll and then destroy the American carriers when they sortied out to dislodge Japanese forces from the area. He then planned to move against the Hawaiian Islands, and some of his staff hoped the Americans might then accept something of an armistice with Japan. Again, Yamamoto had his way because of the force of his personality, although the Coral Sea operation, to conquer the southern half of New Guinea and thus further isolate Australia from the United States, would have to come first.

This time the Japanese would not enjoy the advantage of surprise. Admiral Yamamoto confided his most secret communications from his new flagship, *Yamato,* to and from Tokyo, to enshroudment in the JN–25 fleet code. This was the American name for the cipher, for it represented the twenty-fifth major version or variation of that code since the American Navy had been monitoring it (JN stood simply for Japanese Navy). Intelligence staffs in both Washington and Pearl kept a record of the cipher and attempted to probe its secrets, but it had not been sufficiently penetrated by Pearl Harbor to give warning of the attack.

At Pearl, Commander Joseph Rochefort held the title of combat intelligence officer. By utilizing in part men taken from the crew of the battleship *California* and information passed on from British code-breaking experts, bits and pieces of the JN–25 code could be read by early 1942. Since the Americans were not capable of producing complete, exact translations of each decrypt, the officers in Pearl and in Washington often came up with differing explanations of the content and import of the same messages. By April, Rochefort had been able to deduce that a major Japanese operation was about to take place in or around Port Moresby.

New Guinea is the world's second largest island. The Japanese had invaded the northern half early in their initial offensive, securing the coastal areas. The island, which the Australians regarded as something of a colony, was inhabited by about 600 tribes and a very few white copra (coconut) traders. Almost half of this globe's 1,200 languages are spoken on New Guinea, so dense is the jungle that isolates its tribes. The only means by which the Japanese could cross from the coastal areas of the north to Port Moresby in the south was by transversing the formidable Owen Stanley mountain range by using the Kokoda Trail, a native passageway that could be crossed only with extreme difficulty. The Japanese opted to launch a seaborne invasion instead.

Operation MO was to be led by Admiral Shigeyoshi Inoue, sailing from Rabaul on New Britain in the Bismarcks, and was to contain three fleet carriers for air support. The light carrier *Shoho,* which was part of the Japanese South Seas Fleet, was to be joined by *Shokaku* and *Zuikaku* from the First Air Fleet, as they returned from duty in the Indian Ocean. The force would escort Japanese invasion troops from the north around the southeastern tip of New Guinea through the Jomard Passage and into Port Moresby. Although the Japanese felt certain that the Americans had one carrier operating in the vicinity, they thought three fleet carriers more than sufficient to deal with it.

In fact, the Americans had two carriers, *Yorktown* and *Lexington,* operating together as Task Force Seventeen, under the command of Rear Admiral Frank Jack Fletcher, in the waters east of Australia. Admiral Nimitz instructed Fletcher to interdict the Japanese operation but gave no further tactical instructions. After gaining antiquated maps of the area from the British admiralty, some dating from the eighteenth century, Fletcher proceeded to a point from which he believed he could intercept the Japanese invasion fleet.

The waters off the southeastern coast of New Guinea are treacherous. Indeed, there were only three safe routes for the Japanese to select. The first ran dangerously close to shore and threatened the fleet with the possibility of running aground. The second was quite safe but required a great deal of time, and the Japanese were not that patient. The final option was the Jomard Passage, a narrow corridor in the coral reefs where the ships could round the cape in good order and proceed rapidly to Moresby. This was the choice that Admiral Inoue made and that Admiral Fletcher had anticipated.

Each admiral was cautious and maintained constant aerial search patterns in attempting to determine the location of his adversary. On the morning of May 7, 1942, the two forces spotted one another almost simultaneously. A Japanese scout plane sighted what it reported to be an aircraft carrier and escort that was in reality the oiler *Neosho* and destroyer *Sims*. The mistake was not discovered until Inoue had sent an attack force, which crippled *Neosho,* which had survived the Pearl Harbor attack unscathed, and sank *Sims.*

The Americans responded by sighting *Shoho,* which was operating independently from *Shokaku* and *Zuikaku,* and launched a full attack against her. *Shoho* initially avoided the American planes, but soon they were able to report their greatest victory at sea since the sinking of a Japanese destroyer at Wake. "Scratch one flattop" was the message received by Fletcher aboard his flagship, *Lexington.*

The next morning the two forces closed on each other again. The American forces concentrated their attack on carrier *Shokaku,* as *Zuikaku* found refuge in a convenient rain squall. Two bombs found their mark, but did not mortally cripple *Shokaku,* and she was able to escape to the north.

The Japanese found the Americans in open water and attacked both carriers. *Lexington* took two torpedoes on her port side and also suffered two hits from dive bombers. *Yorktown* received one hit from a dive bomber and escaped the action, but with her fuel tanks fractured. *Lexington* was on fire but was still afloat several hours after the attacks ceased. Initially fire control teams were able to control the initial damage, but *Lexington* suffered fatal damage when sparks from an electric generator motor, which had accidently been left running, ignited gasoline fumes traveling through the ship's ventilation system. This critical error in judgment cost the American fleet one of its desperately needed carriers, as the fires that resulted were beyond control. Rear Admiral Aubrey Fitch was forced to order that *Lexington* be abandoned.

Thus, the battle, which had been fought primarily in the Solomon Sea, was quite costly to both sides. The Japanese Navy lost seventy-seven aircraft, 1,074 men killed and wounded, and one light carrier sunk. Admiral Inoue, in something like a state of controlled panic after the loss of the carriers, called off the Port Moresby invasion force, and so for the time being the Japanese Army abandoned their designs on Port Moresby. The Americans had lost sixty-six aircraft, 543 men killed and wounded, and one fleet carrier sunk. But they had saved Port Moresby and southern New Guinea for the Allies, and had gained a strategic victory. Thus ended the first naval battle in history in which the opposing naval vessels had not actually seen one another.

The most significant development in this battle may not have been what was lost, however, but what was damaged. Admiral Yamamoto chose to scratch the carriers *Shokaku* and *Zuikaku* from his pending Midway, or *Operation AF*, plans to allow them time to expedite repairs and train new flight crews. He could have kept one ready for the Midway battle by taking air crew from the other but chose not to. The Japanese Navy was wedded to the concept of operating ships, especially carriers, in pairs, and Yamamoto may have made a very costly mistake in doing so. The presence of even one of those two carriers might well have swung the balance in Japan's favor at the forthcoming battle of Midway.

Conversely, Admiral Nimitz ordered the estimated ninety days of repairs slated for *Yorktown* to be accomplished in seventy-two hours and sent her along to Midway. *Yorktown*'s presence at Midway allowed the Americans to achieve a victory that might otherwise have been beyond their grasp.

Yamamoto was confident that he could annihilate the American carrier forces because his intelligence had reported that there were only three American carriers in the Pacific. His strike fleet alone boasted four flattops. Also, Japanese air forces had scored some major victories over mobile naval forces near Singapore and in the Indian Ocean.

Even though the Coral Sea fight had not been planned as a major surface-to-air conflict through which naval hegemony could be achieved, it had a great impact on the way naval conflict would take place in the future. The Japanese sought a decisive naval action to eliminate American carrier strength before it could recover, but that victory would never come.

The entire face of naval warfare changed after the Battle of the Coral Sea. The once mighty battleships would become mere screening vessels for the precious carrier forces, which was the true offensive weapon of any task force. The operational tactic employed in sea battles would be to close to a range of approximately 100 miles and fly off waves of bombers and fighters to destroy the enemy's force while attempting to defend one's own from counter strikes.

Attacks would center on the carriers. Only after they had been destroyed would the bombers turn their attention to the supporting vessels. Torpedo bombers would launch their strikes from all points of the compass, assuring that the captain of the ship would not be able to evade all the deadly fish. Dive bombers would plummet down on their prey and attempt to hole the flight deck, or better, knock out the elevators that brought the planes up from the hangar decks. Fighters would accompany the bombers and attempt to clear the skies of enemy combat air patrols (CAP) that might disrupt the attacks. Luck and timing would have a lot to do with the success of these strikes, as will be seen, but the pattern would always remain the same.

The aviators were more important than the planes, and both navies went to great lengths to secure the safe return of their pilots, often running great risks to their vessels and their crews in attempting to retrieve pilots returning after dark. The Japanese, however, made the critical error of not securing a seed crop of these experienced pilots to provide for the training and equipping of future fliers. This was done out of a fear that breaking up a carrier's flight team would lower morale. The Americans realized the potential danger of depleting their experienced aviator stockpile and took pains to provide for the future of their naval aviation. In the upcoming battle of Midway, had either side had more carriers and aircraft, it would not have been able to have manned the additional planes, with the single exception of one Japanese carrier, *Shokaku,* which was sent back to Japan with many of her aviators, the ship itself intact but damaged. As stated above, aviators could have been taken from her and given to her sister ship, *Zuikaku,* which was undamaged but had suffered heavy loss of aviators.

Considerable disagreement erupted between the naval intelligence structures in Pearl and in Washington. Captain Joseph Redman and Commander John Redman, then the de facto bards of naval intelligence in the capital, did not believe that Commander Rochefort's analysis of Japanese intent was correct. They informed Admiral King that the next Japanese target was not Midway, as Rochefort believed, but Pearl itself. Nimitz, however, believed Rochefort's staff had made the correct estimate. The United States had acquired the Midway Atoll in 1867 as a communications relay station for the telegraph cable that ran from Hawaii to the Philippines. The atoll is composed of two small land masses, Sand and Eastern Islands, and is surrounded by a coral reef. The United States had reinforced the atoll following the Japanese attack on Pearl, and had built three runways on Eastern Island, in a triangular configuration.

Rochefort compiled an impressive array of Japanese decrypts that referred to a forthcoming attack against an objective named simply "target AF." Both Rochefort and the Redman brothers were aware that on at least three separate occasions since December 7, 1941, Pearl Harbor had been reconnoitered by search planes flown from Japanese forward bases and refueled by submarines. On March 4, 1942, Pearl was actually subject to a second, if much smaller, Japanese air raid. Two high-altitude Japanese scout planes, flying from the Marshall Islands and refueled at French Frigate Shoals by tanker submarine, proceeded to scout the harbor and dropped small bomb loads in the process. The bombs caused no damage, but greatly embarrassed Nimitz. His staff, after much study, concluded that French Frigate Shoals had been used by the Japanese planes as a refueling point, and the area was thereafter garrisoned by such American warships as Nimitz could spare. These facts led naval intelligence in Washington, however, to conclude that target AF was most probably Pearl itself.

Rochefort disagreed, although he subsequently suggested a means of testing his conclusion. Knowing that Midway obtained its fresh water supply by distilling sea water, he planned to have that garrison send a message in its routine housekeeping reports to Pearl stating that its fresh water condenser was malfunctioning. If this were the case, the Japanese would be interested, assuming that target AF was indeed Midway Atoll, and would almost certainly relay such information to Yamamoto himself. Rochefort received permission from Nimitz to implement his plan. He used the cable as a means of communication with Midway, knowing that the Japanese could not have tapped it. Via this route, Midway received orders to report in the clear that its fresh water condenser was malfunctioning. On May 12, two days after Midway sent the fake message, a Japanese listening post on Kwajalein Atoll notified Admiral Yamamoto that objective AF was short of fresh water, and Rochefort's intelligence unit duly monitored this transmission.

On May 14, 1942, Nimitz, siding with Rochefort, put the fourteenth naval district into a state of readiness to oppose the Japanese invasion of Midway. Rochefort intercepted a message on May 25 detailing the make-up, courses, and probable dates of the invasion forces. His best estimate was that the invasion of Midway would commence on the third of June. Naval intelligence in Washington still believed that Pearl or possibly the West Coast was the real Japanese target but allowed Nimitz to proceed.

To placate Admiral King, a separate force of two heavy cruisers, three light cruisers, and thirteen destroyers under the command of Rear Admiral Robert Theobald was sent north to protect Dutch Harbor in the Aleutians, which Rochefort's staff correctly believed to be a secondary, diversionary Japanese target, scheduled for bombing by a small Japanese carrier force. Theobald believed that the Japanese meant to *invade* Dutch Harbor, so he positioned his fleet 500 miles south and west of Dutch Harbor, near Kodiak, to intercept the Japanese. Hence, he failed to see any action, while leaving Dutch Harbor unprotected from an air raid. And the Japanese were able to follow up by occupying the islands of Kiska and Attu, westward in the Aleutian chain.

The Japanese Midway plan was as follows: a diversionary force under Vice Admiral Hoshiro Hosogaya would attack Dutch Harbor in the Aleutians by air the day before the planned assault on Midway. That same day, a small force of midget submarines would also penetrate Port Darwin and attempt to divert attention from the central Pacific. This would attract American attention away from Midway Atoll, which was to be neutralized and then occupied by the Japanese. Yamamoto had specified that neutralization of Midway's defenses was to be accomplished by the First Air Fleet alone. He had been chagrined by the lack of respect his carriers still engendered in Tokyo (among other annoyances, the naval general staff still credited one of the midget submarines with the destruction of *Arizona*), and he was determined to demonstrate that alone they could soften up the atoll preparatory to actual invasion. Hence he split his forces further. On the day after the diversionary attacks, the First Air Fleet was to launch an air strike that would obliterate Midway's defenses. The First Air Fleet would be comprised of four carriers, *Akagi, Kaga, Soryu,* and *Hiryu,* with a total of 261 aircraft, and two battleships, two heavy cruisers, one light cruiser, eleven destroyers, and assorted support vessels.

The next day, Admiral Yamamoto's force (which Nimitz did not know about), 300 miles behind the First Air Fleet, would arrive, containing seven battleships, including the super battleship *Yamato,* two light cruisers, twenty-one destroyers, one light carrier, and two seaplane carriers filled with midget submarines, as well as the usual support craft. At the same time the Midway invasion force under Admiral Nobutaki Kondo would arrive. It was to have sortied from Truk Island in the Carolines and would approach Midway from the south. It contained one light carrier, two battleships, eight heavy cruisers, two light cruisers, eleven destroyers, and twelve transports that contained the Midway invasion troops. Kondo's force also contained various and sundry other support ships including two seaplane carriers and three converted destroyers that would also carry marines.

As insurance that the American carriers would not be in the Midway area when Nagumo launched his air strike against the atoll, Yamamoto ordered one final force to American waters. A group of 15 *I*-class submarines were to patrol the waters between Pearl and Midway. Unfortunately these submarines did not receive correct orders (an error in encrypting was evidently responsible) and arrived two days late at their patrol stations, *after* the American carrier force had sailed past on its way to Midway. Finally, Yamamoto had authorized a second reconnaissance of Pearl Harbor to make certain that the American carriers were still in port. This plan, known as *Operation K,* was aborted when the Japanese tanker submarine failed to make its appointed rendezvous with the two high-altitude seaplanes at French Frigate Shoals, because a small American warship was anchored there. Admiral Nagumo did not know that *Operation K* had to be canceled. His task force was sailing through a storm front at the time of the report, and his radio receivers were not capable of penetrating the static. Yamamoto mistakenly assumed that if he had heard the report, Nagumo had heard it also. Hence he did not break radio silence to relay the message. Had they received the report, Nagumo's staff might have been a bit less confident and more wary.

Admiral Nimitz was aware of the strength of the Japanese forces opposing him. He knew that the Japanese expected that he would sortie his carriers to oppose the Japanese strike after Midway had been taken by them and that the Japanese intended to destroy them and hopefully force Washington to sue for peace, since the destruction of America's last three carriers would leave Hawaii and even the West Coast open to invasion. He determined to strike the Japanese carriers *before* Midway was invaded, a situation the Japanese had barely considered possible. His major problem was that he had only three carriers to oppose the enemy forces. Further, Admiral Halsey could not command the American carriers. On the return voyage from the Doolittle Tokyo raid he had contracted neurodermatitis, a skin disease severe enough to require hospitalization. Nimitz chose Halsey's cruiser commander, the elegant Admiral Raymond Spruance, as his successor. Admiral Fletcher was also detailed to the forthcoming operation and would function as overall American commander.

Spruance, flying his flag from *Enterprise,* sortied from Pearl on May 28, 1942, in command of Task Force Sixteen, which also included *Hornet,* six cruisers, and nine destroyers; Fletcher, commanding Task Force Seventeen using *Yorktown* as his flagship, cleared Pearl Harbor two days later, accompanied by two cruisers. Between the three carriers, 228 carrier-borne aircraft were available, while on Midway itself were nineteen B–17s, thirty-two Catalina flying boats, sixteen Dauntless Dive bombers, six Avenger torpedo bombers, and some hopelessly outdated fighters.

Nagumo, who had sortied from the Inland Sea on May 27, seemed little happier over the upcoming Midway operation than he had been when he sailed for Pearl Harbor six months before. But unlike the Pearl operation, he was embarked on an operation whose authors rather blithely assumed that surprise would be almost automatically achieved. Since sailing for Pearl, Nagumo had navigated his fleet over 50,000 miles, and he did not like the condition of many of his aviators. Like Rochefort's combat intelligence team at Pearl, they were using amphetamines to maintain their alertness, and many evidently did so to excess, for no few actually reported encountering ghosts of dead relatives, among other oddities, to their flight surgeons. The same physicians noted low red blood cell counts and often elevated white blood cell counts as well among the flyers. There can be no doubt that Nagumo's aviators were suffering from exhaustion.

Further, Nagumo's trusted right-hand man on the voyage to Pearl, Kusaka, had been eclipsed in influence by Genda, who now gave indispensable advice on air operations, so much so that some wags referred to the First Air Fleet simply as "Genda's Fleet." But Nagumo also had very practical reasons for concern. The entire Japanese military and naval establishment was suffering from what was later termed victory fever. Overconfidence seemed pandemic. Against all odds in the book, the Japanese had conquered the Eldorado of the South in record time, and despite a strategic defeat at Coral Sea, they seemed unstoppable. This led to overconfidence, which worried Nagumo. Also, his two most experienced commanders would probably not be available at Midway. Fuchida, who had for several days been ignoring right abdominal pain, reported to a flight surgeon on May 27, and was promptly diagnosed as suffering from appendicitis and prepared for surgery. And on the first of June, Genda reported to the sick bay; his temperature indicated a viral infection, either pneumonia or influenza.

Further, Nagumo soon found himself sailing in a storm front. On one occasion he had to break radio silence to indicate a course change to all of his vessels. Contrary to the version of events found in Hollywood movies, Nagumo did *not* decide to fight the battle as if the Americans had anticipated his battle plan, but he was determined to leave nothing to chance. At the last moment, early on the morning of June 4, Genda discharged himself from sick bay and participated in a conference that decided that as the Midway-bound aircraft were launched, scout planes would also be sent aloft to seek out any enemy vessels in the vicinity, particularly to the north of Midway, which was exactly where the three American carriers were lying in wait.

Although Nimitz remained at Pearl, he had also left nothing to chance. As of May 30 he instituted aerial reconnaissance out of Midway by PBY Catalina flying boats. Each day twenty-two of these aircraft flew in a spoke pattern 700 miles out from Midway to the northwest, alert for the Japanese. On June 3 one PBY sighted Kondo's invasion fleet rapidly closing on Midway from the south. But the pilot did not know which force he had sighted; he radioed Midway that he had sighted Nagumo's "main body" of ships, which had to mean the First Air Fleet. For the first and only time during the Midway operation, Nimitz gave his commanders at sea tactical instructions. He sent them an urgent message, assuring them the PBYs had sighted *Kondo*'s invasion fleet, stating Nagumo would strike from the northwest the next day, as anticipated. Fletcher and Spruance closed to a position almost exactly 200 miles north of Midway Atoll.

At 4:30 AM, June 4, 1942, Nagumo began launching his Midway attack force. In fifteen minutes the entire attack force was in the air, led by Lt. Joichi Tomonaga. Three of the Japanese scout planes left on schedule, but four were delayed for reasons that still are not evident. In particular, the cruiser *Tone* was delayed in catapulting off both of her scouts, which were coded as Scouts Three and Four. Both were delayed by precious minutes, and number four was launched only at 5:00 AM. Now Nagumo had no choice but to wait.

At 5:45 AM a PBY radioed in the clear "many planes heading Midway." Nimitz was finally absolutely certain that he had been correct and Washington mistaken concerning the ultimate objective of *Operation AF*. Midway launched its fighters to stop the oncoming

Japanese. Midway's Wildcats did their best, but they could not match the Japanese Zeros, and the antique Brewster Buffaloes did not fare all that well either. At 6:30 AM Tomonaga's planes began bombing Midway. Despite the fact that Midway's airfield was on Eastern Island, Sand Island received much more Japanese attention. The oil storage tanks were set on fire, and many buildings were completely gutted. About twenty men on the ground were killed in the raid. Nagumo lost eight aircraft, while the Americans lost seventeen planes. But the air strips remained intact, as did numerous antiaircraft guns. Thus, at exactly 7:05 AM Tomonaga radioed *Akagi* that "a second attack wave is needed over the target."

Meanwhile, at 5:20 AM, the Americans had learned the position of Nagumo's carriers. Spruance decided to attack the carriers roughly two hours earlier than he had initially planned, in the hope that he might catch Nagumo's flattops while they were refueling their Midway attack force. He was at maximum range, and began launching his aircraft piecemeal at 7:02 AM. Spruance believed he had been sighted by a Nagumo scout plane by then, but he did not know his luck. *Chikuma*'s Number Five Scout evidently flew directly over the American carriers, but somehow did not observe them. Scout Four, the longest delayed in launching, sighted the American ships initially at 7:28 AM, but only at 8:20 AM was he able to report that a carrier was among the American vessels.

Nagumo had been in a quandary since he had received Tomonaga's request for another strike. Initially, half of the remaining aircraft had been brought on deck, on two of his four carriers armed with torpedoes, and manned by the most experienced pilots in Nagumo's fleet in case American warships suddenly appeared. But at 7:15 AM Nagumo ordered all planes to switch to contact bombs; then at 7:45, he ordered torpedoes left on those planes so equipped. Meanwhile, attacks against the Japanese carriers had begun at 7:08 AM. These first attacks were executed by Midway-based aircraft.

At a little past 8:30 AM Tomonaga requested permission to land his returning Midway strike force. Genda made the decision: land the Midway strike force, rearm it with torpedoes, and then dispatch all aircraft to the just-sighted American carrier. At 8:37 AM *Akagi* began landing Tomonaga's planes. But Rear Admiral Tamon Yamaguchi, in command of *Hiryu* and *Soryu,* argued that all remaining aircraft, however they were armed, should be launched at once against the American carrier, which would have meant letting Tomonaga's 100-odd planes fall into the sea. Nagumo refused Yamaguchi's request. On Genda's advice, he made a more humane decision, albeit, as will be seen, an incorrect one.

It had been an exceedingly hectic morning for Nagumo's hangar crews. The frequent changes of armament for the planes had been ordered in language that did not admit of delay, and they had complied. As a result, after Tomonaga's Midway strike force had returned, they were equipped primarily with long-lance torpedoes, as were most of the remaining aircraft.

Nagumo now turned to close distance with the sighted American carrier. He first came under attack from carrier planes, flying from *Hornet,* a moment or two after his course change, about 9:18 AM. American steam-driven torpedoes were antiquated models, little different from Whitehead models of World War I. They did have magnetic detonators, but these tended to malfunction, and in any event they usually ran deeper than their preset running depth. Several American torpedo squadrons attacked Nagumo's force that morning; but not one American torpedo exploded against the hull of a Japanese ship. They did, however, draw Nagumo's Zero fighter umbrella to low patrol altitudes, where they temporarily remained. Then, at 10:20 AM, Nagumo received word that all his aircraft had been refitted with torpedoes and were nearly ready to attack the American carrier. He ordered his carriers to turn into the wind and commence launching at once. Seconds after the first plane left *Akagi'*s flight deck, American dive bombers found the Japanese. A carrier at sea with freedom to maneuver would ordinarily least fear a dive bomber attack, but Nagumo's carriers had no fighter umbrella left to protect them. The prior American air attacks had drawn his Zeros down to wavetop level.

Further, Nagumo's flight decks were filled with fully armed and fueled aircraft, while the hangar decks of all four carriers were littered with contact bombs, left in the rush that allowed no time for them to be returned to the ships' magazines. At 10:24 AM the dive bombers swarmed in. Someone on the deck of *Akagi* cried, "Helldivers!" (the Japanese had used this English term since a 1931 Hollywood production had glorified such pilots) as a warning, but Nagumo's carriers could only engage in violent evasive maneuvers as protection.

Within six minutes, three of his four carriers were stricken. *Kaga* was hit first, then *Akagi,* and finally *Soryu.* Induced explosions followed the initial impact by American contact bombs on the flight decks, as flaming gasoline reached the contact bombs scattered on the hangar deck floors. Only *Hiryu* escaped. Nagumo barely managed to escape the bridge of *Akagi,* transferring his flag to the cruiser *Nagara.*

Yamaguchi, a Princeton graduate noted for his aggressiveness but also for a penchant for theatrics, struck back as soon as he was able. At 10:54 AM, his carrier *Hiryu* still unscathed, he launched twenty-four aircraft against the sighted American carrier. At noon the aircraft found *Yorktown* and put several contact bombs into her. Yamaguchi now learned from a scout that a total of three American carriers were north of Midway. He launched his planes again, assuming they would damage or sink a second American carrier. Instead, they found *Yorktown* again and put two torpedoes into her. At 2:55 PM, Captain Elliott Buckmaster of the *Yorktown* was forced to order abandon ship. Then, repaying the score, American carrier planes found *Hiryu* just after 5:00 PM and left her ablaze. Yamaguchi was late in releasing his men to abandon ship, however, indulging his penchant for the dramatic in traditional *Samurai* ceremony.

The remainder of the combat action was incidental. At about 3:00 AM, after receiving reconnaissance photographs of what was left of the First Air Fleet, Yamamoto ordered it to be sunk by its own destroyers. He then ordered a general withdrawal, admitting defeat. On June 6, a Japanese *I*-class submarine penetrated a protective destroyer screen and sunk the *Yorktown,* whose damage was under repair. Finally, two of Kondo's retiring cruisers, *Mogami* and *Mikuma,* collided, and Spruance's planes sunk the latter. There was no further action of consequence.

At Midway, the scoring punch of the Japanese Navy had been blunted: four carriers and one cruiser were sunk, 5,000 Japanese had lost their lives, and 322 planes were lost. Worse, the pilots who were lost—many of whom had a thousand hours in combat experience over the skies in China, not to mention experience gained since—were irreplaceable. American losses comprised ninety-nine carrier-based aircraft, thirty-eight Midway-based planes, and the *Yorktown.* As it was, if Nimitz had had *Saratoga* available, he would have experienced difficulty in rounding out their squadrons, and after the battle many of the remaining pilots were in a state of acute fatigue. Nimitz and King realized that something had to be done to ensure that there would be properly trained and experienced pilots on all of the American carriers.

They decided to break up the veteran crews of *Yorktown, Enterprise,* and *Hornet,* and reassigned them. Some veteran pilots were transferred to new squadrons to act as leavening, others became instructors. More to the point, steps were taken to ensure an increased flow of new pilots, particularly from San Diego. No such steps were taken by the Japanese, who stoically endured their losses as part of the cost of war, and evidently gave no thought to ensuring a flow of new pilots for what was surely to be a protracted conflict. They made no prognosis for the future, as Nimitz and King did. The results would be disaster for the imperial forces.

The Japanese lost at Midway for reasons as complex as the Japanese order of battle for the action. They were overconfident of victory and, although it had no effect on the battle's outcome, security had been very lax. Their pilots were probably even more exhausted than their American counterparts, and the Japanese failed to anticipate that the United States would substantially penetrate their JN–25 fleet code cipher. (Later they assumed that the United States had probably known their intent via a chance submarine sighting of the First Air Fleet.) Yamamoto's plan hinged on surprise, even more than was the case at Pearl Harbor. Obviously, the American carriers could be drawn out for battle successfully only if they were at Pearl, or heading northward toward Dutch Harbor, when Nagumo made his first air strike against Midway. Failure to search properly for the U.S. fleet with a significant number of planes at the outset played its role in the disaster.

Yamamoto has also frequently been criticized for splitting his fleet. There is merit to this observation, but Yamamoto had his reasons: he wished the battleship admirals in Tokyo to appreciate properly the value of carriers in neutralizing a shore target; he did not wish his presence in the immediate vicinity to hinder command structure, and his older battleships would have impeded the mobility of First Air Fleet. And, because of faulty intelligence, the Japanese estimate was that no more than two American carriers could be called upon to retaliate, which still gave Nagumo a two-to-one advantage.

Still, the basic Japanese plan, while overly complicated, was sound. If Rochefort and his staff had not read and correctly interpreted the JN–25 fleet code, Midway probably would have fallen, and the American carriers would probably have been drawn into a battle fought more on Japanese terms than it was. The fact that Plan Midway did not fit in with the classic rule for sea engagement as outlined by Alfred T.

Mahan means little. (Mahan himself was the son of a West Point instructor.) Mahan did not write in the age of naval air power. And of course, hindsight is twenty-twenty as usual. The point is that Japan did lose at Midway, and from this battle to the end of the conflict, it reacted to American advances, rather than the opposite. Midway was the turn of the tide, and Yamamoto knew it.

The average Japanese and indeed the emperor himself did not know this. Premier Tojo was actually pleased that the Imperial Navy had lost at Midway. But rather than admit a national defeat, Tojo announced a victory, although his announcement gave no details. But all the rhetoric in the world could not restore Japan's four lost carriers, or their pilots. Midway belongs to that very small group of truly decisive naval engagements.

Suggestions for Further Reading

There are several recent studies of Doolittle's exploit, including Carroll Glines, *The Doolittle Raid* (New York: Orion Books, 1988) and James M. Merrill, *Target Tokyo: The Halsey-Doolittle Raid* (New York, 1964). The best study of the Coral Sea campaign is John B. Lundstrom, *The First South Pacific Campaign: Pacific Fleet Strategy, December 1941–June 1942* (Annapolis, MD: Naval Institute Press, 1976), but see also Bernard Millot, *The Battle of the Coral Sea* (Annapolis, MD: Naval Institute Press, 1974). For the Midway engagement, we have relied on the following: H. P. Willmott, *The Barrier and the Javelin: Japanese and Allied Pacific Strategies, February to June 1942* (Annapolis, MD: Naval Institute Press, 1983); Gordon W. Prange, *Miracle at Midway* (New York: McGraw-Hill, 1982); Mitsuo Fuchida and Masatake Okumiya, *Midway: The Battle that Doomed Japan* (Annapolis, MD: Naval Institute Press, 1955), written by Japan's Pearl Harbor hero; William W. Smith, *Midway: Turning Point of the Pacific* (New York: Crowell, 1966); Department of the Navy, *The Japanese Story of the Battle of Midway* (Washington, DC: Government Printing Office, 1947); George H. Gay, who wrote *Sole Survivor* (Naples, FL: Naples Graphics Services, 1979), survived a torpedo squadron at Midway; S.E. Morison, *History of United States Naval Operations in World War Two*, vol. 4, *Coral Sea, Midway and Submarine Actions* (Boston: Little, Brown, 1949); Pat Frank and Joseph Harrington, *Rendezvous at Midway: USS Yorktown and the Japanese Carrier Fleet* (New York: John Day, 1967); Edmund Forrestal, *Admiral Raymond A. Spruance, USN: A Study in Command* (Washington, DC: U.S. Government Printing Office, 1966); Tameichi Hara, *Japanese Destroyer Captain* (New York: Ballantine Books, 1961); Robert Heinl, *Marines at Midway* (Washington, DC: Historical Section, USMC, 1948); and Thomas Buell, *The Quiet Warrior: A Biography of Admiral Raymond A. Spruance* (Boston: Little, Brown, 1974). The best overall study of this period is H.P. Willmott, *Empires in the Balance: Japanese and Allied Pacific Strategies to April 1942* (Annapolis, MD: Naval Institute Press, 1982).

5.   First Allied Land Victories

Fighting on New Guinea
Guadalcanal and Related Actions
The Japanese Are Driven from New Guinea
American Strength and the New Technology of War
U.S. Strategy
Island Hopping

The initial Allied landings on Guadalcanal and New Guinea in 1942 were, like Midway, reactions to Japan's attempts to secure outer bases from which to defend its empire. After MacArthur escaped from Corregidor, he sought refuge in Australia, where he believed he would find an American Army with which he would soon return to liberate the Philippines. When he arrived, he found the Australians in a state of acute anxiety, with virtually no American troops in the country. Mac-Arthur had to convince Prime Minister John Curtin and General Thomas Blamey, commander of the Australian Army, to forsake the Brisbane Line. That line of defense would have left northern Australia open to Japanese invasion, with the defense of the continent established in the large cities of the southeast.

MacArthur convinced Curtin and Blamey that the defense of Australia should in effect be in New Guinea, which Australia had always regarded as something of a colony. American as well as Australian troops would be employed. It was agreed that MacArthur would command Australian units so long as they operated south of the equator. The arrangement worked well, but the occasional difficulties were not insignificant. At one point, disembarking American troops at Brisbane told their Australian counterparts, who were embarking, of their intentions toward Australian women when they received leave. More than words were exchanged. In this, the "Battle of Brisbane," gunfire ensued and several dozen lives were lost. For the sake of Allied unity the matter was quickly hushed up.

The Japanese Army on New Guinea had decided to attempt to force the Kokoda Trail and proceed to Port Moresby without the aid of the navy. Major General Tomitaro Horii was placed in charge of a dual offensive aimed first at capturing the coastal city of Buna for its aerial support value; after this he was to cross the Owen Stanley Mountain Range and capture Port Moresby, the colonial capital of the island. This second feat would indeed have been impressive, for the New Guinea jungles, located directly south of the equator, are very probably the most dense, impenetrable jungles on this planet. The Kokoda Trail itself is hardly a readily passable route, and the Owen Stanley Range has peaks as high as 15,000 feet. Even the local inhabitants thought the Japanese foolish to attempt so challenging an undertaking.

Meanwhile MacArthur had begun to commit the remaining Australian forces to Port Moresby and the defense of New Guinea. The Australian Seventh Division was the first to arrive, and was eventually joined by the American Thirty-Second, or Red Arrow Division, from Wisconsin and Michigan. The Australians had deployed troops along the Kokoda Trail as delaying or skirmish forces. None of the groups was large enough to stop the Japanese advance, but they could buy the defenders of the port enough time to establish a line of defense that would hold. The Australians also built airfields around Port Moresby and were supplied with sufficient aircraft to cut Japanese supply lines and interdict the advance.

General Horii pressed his men on after the rapid fall of Buna and began pushing back the Australians in an attempt to cross the mountains before the onset of the rainy season. The Japanese pressed to within twenty-five miles of Moresby. They could actually see the port before the Australian defenders were able to turn them back on September 24, 1942. Because they had intended to take the city and subsist on supplies garnered there, the Japanese found themselves forced to retreat with limited supplies and no prospect of resupply. Consequently, attrition by natural factors, particularly climate and disease, was as great as that caused by fighting. And the rainy season had begun in the mountains. What had been small streams during the Japanese advance were now raging torrents, each of which posed a different obstacle to the Japanese retreat. It was while attempting to cross one such swollen river that General Horii drowned, when his makeshift raft overturned. The Australians were able to push the Japanese back to their defensive positions at Buna while inflicting heavy casualties on them as well.

On July 3, 1942, an Allied reconnaissance aircraft, while on a routine patrol, had discovered an airfield under construction on the small is-

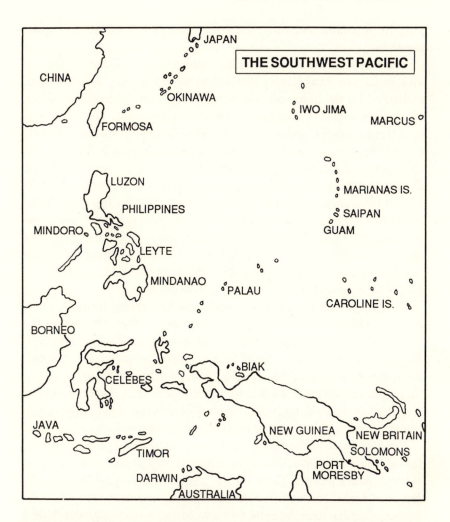

land of Guadalcanal, in the Solomon Island chain. The Japanese name for this then virtually unknown parcel of real estate was *Gadarukanaru*. Until this time the island had little significance, other than having served as the location of a Lever Brothers copra planta-tion. The Americans, aware that Guadalcanal had been part of the British Empire, again turned to antiquated British admiralty maps and Australian charts to plan their landings. Obviously the Japanese were building a landing strip to provide fighter and bomber strength to aug-ment the reconnaissance plane base already established at nearby Tulagi, on Florida Island. With these, they could interdict U.S. shipping to Australia and deny the Allied forces "down under" much needed supplies.

The First Marine Division, which had trained at Quantico for service in Europe, was hastily dispatched to San Diego, where its men embarked for the Solomons via New Zealand. On August 7, 1942, the Marines landed on Guadalcanal, virtually unopposed. The only Japanese troops present, about 2,200 (probably Korean) construction workers, evidently unarmed, fled into the interior as the leathernecks approached. Later the Japanese sent in regular army troops. The airfield was quickly secured by the Americans and renamed for Major Lofton Henderson, a Marine dive bomber who lost his life in the Battle of Midway. The ice manufacturing facility, also captured intact, was rechristened as the Tojo Ice Plant (under new management). Eleven thousand marines under the command of Major General Alexander Vandegrift landed during the initial invasion and took up defensive positions around the perimeter of the air strip.

Fletcher gained permission to withdraw his carriers from the vicinity late on the afternoon of August 8 in order to refuel. He commanded two of America's remaining three carriers in the Pacific. Evidently Fletcher did not wish to place them in undue jeopardy. The marines thought very poorly of this decision, however, and some opined aloud they believed Fletcher wished to add a fourth color to the American flag. His decision delayed the landing of much-needed supplies and probably cost Marine lives by depriving them of naval air cover.

Rear Admiral Richmond Turner was posted to the straits off Savo Island, north of Guadalcanal, to intercept any Japanese resupply or surprise attack efforts. Early on the morning of August 9, 1942, the Japanese sent a force of five heavy cruisers, two light cruisers, and a destroyer under Rear Admiral Gunichi Mikawa to engage the American forces at Guadalcanal and destroy their transport and supply vessels if possible. At 1:00 AM the Japanese met a force of five heavy cruisers and several destroyers commanded by Rear Admiral Victor Crutchley, which was guarding the northern passage to Guadalcanal.

Although the Americans actually had some prior warning, including unidentified radar contacts, it was not credited and so the attack came as a complete surprise. Within thirty minutes, the Japanese inflicted on the American Navy the worst defeat it ever suffered in a conventional, "textbook" fight. The Allies lost four of their five heavy cruisers, including the Australian cruiser *Canberra,* and a destroyer, along with

1,270 officers and men killed, and 900 more wounded. In return, Mikawa had lost thirty-seven men killed and fifty-seven wounded. Mikawa, afraid of American carrier plane air strikes, withdrew, unaware that Fletcher's carriers had already left the area. Mikawa lost one of his heavy cruisers, *Kako*, to a submarine during the withdrawal but still achieved a stunning victory. After the action ended, Captain Howard D. Bode, commander of the cruiser *Chicago*, committed suicide, even though his ship had survived, albeit seriously damaged, the night's fighting.

The Battle of Savo Island was only the first in a series of colorful and bloody naval actions that were to take place in the waters around Guadalcanal. The American Navy had a natural advantage in that it possessed radar, while hardly any of the Japanese ships were so equipped. But the Imperial Navy ensured that the men who served aboard its ships had night vision, the ability to see extraordinarily well in the dark. As radar itself grew more sophisticated and the Allies learned how to use and evaluate its findings better, the balance shifted to the American side, but only after many costly attempts to engage the Japanese in night combat where the latter's reliance on their men's ability gave them the edge.

In subsequent encounters the Japanese and the Americans both suffered substantial losses. The American carrier *Wasp*, recently transferred from the Atlantic, and the Japanese light carrier *Ryujo* were sunk, along with countless other vessels. Probably the greatest loss for the Japanese was the battleship *Kirishima*, sunk by the battleships *Washington* and *South Dakota* on November 12, 1942, in the sort of surface engagement between battleships that had been anticipated before Pearl Harbor by both the American and Japanese naval establishments. Both sides had determined that Guadalcanal was to be a significant, highly publicized campaign. The victor would at the least have a significant propaganda advantage. But the Japanese fought the battle in a piecemeal fashion, both from a naval standpoint and in reinforcing Guadalcanal. The enormous cost in lives and vessels led the narrow body of water separating Guadalcanal from Florida Island to be christened unofficially Ironbottom Sound.

The last significant naval battle was be that of Tassafaronga Point, fought on November 30, after which the Japanese imperial command determined that Guadalcanal was no longer worth the great expense required to hold it. They did not, however, convey this message to the ground soldiers on the island. All told, the Americans had lost one carrier, seven cruisers, and five destroyers; the Japanese had lined Ironbottom Sound with one carrier, two battleships, one cruiser, and six destroyers. The Americans had failed to press the advantages that radar gave them, while the Japanese Navy had used its night training to great effectiveness. In numbers it was a tactical draw, but it was a strategic victory for the Americans, who had started the rollback of the Japanese empire. Although the Japanese had lost the battle at sea, the struggle on the ground continued for several more months.

In the interim, the aggressive Halsey replaced Admiral Robert Ghormley as overall commander in the South Pacific, Rear Admiral Thomas Kinkaid relieved Fletcher, and Major General Alexander Patch, commanding the so-called Americal Division, replaced Vandegrift and his exhausted First Marine Division. Life on Guadalcanal was putrid in every sense for both sides. In part because Fletcher had pulled out before all the necessary supplies were landed, shortages were endemic. Many nights the "Tokyo Express" would proceed down "the Slot," the channel between the northern and southern Solomons, essentially unopposed, and shell the Marine positions and Henderson field. Although these attacks did not kill a substantial number of marines, they had considerable harassment value and were quite effective as a psychological weapon. Every marine on the island came to dread twilight.

The marines subsisted on rations that had been condemned but saved as an economy measure in 1931. Vile as these foodstuffs were, they were a virtual feast compared to the Japanese soldiers' diet of roots, berries, and the occasional odd insect. And on rare occasions individual Japanese actually practiced cannibalism. The average marine on Guadalcanal lost eighteen pounds; the average Japanese lost forty. For both sides disease was as deadly as the opposing enemy. Dysentery, severe malaria—including the cerebral variety, which was much harder to prevent or to treat since it resulted in convulsions, or *status epilepticus*—and beri beri took a heavy toll on the troops. The Japanese suffered more because they received virtually no supplies and had little means of combating illness, but even the marines were forced to remain in line positions unless they ran a fever of over 102 degrees. Guadalcanal was a supreme test of will for all involved.

The Japanese attempted to supply their forces by tying half-filled drums of supplies together and towing them behind destroyers, then cutting them loose as they approached the coastline in the hope that the tide would wash them ashore. They did not anticipate the irregular neap and dodging tides that bathed the Solomons. These unpredictable currents often washed the supplies back out to sea or, on more than one occasion, down to the marines near Henderson Field. The only thing the Japanese were able to pour into Guadalcanal with regularity were reinforcements. While a total of 39,000 Japanese fought there, they never could muster at any one time a numerical advantage over the Americans, who committed 24,000 men to the island.

During the first week of February 1943, 13,000 Japanese soldiers were evacuated from Guadalcanal after being promised that they were being transported for a direct amphibious assault against Henderson Field. The evacuation was handled extremely well and was unknown to the Marines until after its completion. It did not, however, conform to the warrior code of *Bushido,* which dictated that one should die rather than withdraw (or surrender). Most of the soldiers evacuated were never again fit for front line duty.

The Marines had now surmounted the first obstacle in the reconquest of the Solomon chain. The ensuing battles would be fought against an enemy instructed to stand with the materials available or die in the service of their emperor. The U.S. naval strategy of island hopping was first executed, albeit on a relatively minor scale, in the Solomons, since the marines only assaulted the vital islands in the chain, including New Georgia (June 21–August 27, 1943), Rendova (June 30–August 27), Choiseul (August 27–28), and Shortland (August 27) until they reached the final link in the chain, Bougainville. The practice of isolating potential Japanese strongholds and bypassing them to strike where the enemy was weaker became an integral part of the navy's plan for prosecuting the war.

The first manifestation of this strategy became *Operation Cartwheel,* which dealt only with the Solomon Islands and New Guinea. The goal of *Cartwheel* was to conquer the small enemy positions on the islands surrounding the Bismarck Archipelago, thereby isolating the major enemy naval base of Rabaul, located on the northeast tip of the island of New Britain. The navy had gained permission to execute this strategy over the complaints of Douglas MacArthur, who argued that in order to win one must fight the enemy wherever he is found, which would in effect have meant an invasion of every Japanese stronghold. As an unanticipated benefit of its strategy, the navy had the opportunity to remove one of Japan's greatest leaders from the conflict.

After Midway, Rochefort was dispatched to Washington to be decorated for his contribution to the Midway victory. But there he fell afoul of the Redman brothers. He was not decorated. Instead, Rochefort finished his wartime years in command of a drydock on the West Coast. Apparently his superiors were embarrassed and/or envious of his stellar performance, and since the navy then regarded intelligence work as far inferior to sea duty, this decision, in a sense, should not have been surprising. Luckily, though, even with Rochefort gone the decrypting staff at Pearl, which he had assembled, was still functioning well, for in early April of 1943 a message was intercepted that revealed that Admiral Yamamoto intended to visit aviators on Bougainville as part of a series of front-line inspections undertaken to raise morale. This message, with its precise timetable, was passed on to Washington, where it was read by Admiral King, who realized its potential import. Had the message concerned any other commander, probably nothing would have been done. But knowing Yamamoto's penchant for promptness, and realizing how important he was to Japan's war effort, Washington decided that an attempt should be made to eliminate him.

On April 18, 1943 Cactus air group, as the Marine and Army Air Corps air arm on Guadalcanal was code-named, dispatched a squadron of American P–38 Lightning fighters to intercept and ambush Yamamoto and his entourage. The Lightnings caught Yamamoto's two transport bombers just after their Zero escort had turned away. Captain Thomas Lanphier found himself the only pilot within range of the lead bomber, which was at treetop level and about to land at Bougainville. Lanphier, who was approaching from the rear at an oblique angle, believed his target would escape, but since he had not yet tested his guns, he fired a burst into the bomber. The bomber, like all other Japanese planes, did not have self-sealing wing tanks, and it burst into flames, then fell into the jungle. In it was Yamamoto, who probably never even realized what had happened, since two bullets were found in his body, one in the skull, the other at the base of the spine.

Yamamoto's staff, who always traveled in a separate plane, crashed into the surf just off shore but survived the attack. Commander Kaysuji Watanabe, perhaps Yamamoto's closest friend, retrieved the admiral's body, which was cremated in the jungle. The ashes were transported back to Japan. After a full state funeral, they were buried next to Admiral Togo and the emperor Taisho.

The Japanese Navy now faced a crisis in its leadership structure and a blow to its morale from which it would never fully recover. Yamamoto was replaced by Admiral Mineichi Koga, one of his ardent disciples. Like Yamamoto, Koga was loath to cooperate with the army but fervently believed in the primacy of naval aviation over battleships. But he lacked Yamamoto's forceful personality. While Koga commanded the combined fleet, little initiative against the Americans was taken.

Roosevelt, always the consummate politician, insisted that the next American offensive action take place in the northern Pacific. Here actual U.S. territory was under Japanese occupation. During the Midway operation, a subscript of Yamamoto's plan had been to capture several of the outermost islands in the Aleutian chain and establish outposts there to use as bases for raids on Dutch Harbor. The islands of Attu and Kiska had been taken without opposition on the sixth and seventh of June 1942. The Japanese had established garrisons there and used them as their northern and westernmost outposts. While the Aleutians, like the Solomons, had been written off as too costly to retain if their occupation were seriously contested by the Americans, they still constituted something of a prestige item. Tokyo had in effect told the commanders involved to stand with what they had at their disposal.

This had come on the heels of a naval battle off the Komandorski Islands on March 26, 1943, in which a small American cruiser force engaged a Japanese supply force attempting to reach the Aleutians; in a long-range gun battle, the Americans damaged the Japanese cruiser *Nachi* while an old cruiser, *Salt Lake City,* was crippled. After that the Japanese resorted to submarines to supply the outposts. When the Americans invaded on May 11, 1943, the Japanese put up a stiff but doomed defense. On May 29, after losing 516 men killed and 1,136 wounded, the Americans once again flew their flag over Attu. Of the 2,150-man Japanese force, all but nineteen perished. When a joint Canadian-American force landed on Kiska on August 15, they found the island deserted, much to their embarrassment. In less than one hour on July 28 the Japanese had executed a textbook withdrawal of their 5,000-man garrison.

To return to New Guinea, much to the delight of the Australians the campaign there had been going well for the Allies. By November 1942 the Australian Seventh and American Thirty-Second Infantry Divisions had driven the Japanese back within their defensive positions around the coastal villages of Gona and Buna. Their progress had stalled, however, because of a lack of proper supplies and the effects of tropical/jungle illness. MacArthur and his headquarters a thousand miles away had no concept of the difficulties involved. But MacArthur did place Lt. General Robert Eichelberger in charge of the combined force, and Eichelberger immediately set about correcting the logistical and morale problems that had been inherent in the command. The Allied offensive progressed again. Gona and Buna fell to the Allies by January 21, 1943, at a cost of more than 8,000 Australians and Americans killed and wounded. This victory opened the way for an expanded campaign on the northern coast of New Guinea. While Midway had been the first decisive victory over the Imperial Japanese Navy, Gona and Buna had proven that the Imperial Japanese Army was vulnerable as well in a jungle milieu.

While MacArthur was massing troops in Australia for a series of amphibious assaults on the northern coast of New Guinea, a battle was raging for air supremacy. The air bases established by the Allies at Port Moresby and by the Japanese in the northern villages were in constant aerial combat, highlighted by bombing raids on each other's fields, with the Japanese flying not only from air bases on New Guinea but from the fortress of Rabaul as well. During a battle fought March 2–4, 1943, the air forces of the Allies discovered and destroyed a force of destroyers and transports steaming in the Bismarck Sea from Rabaul to New Guinea. Using a tactic known as skip bombing, medium U.S. bombers flew in at masthead level and released their bomb loads short of their target. The effect was the same as skipping stones across a pond. The bombs bounced across the water and slammed into the sides of the support vessels at water level, effectively sinking them. During the ongoing battle, the Japanese lost seven transports and four destroyers. The Americans also managed to shoot down twenty-five Japanese planes, while themselves losing only three bombers and two fighters.

In an attempt to regain air superiority in the Solomons and New Guinea, Admiral Yamamoto had stripped the South Seas Fleet in Truk of its remaining planes and pilots and sent them to Rabaul. He was not, however, able to supply Rabaul with properly trained replacement air crews. As previously mentioned, the Japanese had made no effort to husband their trained pilots to use as instructors and leaven for the raw recruits. The results were devastating to the Japanese, who lost almost *3,000* planes from November 1942 through December 1943. The Japanese were unable to sustain losses at this rate, and so the Allies were able to establish air superiority by mid-spring of 1944.

By June 1943 MacArthur was ready to launch amphibious assaults along the coast of New Guinea. The pattern these landings followed became a recurring theme. First, American fighters and bombers would soften up the intended landing sight and provide sufficient cover for the Allied troops to come ashore. Next, army engineers and navy Seabees would build air strips or repair existing facilities to allow aircraft to operate from them on advance missions against future assault locations. This procedure was then repeated. By March 1944 the Allies had reached what would be the decisive battle for control of New Guinea.

The Japanese Eighteenth Army, among other Japanese units, had massed nearly 65,000 battle-ready troops at the twin villages of Wewak and Madang. MacArthur wisely opted to bypass that stronghold. He proceeded to the strategically important city of Hollandia, to the rear of the Eighteenth Army. In order to be successful, though, MacArthur would need air support, which his land-based aircraft would not be able to supply. Thus, Nimitz agreed to allow MacArthur to use his fast carrier fleet to provide the necessary air cover, while the engineers and Seabees carved out air strips on several nearby islands that MacArthur intended to secure.

On March 30, 1944, the Allies began their preliminary bombardment. Two two days later the Australians engaged a portion of the Eighteenth Army near Madang. On April 22, MacArthur surprised the Japanese by attacking Hollandia and taking the village of Aitape, in the rear of their lines. Airfields were constructed at Aitape. Within two days the Allies were conducting air attacks on the Japanese force from both sides. Nearly all Japanese air power had been destroyed as a result of the preliminary invasion bombardments, and the Eighteenth Army was forced to retreat into the jungle. The Eighteenth Army did launch an offensive against Allied positions in Wewak in late June, but suffered heavy losses and was pushed back once again into the interior. The Allies easily overran Hollandia and proceeded northward. In hard-fought battles, the Allies took the islands of Wakde and Biak in mid-May. When Noemfoor and Sansapor were taken at the end of July, Japanese strength in New Guinea had effectively been destroyed.

The battle for the island of Biak, May 27–July 29, 1944, was a turning point in Japanese military strategy. Up to this time, it had been the practice of Japanese forces to meet the invaders on the beachhead, and if unsuccessful, proceed to launch suicidal *Banzai* charges at the enemy's position in an attempt to drive him back into the sea. At Biak, the Japanese commander opted to withdraw his forces inland and set up a defensive network that would exact a heavy cost in Allied lives, which the suicide charges had failed to do. This would frequently be the pattern for further land engagements during the war. By early August 1944, MacArthur could state that New Guinea had been secured.

Admiral Yamamoto had voiced concern long before the war began about America's overwhelming industrial potential. Even then he had realized that in a conflict with America victory must be achieved before full use could be made of the military construction capacity of Detroit, the Brooklyn Navy yard, and countless other industrial complexes he had personally inspected during his sojourn in the United States. Indeed the Sparrow's Point plant of the Bethlehem Steel Company, in Baltimore, working round the clock, produced more steel during the conflict than Japan, Germany, and Italy combined.

The pendulum swing of military advantage became complete by late 1943 as a result of newly developed technologies. The new weapons that were introduced placed the Allies in a position of superior power that they never relinquished. First proposed and blueprinted in 1939, the *Essex*-class aircraft carrier was introduced en masse in 1943. These carriers were larger, faster, and had a greater aircraft capacity than anything built before. The new carriers displaced 36,380 tons fully loaded and were some 880 feet long. The *Essex*-class carrier typically carried eighty-seven aircraft and could make well over thirty knots. Twenty-four of these carriers were built. Only in 1970 were the final two of this class, *Hornet* and *Bennington,* retired from active sea duty. (As of this writing, the carrier *Lexington,* although extensively rebuilt from its original *Essex*-class design specification, still serves the Naval Air Station at Pensacola as the navy's only permanent training carrier.)

New subclasses of aircraft carriers were also introduced in 1943. The light carrier and the escort carrier became prominent new additions to the navy. The *Independence*-class light carrier was smaller and faster than the old *Lexington, Yorktown,* and *Hornet,* although it could carry only half the aircraft of the *Essex* class. Finally, the escort, or jeep, carriers, constructed partially of plywood, were lighter still and provided efficient, rapid, and inexpensive transport of aircraft. The jeep carriers were nearly disposable because they could be built so quickly, but they rendered invaluable service in, for example, Leyte Gulf.

Also developed in 1943 was the Grumman F6F Hellcat. The Americans had always suffered because of the inferior quality of their aircraft, especially the fighters. When the Americans retook the Aleutians, however, they managed to capture intact a Japanese A6M3-type Zero. Lord of the skies, the Zero had devastated American fighters. It could only be bested when American pilots used "hit and run" tactics (sometimes known as the "Thatch Weave"), or enjoyed numerical superiority. The American designers tested and almost literally dissected the Zero, designing and building a plane that would outperform it in almost every respect: the F6F Hellcat. Faster, nearly as maneuverable, and much more heavily armored, the Hellcat was for the most part a superior plane. This, coupled with the fact that after Midway Nimitz and King had provided for a cadre of properly trained combat pilots—which the Japanese had not—made the Hellcat a true killing machine.

The development of new aircraft was not limited to fighters alone. Although its potential would not be recognized for many months, a new aircraft made its appearance in early 1944, courtesy of the Boeing corporation. The B–29, or "Superfortress" as it came to be known, was the largest plane ever built. It had fuel-injected engines and a pressurized cabin that, in part, allowed it to fly much higher than any of its Japanese counterparts. Its cruise speed was approximately 290 mph and it was capable of traveling up to 3,000 miles. It had a payload of 20,000 pounds and was heavily armored. For self-defense, the B–29 was armed with twelve .50-caliber machine guns and a 20 mm cannon. The first of these planes were given to bomber command in China to be used against the Japanese home islands, but they did not work out when employed from Chinese bases, as will be seen. When eventually stationed on the Mariana Islands and used for attacks on the home islands, the B–29's became a devastating weapon in the American arsenal. The Japanese came to regard the B–29 with a mixture of fear and awe especially after they saw several at first hand. Particularly impressive was the strength of its basic air frame and its payload capacity, but the Japanese were also puzzled by the extent to which the Americans took steps to protect their aircrew.

There were other, less conventional approaches to bombload, however. At the beginning of every major war, inventors, professional and otherwise, besiege their military establishments with ways to do in the enemy efficiently. In 1941, a Pennsylvania dental surgeon managed to convince President Roosevelt that bats armed with incendiary devices could be dropped on the Japanese. Part of the active warhead device to be affixed to the bats is still classified by the CIA, but it is estimated that two million dollars was expended on the idea by the army, then the navy, before the project was abandoned.

More to the point, the Americans did implement a new type of warfare, one that some experts claimed could not be done as desired. Amphibious assaults called for special tools to ensure success. The Marine Corps, the navy's specially trained assault troops, were assigned to lead the island-hopping campaign as it reclaimed the vital islands of the Pacific. In 1941 they did not possess any special sort of boat or craft that would allow them to travel from their home vessels to the shore and launch an invasion.

The navy's marine architects reputedly proclaimed themselves incapable of producing a boat of the sort the Corps desired: lightweight, so it would draw no more than four feet of water and thus be able to cross coral reefs; equipped with a landing ramp, which would allow its occupants to step out onto the beach itself; reasonably spacious, if open to the weather, capable of carrying several dozen men and some equipment. When the navy responded, in effect, that such a vessel was impractical, a reputed one-time Louisiana bootlegger and highly skilled shipbuilder produced the Higgins Boat, which the marines waggishly claimed had been used by its builder to elude Federal Revenue agents. Regardless of the truth of this claim, the Higgins Boat, although without armor, was the Corp's workhorse landing craft for the better part of the Pacific war (almost all other landing craft used in the Pacific were of British design).

Officially designated as an *LCPL,* the Higgins boat, constructed of wood, was thirty-six feet long, ten feet wide, and, fully loaded, weighed 18,000 lbs., and drew three and one-half feet of water. It could carry, at the most, thirty-six fully loaded marines. It was built almost exclusively of wood and possessed no armor.

Finally, the American submarine warfare effort underwent dramatic changes in late 1943. American skippers had complained from the outset of the war that there were problems with the torpedoes carried by both the American submarines and torpedo planes. The torpedoes tended to run too deep, or detonate too early, or not detonate at all. Torpedo improvements, particularly in the form of the Mark XVI electric-driven torpedo, and wolfpacking vessels caused a dramatic increase in submarine effectiveness. The submarine campaign will be dealt with in greater depth in chapter 7.

By this time, Washington had witnessed a heated debate over strategy between the army and the navy, with mixed results. MacArthur, who originally had the Solomons in his bailiwick, had at first opposed the bypassing of Rabaul, but his public relations staff now claimed that island hopping was a MacArthur invention. The effect in Washington in general and in the naval establishment in particular of his fraudulent claim may be imagined. While both the army and the navy agreed that island hopping was the strategy of choice for the reconquest of the Pacific, two very distinct and different ideas began to form about how best to accomplish this advance. General MacArthur proposed a direct route of attack from New Guinea through the Philippines to the Japanese home islands. If he were given control of the naval forces in the Pacific, he felt this drive well within his abilities. Pointing out that his plan left the Allies' flanks open to attack, the navy proposed an equally direct route to the home islands that called for skirting the center of the Japanese empire and advancing northward through the Marshall, Gilbert, and Mariana island chains.

The two sides had reached an impasse. Largely by default, it emerged that both strategies would be implemented. But no one at first knew this would be so, for many believed that given the overall Europe-First commitment of the war effort, such could not be the case. It was only America's industrial strength, which was at first unrealized, that permitted the twin-pronged Asian strategy, as it came to be called, to be implemented. Thus, MacArthur was given enough naval support to initiate his plan while the navy was to use the marines and proceed with its strategy. The two would link up at the base of the home islands in a joint assault on Okinawa, some time in the future. All told, six marine and twenty army divisions would participate in the Pacific conflict.

Some have claimed that the two prongs supported one another and kept the Japanese off balance. Perhaps they did. But had Japanese intelligence ever been capable of breaking American ciphers and determining how uncoordinated the two advances were, the Japanese could have concentrated their strength first on one prong and then could have shifted to deal with the other, thereby possibly lengthening the conflict. This is the primary danger when commanders divide their forces. As it was, Halsey and the navy far outpaced MacArthur, who became bogged down with his New Guinea campaign. The Japanese never were capable of predicting the Allies' next move, though. They were forced to rush to countermeasures and never had the initiative. By maintaining the element of surprise, the Allies were able to keep the Japanese guessing and always had the numerical advantage when and where they chose to fight.

Had the United States chosen to name a single supreme commander in the Pacific, rather than relying on the considered opinion of divergent personalities, the chance of Japanese intelligence surprising the Allied forces could have been reduced practically to nil. One overall military leader, such as Admiral Nimitz, perhaps the most gifted and talented admiral in this nation's history, could have kept the advance through the Pacific on an even keel and perfectly organized. This was not possible, though, because of the personalities involved. The painful fact is that Douglas MacArthur had many enemies in Washington because he treated the staff officers there, both army and navy, as if *they* were his enemies; in doing so, he gave life to what was at first true only in his imagination. He even claimed that while chief of staff in the early 1930s, he had uncovered secret navy plans to isolate the army commanders in the Pacific and win the war unaided. MacArthur himself did not understand, at least at first, the basic principles of island hopping, and no one in the naval establishment from Washington to Pearl would have tolerated serving under him had he been made Pacific commander in chief. If a joint command was possible in Europe, where different nationalities were present, it should have been possible at least among American forces in the Pacific. But it was not to be. As Army Chief of Staff George Marshall remarked after the conflict, the personalities involved, especially MacArthur and Claire Chennault (who will be profiled in chapter 7), made a single commander neither possible nor practical.

In November 1943 Admiral Nimitz was prepared to take the next step in his planned reconquest of the island chains leading to Japan. The first of these landings, code-named *Operation Galvanic,* was to take place in the Gilbert Island chain, a former New Zealand colony. The islands of Betio in the Tarawa Atoll and Makin were designated as necessary to control the Gilberts, which stood directly athwart the American supply route to Australia.

Galvanic was to be the first of the navy's central Pacific drives. But the Japanese had begun reinforcement of the islands long before the evacuation of Guadalcanal in February 1943. In order to relieve pressure on the Solomons, Lt. Colonel Evans Carlson's Second Marine Raider Battalion had staged a raid in the Gilberts in mid-August 1942, which caused the Japanese to strengthen its defenses. Nimitz spent the greater portion of the year 1943 husbanding his strength for *Galvanic* in Oahu, the Fijis, and the New Hebrides.

Makin Atoll, in particular Butaritari, was the first American target. Very early on the morning of November 20, 1943 the One Hundred and Sixty-Fifth Infantry Regiment of the army's Twenty-Seventh Division landed on Makin, where they were opposed by 250 Japanese and some construction workers, many of whom were Korean and could have had little love for the Japanese. Whatever the case, Makin was secured by twilight of November 23, 1943.

Tarawa Atoll was another matter. Like many of the islands the navy would have to seize, Tarawa was surrounded by a coral reef. Betio (pronounced *Bashio*), the selected target island, is a little less than 300 acres in area, but has caves; the island's neap and dodging tides, which are irregular and almost impossible to predict, complicated the landings. The Japanese had also placed there a few of the eight-inch guns captured when Singapore surrendered, although these did little to help or hinder either side. Several British advisers warned that the marines' Higgins Boats would not be able to cross the reef at high tide, as did a native, who risked his life to inform the Americans that the tides would not permit an invasion the next day, November 21.

Obviously believing they had better information, the navy proceeded on schedule. Many marines had to wade when their boats grounded on the coral reef, which was 400 to 500 yards offshore. And no one had realized that Betio's alkaline sand, if mixed with concrete, would form a substance harder than concrete itself. Betio's defenders were largely Japanese marines, commanded by Rear Admiral Keiji Shibasaki. Indeed, many of his men were positioned in deep, if damp, underground caves that even naval shells had not penetrated. And, although the Japanese did contest the beach area landing, they chose to wait inland to inflict maximum casualties on the Americans. The marines' answer to this was to pour or pump gasoline into caves or very heavily fortified pillboxes and then ignite it. The island was declared secure on November 23, but pockets of enemy resistance continued for many days. Well over 900 marines died capturing the island, while about 4,200 Japanese combat troops perished defending it. Several days later, other islands in the atoll chain were seized to negate the threat of air strikes that might cut the great circle (shortest) route from the U.S. West Coast to Australia and New Zealand.

Several lessons were evident. A longer naval and air bombardment was needed, along with greater aerial reconnaissance to pinpoint enemy strongholds. But the United States had gained an excellent base to build up strength for its next objective, the Marshalls.

In January 1944, at the same time that MacArthur was beginning his campaign in New Guinea, the navy was readying itself for forthcoming operations in the central Pacific. Admiral Halsey had acquired a well-coordinated, fast carrier force of six heavy and six light carriers, with fast battleship, cruiser, and destroyer escorts. Designated Task Force Thirty-Eight and commanded by Vice Admiral Marc Mitscher, the force used lightning strikes against Japanese strongholds. This carrier force was called upon to establish air superiority over the Marshalls before the invasion force arrived.

Nimitz made a bold gesture by insisting that the marines take only the Kwajalein and Eniwetok atolls, bypassing the numerous other Japanese strongholds in the chain. Kwajalein was a key Japanese communication center, and Nimitz evidently perceived it as a priority target. After Mitscher's force had reduced the Japanese air power in the vicinity, the big ships approached and initiated a three-day saturation bombardment of the atoll. The Japanese had 8,000 men on Kwajalein under Rear Admiral Monzo Akiyama. When the Seventh Infantry landed on Kwajalein, they found the Japanese dug in as they had been at Tarawa, but the Americans put their experience with this style of warfare to good use and suffered comparatively light losses. In the meantime, the Marine Fourth Division had landed on the nearby islands of Roi and Namur. In all the United States used some 41,000 men to take the atoll and lost only 372 killed, 1,000 wounded. The Japanese, in comparison, had lost all but 130 of their original force. By February 7 the atoll was declared secure; the Americans had denied the Japanese an important communications center.

On February 17, 1944, Mitscher's fast task force was used once again, this time in a raid on the redoubtable Japanese garrison at Truk. Knowing that the Japanese had a sizable force on the island, and that the true importance of Truk was its port facility, Halsey opted to launch an air strike in order to neutralize the base. Admiral Koga, commander of the Japanese combined fleet stationed at Truk, managed to get his warships out intact. Mitscher's pilots did sink fifty merchant vessels in the harbor while destroying 275 aircraft as well. Later, while patrolling the waters around Truk, Admiral Spruance managed to sink a light cruiser and a destroyer. The myth of Truk's invincibility had been destroyed, as had its usefulness as a Japanese staging area.

At the same time that Mitscher was attacking the base at Truk, the U.S. Army and Marines were reducing the Japanese garrison at Eniwetok. The three main islands of the Eniwetok Atoll were defended by the 2,200 men of the Japanese First Amphibious Battalion. All three islands were secured by February 21, at a cost of 339 American dead. The entire Japanese garrison was wiped out in deadly hand-to-hand warfare, supplemented by the Americans' extensive use of flame-throwers. With the fall of Eniwetok the way was open for the American advance to the Marianas.

From the standpoint of the average Japanese soldier, it may have been just as well that so few of them survived. The code of *Bushido* held that the highest disgrace for a soldier was capture. "Save the last bullet for yourself," read the opening statement of most training manuals for enlisted personnel in the Japanese Army. If a soldier were captured, the Red Cross would report that fact to the Japanese government, and the soldier's family, friends, and neighbors would very probably literally pretend that he had never existed.

The few Japanese taken prisoner were captured under unusual circumstances. Some were rendered unconscious by bursting shells, only to regain consciousness in an American medical facility. Seeking information on enemy dispositions, American commanders would occasionally call for prisoner capture. The prisoners were usually plied with "medicinal" alcohol, for which Japanese soldiers seemed to have little tolerance, apparently due to the lack of a certain enzyme in their blood stream. In any event, Japanese captives usually gave false names, or pleaded that their families not be told of their captivity. The Japanese occasionally took prisoners for the same reason. But essentially, for the man actually in the front line, the war was one of racial extinction, similar to many of the campaigns against the American Plains Indians. No quarter was ever asked. Only rarely was any given.

By the end of 1943 the Japanese were in a very different posture and position than in 1941. Their navy especially lacked key personnel, particularly aviators. Many had perished by the end of the year. True, the Japanese had accumulated an impressive cadre of naval aces. The greatest was Lt. Hiroyoshi Nishizawa, who accounted for *at least* eighty-seven enemy aircraft, before perishing in 1944. (His record makes him the most prodigious ace of the Pacific theater of the war.) But the later aces tended to have less impressive records and were professionally short-lived, as a recent Japanese study (see the reading list below) indicates. Star or flag-grade commanders had also been lost, and veteran soldiers as-well as pilots who could remember the first combat actions were now exceptions. The impressive aggressive posture of the imperial forces was depleted. Morale remained high, but the resources necessary to maintain the war machine were growing scarcer with the passing of every day.

On the other hand, America had mobilized impressive military and naval might that dwarfed what Japan had marshalled in 1941. At least 110,000 Japanese fighting men had been bypassed on islands, left to spend the remainder of the conflict squinting at the horizon for a relief fleet that would never arrive. The decisive battle between battleships anticipated by the Japanese Naval General Staff had not come, but the tide of war had turned. Japan's outpost sentinels were gone and there was no hope of recapturing them.

The Americans, with their new technology, manpower, and industrial resources, had gained the upper hand. The conflict would now be fought largely on American terms. Time was now an American ally. The Japanese leaders in Tokyo could only watch and wait for the time and location of the next American blow.

Suggestions for Further Reading

Walter Lord's *Lonely Vigil: Coastwatchers of the Solomons* (New York: Viking Press, 1977) is a very worthwhile history of the Australians who stayed behind after the Japanese conquest as unknown observers; a second good study on the same topic is Eric Feldt, *The Coastwatchers* (New York: Oxford University Press, 1978). Dudley McCarthy, *South-West Pacific Area—First Year, Kokoda to Wau* (Canberra: Australian War Memorial, 1956), is one of a series of official Australian histories of the war south of the equator. John Miller, Jr. *Cartwheel: The*

Reduction of Rabaul (Washington, DC: Army Historical Office, 1959); and Samuel Miller, *Victory in Papua* (Washington, DC: Army Historical Office, 1957) are two useful official U.S. Army studies. Brian Garfield, *The Thousand Mile War: World War II in Alaska and the Aleutians* (Garden City, NY: Doubleday, 1969) is the best study so far of the war in the Aleutians; John Lorelli, *The Battle of the Komandorski Islands* (Annapolis, MD: Naval Institute Press, 1984) is a recent account of that relatively neglected engagement. A good account of MacArthur during this period appears in chapter eight of Ronald Lewin, *The American Magic: Codes, Ciphers, and the Defeat of Japan* (New York: Farrar Straus Giroux, 1982). For amphibious warfare see Daniel Barbey, *MacArthur's Amphibious Navy: Seventh Amphibious Force Operations, 1943–1945* (Annapolis, MD: Naval Institute Press, 1969), especially useful for the development of landing craft and interservice rivalry; James Ladd, *Assault from the Sea: The Craft, the Landings, the Man* (New York: Hippocrene Books, 1976); and Peter Iseley and Philip Crowl, *The U.S. Marines and Amphibious War: Its Theory and Its Practice in the Pacific* (Princeton, NJ: Princeton University Press, 1951). Jack Coggins, *The Campaign for Guadalcanal* (Garden City, NY: Doubleday, 1972) is very worthwhile; Eric Hammel, *Guadalcanal: The Carrier Battles* (New York: Crown Publishers, 1987) is also useful. Thomas Miller, *The Cactus Air Force* (New York: Harper and Row, 1969), explores the adventures of the Marine aviators on Guadalcanal. The definitive work on the "black sheep" squadron is Frank Walton, *Once They Were Eagles: The Men of the Black Sheep Squadron* (Lexington: University Press of Kentucky, 1986). Stanley Smith, *The Battle of Savo* (New York: Macfadden-Bartell, 1962), is a passable account of the naval action. Peter Phinney, *The Barbarians: A Soldier's New Guinea Diary* (St. Lucia: University of Queensland Press, 1989), is an Australian's diary which reveals a little-known side of the enlisted Allied soldier who fought "down under." Similarly, *To Kokoda and Beyond: The Story of the 39th Battalion* (Melbourne: Melbourne University Press, 1988), ed. by Victor Austin, includes Japanese as well as Australian materials on a "scratch" unit that suddenly found itself in the first line of defense after Pearl Harbor. For Tarawa, see especially Eric Hammel and John Lane, *Seventy-Six Hours: The Invasion of Tarawa* (New York: Tower Books, 1980), which is in part a study via oral history. The definitive Japanese study of naval aviator aces is Ikuhiko Hata and Yasuho Izawa, *Japanese Naval Aces and Fighter Units in World War Two* (Annapolis, MD: Naval Institute Press, 1989); on the same topic see Rene J. Francillon, *Japanese Aircraft of the Pacific War* (New York: Funk and Wagnalls, 1970); and Jrio Hirokoshi, *Eagles of Mitsubishi: The Story of the Zero Fighter* (Seattle: University of Washington Press, 1981), which speak to the matter of Japanese aircraft production and performance. For American aces, see Edward Sims, *The Greatest Aces* (New York: Harper and Row, 1967). Material on the bat incendiary scheme is in Joe M. Feist, "Bats Away," *American Heritage 33* (April–May 1982); 93–95.

6. The Marianas and the Philippines

The Marianas
MacArthur Returns to the Philippines
The Battle of Leyte Gulf
The Kamikazes
Leyte and Luzon Islands
Western Prisoners of War
The Liberation of the Philippines

Having secured the Marshall and Caroline island chains, the U.S. Navy prepared to climb the next rung of the ladder leading to the Japanese home islands. The Mariana Island group was dominated by three islands in particular: Saipan, Tinian, and Guam. Saipan had been mandated to Japan under the Versailles Treaty in 1919 as reward for its nominal participation in World War I. The Japanese had intended eventually to annex the island and had initiated a rather substantial colonization effort on it. Thus for the first time Japanese civilians would be eyewitnesses to the American conquest of an island.

Tinian, a sister island to Saipan, was the site of a large Japanese air facility. From the runways on Tinian, the Japanese could venture as far south as Truk, or, conversely, as far north as Tokyo. These runways were a primary target of the Allied advance. Possession of them would place the Japanese home islands well within the range of the new B–29 bomber. Finally, the southernmost island of the chain, Guam, had been a U.S. possession since 1898. Although the Americans had never effectively developed Guam in a commercial sense, its inhabitants were fiercely proud American citizens. Thus, it was both psychologically and politically important that Guam be liberated at an early date as a token of faith to other captive indigenous populations to demonstrate American good will—most especially to the Filipinos.

The Marianas were essential to the maintenance of the Japanese empire for the same strategic military reasons that the Americans desired them. The military leaders in Tokyo determined to pursue an all-out effort to insure that they remained in Japanese hands. On the first of April 1944, Admiral Koga, commander of Japan's combined fleet, perished when his plane was lost at sea. His successor, Admiral

Soemu Toyoda, was both more aggressive and more persuasive. He initiated *Operation A-Go* in an effort to deal a crippling blow to the American Navy. He set his staff planners to work almost as soon as he took command, but the battle may have come sooner than he had anticipated because of the arrival of an American task force off the island of Saipan.

Saipan would be a difficult objective. Twelve miles long, it had a curving mountainous spine and was located 100 miles north of Guam. Nimitz and King both regarded Saipan as the key to the Marianas, and so the Guamanians would have to wait until Saipan fell for their own liberation from the Japanese. Saipan is honeycombed with caves, perhaps more per square mile than any other island of its approximate size in the Pacific. Lt. General Yoshitsugu Saito commanded the island's garrison. Technically, though, the Japanese command structure was unique on Saipan, for Admiral Nagumo had requested a land command. Nagumo was allegedly in charge of the overall defense of the island, which was to be coordinated with the navy. In actual fact, however, Nagumo was just a bystander, which was as he wished. With no hope of avenging his losses at Midway—only two of the six original carriers of the First Air Fleet *(Zuikaku* and *Shokaku)* and very few of her veteran aviators remaining—Nagumo had undertaken a mission from which he did not wish to return.

Beginning on June 11, 1944, Mitscher's fast carrier task force had begun neutralizing the island's defenses. The Japanese garrison numbered 30,000 men—two full divisions, in effect. Saito contested the islands at the waterline, as the Second and Fourth Marine Divisions discovered when they landed on June 15. Resistance was more than even the marines had bargained for, and the only reinforcements to be had was the Twenty-Seventh Army Division, a national guard unit recruited from the New England states. There is no doubt that the Twenty-Seventh performed below par, probably because of the attitude of some of its senior officers, who had enlisted in peacetime and evidently took their duties too lightly. Individual men fought bravely, but their leadership was sometimes lacking. The Twenty-Seventh helped to turn the tide on Saipan, but its commander, Major General Ralph Smith, was relieved at Marine insistence, and their quality of performance is moot to this day.

Nagumo lived long enough to witness several of the ships his aviators had sunk at Pearl Harbor bombard targets on the island of Saipan.

Fighting was hand to hand, especially after the five days it took the marines to get beyond their beachheads. When the Americans had clearly triumphed, Saito and Nagumo committed *seppuku,* ritual suicide, with the usual wartime twist of having an officer stand behind the suicide to put a bullet into the dying man's head, lest he be captured, sutured, transfused, and made a prisoner of war by the enemy. Before his death, Saito, acting in Nagumo's name, had ordered what would be the biggest *Banzai*—suicide charge—of the war, to be executed the next morning. Marines and soldiers of the Twenty-Seventh Division knew what was coming long before. Saito's remaining troops consumed large quantities of the Japanese rice wine, sake, that evening, on the grounds that it was a vasodilator that would facilitate bleeding, thus ensuring a more rapid death in battle.

At dawn well over 3,000 drunken Japanese swarmed into a gap that opened in the Twenty-Seventh's lines. The Japanese poured through, bearing down upon amazed Marine artillery groups, which had to fuse their shells to fire literal muzzle bursts to stop them. The charge was as colorful, and perhaps frightening, as it was futile. American loses on Saipan were 3,100 killed, 13,160 wounded; Japanese military losses were staggering: 27,000 killed. This latter figure does not include some 22,000 civilians who took their own lives, evidently believing Japanese Army propaganda concerning the American forces about to occupy their homes. They had been told that civilians would be torn to pieces by gorillas brought from the States for this purpose. Whether they accepted such propaganda as literal truth or not, many chose to jump from cliffs rather than submit to life under the American flag.

The marines on Saipan had complained of the lack of proper air support, and with good reason. Vice Admiral Jisaburo Ozawa had promptly executed Toyoda's plan to destroy American air and naval power. Utilizing all of Japan's remaining available carrier strength, he marshalled a force that included five heavy and four light carriers to gain aerial supremacy. He launched four attacks, the first on June 19. He had over 420 aircraft, plus an added 100-odd land-based aircraft from adjacent islands, including Guam, technically under his command.

Admiral Spruance's opposing fleet comprised seven fleet and eight light carriers, giving him almost double the 955 planes available to the Japanese. Here the Hellcat fighter made its most impressive showing against the Zero; 330 Japanese planes were shot down, while the

United States lost a mere thirty planes. Further, American submarines had found Ozawa's carrier force and put their new, improved torpedoes into two of his carriers: the new 34,000-ton *Taiho,* which was serving as Ozawa's flagship, and the veteran carrier *Shokaku* were lost. Mitscher pursued the enemy, inflicting further losses; Japan lost the carrier *Hiyo* (29,000 tons), and sixty-five more aircraft, while 100 U.S. aircraft were lost, the bulk because they ran out of fuel and ditched in the ocean. More than 460 Japanese pilots had perished; Japanese naval air power was now a mere shadow of its former self, and, with the exception of the *Kamikaze* corps, had little more than nuisance value for the remainder of the war.

The Guamanians wondered what American intentions were. At first, life under Japanese rule had not been brutal, but as the tide of war turned, the Japanese grew senselessly and arbitrarily cruel. Leading citizens were executed for no apparent reason. Life became a living hell, but reconquest of the island was delayed by the assignment to Saipan of the only reserve in the area, the Twenty-Seventh Division.

The invaders on Guam enjoyed advantages not heretofore known. There were excellent maps of the area. Also, a small but very effective resistance movement provided last-minute intelligence data. After a sporadic seventeen-day bombardment by naval and air forces, the marines and the Seventy-Seventh Army Division landed on Guam on July 20, 1944. Three weeks of fighting ensued, costing the lives of 1,290 Americans and 10,690 Japanese. Meanwhile, on July 24, Tinian was invaded; 5,700 Japanese and 390 Americans perished.

The Mariana campaign, including the carrier battle, demonstrated to the Japanese ruling elite that all hope of winning the war had disappeared. In Tokyo, the emperor exclaimed, ''Hell is upon us,'' and, after an expression of imperial disapproval of the way he was prosecuting the war, on July 18, 1944, Premier Tojo resigned. Some viewed it as high time for Tojo to step down. For many weeks his household had been receiving generic phone calls, all to the same effect: ''Why hasn't Tojo committed suicide yet?''

This was the last instance in which the emperor appeared to believe that the conflict might still somehow be resolved in Japan's favor. He even briefly considered appointing a general and an admiral as co-premiers, but when the chosen navy candidate, Admiral Mitsumasa Yonai, declined, retired General Kuniaki Koiso replaced Tojo, with Yonai as his navy minister and deputy premier. The emperor, speaking through Kido, urged an end to interservice rivalry and all due speed in reversing Japan's decline.

At the time little was known in Washington of the vicissitudes of Japanese internal politics. The joint chiefs and the president had more pressing matters at hand. Should the next target be the Philippines, which MacArthur was now ready to approach, or should the islands be bypassed in favor of seizing Okinawa, and perhaps Formosa as well, as many in the navy, particularly Admiral King, desired? Never had interservice rivalry been more evident, or the Europe-first decision brought into more question—particularly by Admiral King. And it was an election year. Roosevelt was running for an unprecedented fourth term as president. Stressing his role as commander in chief, he chose to resolve the debate in person, or at least to give that impression. Sailing on the heavy cruiser *Baltimore,* via San Diego, Roosevelt reached Pearl Harbor on July 26, 1944, for a conference with MacArthur and Nimitz. The president brought with him only his White House chief of staff, Admiral William Leahy. They conferred at a former civilian residence on Waikiki beach, where they also spent the night.

Roosevelt must have been conscious of his health as seldom before. He knew it was poor. Further, according to one of his sons, he had suffered an acute attack of chest pain just before he left the West Coast. Perhaps this made him more susceptible to MacArthur's arguments that he had a moral obligation to liberate the Philippine people from the Japanese yoke as soon as possible. Some writers have suggested that during the evening of the 26th, MacArthur secretly sought out the president and offered further arguments; a few have even claimed that the general might have promised to relinquish all presidential ambitions for 1944 if the president would approve immediate invasion of the Philippines. But there is no proof of any of this, and while such speculation is interesting, such bargaining remains improbable.

Nonetheless, MacArthur's largely political argument won the day, backed by the general's suggestion that the electorate might be disenchanted if Roosevelt seemed to desert the Philippine people. On July 27, in the course of an automobile drive, Nimitz sensed from conversation between MacArthur and Roosevelt that the general had indeed persuaded the president. "We've sold it," MacArthur told his staff aboard his own aircraft as they left the islands, referring to the proposed liberation of the Philippines in what must seem, in or out of context, a somewhat flippant manner. Still, Washington in general and King in particular were skeptical. It was several weeks before they agreed to the invasion of Luzon in particular.

In late August and early September 1944 Nimitz sent Halsey on a series of preemptive strikes against the Bonin Islands, Yap, the Palaus, and Mindanao. Halsey's aviators found the southern Philippines and their approaches more lightly defended than they expected. As a result, the first of MacArthur's landings in Mindanao was canceled and MacArthur was authorized to bypass that island and strike directly at the island of Leyte, in the central part of the Philippine archipelago. MacArthur would begin liberating the Philippine people two months ahead of schedule.

Nimitz and MacArthur, however, wanted the Palaus group to be secured before any further advances were made on the Philippines. This would insure that MacArthur's flank would be safe. The marines were very near the area already, so Washington gave its approval and the First Marine Division was slated to conquer the island of Peleliu.

Intelligence had determined that there were as many as 10,000 Japanese on the island, but that only 6,000 were actually battle-ready. The preinvasion reconnaissance of the island had failed to disclose the extensive bunker system that permeated the island, so when the marines hit the beaches on September 15, they were greeted with a most unwelcome surprise. The Japanese had dug in extraordinarily well and evidenced stiffer resistance then was normal even for them. By the end of the first day's fighting, the marines were forced to commit all of their reserves to the battle. This bloody struggle went on for nearly a month before the defenders had been rooted out. One in four of the marines who fought on Peleliu was buried there. The losses suffered by the Americans were horrendous in comparison to the gains they made. All but 200 of the Japanese on the island were killed, and those captured were largely suffering from wounds or shelling that rendered them unconscious. No small number awakened in American field hospitals. A live documentary of the invasion of Peleliu was filmed, and nine combat photographers fell during its shooting. The film, entitled *Fury in the Pacific,* remains a graphic documentary of American and Japanese determination and combat operations.

The real tragedy of Peleliu is that the whole operation may well have been unnecessary. There was an air strip on the island, but

Mitscher's fast carrier force had reduced larger targets before, and with American superiority in the air, what kind of problems could the Japanese have really caused from this tiny island garrison? After the war Nimitz admitted that the campaign in the Palaus area may have been a mistake. In any case, the stage was set for the glorious fulfillment of Douglas MacArthur's promise to return to the Philippines.

MacArthur was on the verge of committing a considerable military faux pas; he had been publicizing his return to the islands for quite some time. The Japanese would surely be prepared to meet his arrival. MacArthur had been air dropping items to the Filipinos with the motto *"I shall return"* printed or otherwise affixed to them. When he ordered a sudden and dramatic increase in the number of objects so dropped, he may not only have destroyed the chances of surprise but also in the end, revealed the actual landing area. Some of MacArthur's staff had misgivings about his propaganda campaign but evidently kept their own counsel concerning the matter.

This propaganda campaign per se had its downside as well. Making such promises publicly, MacArthur had committed his prestige to the forthcoming campaign. In a sense he committed himself to location as well. Army strategy taught that a soldier should attack his enemy wherever he was found and that bypassing strongholds was logistical suicide. These reasons, along with the simple fact that MacArthur wished to make the Japanese in the Philippines pay for the humiliation he had suffered, had motivated MacArthur to propose an invasion of the southernmost island of Mindanao, followed by a stair-step campaign through the entire island chain.

But, as has already been recounted, during their preinvasion strikes on the islands of Yap, Ulithi, and the Paluas, the navy had experienced less resistance than expected. Consequently the navy proposed moving the landings on Leyte up by two months from December 20 to October 20, 1944, and bypassing the Japanese garrison on Mindanao. MacArthur accepted this proposal, averring that it would return him to Philippine soil that much earlier.

The Japanese fully realized that American reconquest of the Philippines would enable U.S. submarines to interdict what remained of their maritime supply lines to the southern resource regions. From the obscurity of retirement they called upon General Yamashita, the "Tiger of Malaya," to command the nearly 350,000 Japanese troops on the islands. Yamashita's task would not be an easy one. The Japanese had made the initial mistake of assuming that the Filipinos would greet them as liberators, not realizing that the inhabitants regarded themselves as an Hispanic-American people. Long before MacArthur's approach, the Filipino underground had been nipping at the heels of the Japanese conqueror, especially in the Moro country, where the Japanese travelled in convoy or not at all. Further, most of Yamashita's air power had been used up in mid-October, in a series of battles over and near Formosa. In Tokyo, a new strategy was formalized: the beaches were not to be contested. Japanese air power, including land-based aircraft, would strike at the American landing craft and/or support vessels on the beaches.

None of this came soon enough to save the island of Leyte from American assault. After a very heavy naval bombardment, the first U.S. Army landings on Leyte began on October 20, 1944. The Japanese at once put the latest revision of their *"go"* (victory) plan into operation. Diesel oil had become so scarce in Japan proper that part of the Japanese fleet had to sail from ports in the southern conquered regions.

Though the plan itself employed a varied and large number of ships, it might well have come from a Japanese naval academy textbook. Vice Admiral Jisaburo Ozawa commanded a northern force that served only one purpose—to lure Halsey and his fleet carriers away from the Leyte area. Ozawa commanded Japan's four remaining carriers, two battleships, three cruisers, and eight destroyers. But he reputedly had only 116 operative aircraft, flown by inexperienced aviators, and divided among his carriers, although Halsey did not know this.

The center force, which had rendezvoused from several southern ports, was commanded by Rear Admiral Takeo Kurita. It included the super-battleships *Yamato* and *Musashi,* both of which when fully loaded displaced well over 70,000 tons. Kurita was to make for the San Bernadino Straits, where they would fire their eighteen-inch guns in action for the first time. Admiral Kurita ringed his giant ships with his three remaining battleships, twelve cruisers, and fifteen destroyers.

To his south, Vice Admiral Shoji Nishimura commanded two battleships, one heavy cruiser, and four destroyers; he was to be aided by Vice Admiral Kiyohide Shima, whose force comprised three cruisers and four destroyers. Nishimura and Shima were to traverse the Surigao Strait. All were to converge on Leyte Gulf, where, if American landing craft were no longer apparent, they would destroy the American supply train and, if possible, direct their fire on American troops ashore.

For the superstitious in the Japanese Navy, plans began to go astray from the first. The submarines *Darter* and *Dace* sighted Kurita's center force, alerted Admiral Halsey, and sank two of Kurita's cruisers (including his flagship) off of Palawan. Two days later Halsey's airmen attacked *Musashi,* and she took at least nineteen torpedoes; clearly lost, all Kurita could do was to order *Musashi* to engage flank speed, either forward or reverse, ground herself, and become a land battery! Since her steering capacity had been impaired, this proved impossible, and at sunset that day, October 24, 1944, she sank. At dusk that evening, Kurita turned westward. It looked as if the central part of the battle had terminated. In fact, Kurita was pulling back to regroup and intended to attempt to force the straits the next day. This should have been evident to the American command structure. Kurita had a reputation for tenacity. Further, signal fires and lighthouses, never before lit by the Japanese in the San Bernadino Straits, glowed that evening, betraying Kurita's intention to return.

Halsey nonetheless evidently remained convinced that the fighting in this area was over; he proceeded to execute a standing order to sink Japanese carriers whenever possible. Along with Mitscher's fast carrier task force, coded as Task Force Thirty-Eight, he turned northward on October 24 to pursue Ozawa's decoy force. He did not inform Rear Admiral Thomas Kinkaid of this decision, and Kinkaid was left alone to guard the Leyte area. The men of Leyte were left with only a light screen of cover provided by the Seventh Fleet's jeep carrier task groups. The Japanese now had the situation they had hoped for. American landing forces at Leyte were compromised and the battleships could proceed nearly unmolested to shell the American supply vessels and troops.

Early on the morning of October 25, Admiral J.B. Oldendorf's PT boat picket line detected Nishimura's force attempting to navigate through Surigao Strait. Oldendorf had his destroyers torpedo several Japanese ships, after which they retired. Nishimura pressed on through the strait in a storm front, which greatly limited his visibility.

When he broke out of the front on the morning of October 25, he did so in the face of Oldendorf's defensive line, essentially placing himself on the wrong end of a T formation. Oldendorf's force of battleships, cruisers, and destroyers decimated Nishimura's force, sinking all but one of his destroyers. Admiral Shima's force managed to escape, but was harassed by American PT boats. In the ensuing confusion, Shima's flagship collided with one of Nishimura's mortally wounded vessels, and one of his cruisers was lost. At this point, Oldendorf broke off contact, fearful of another Japanese advance toward the strait. Shima's few remaining destroyers retired from the battle.

At dawn on the 25th, Kurita reentered the San Bernadino Straits. This time he found American carriers unprotected, unsuspecting, and just within range of *Yamato*'s big guns. Taffy Five, the designation for Rear Admiral Clifton Sprague's jeep carrier force, was protecting the northern approaches to the landing zone and thought that Halsey was still in the area. Sprague's force of six escort carriers, three destroyers, and four destroyer escorts was the only unit in position to stop Kurita's advance. But Kurita did not know that he faced only the light carriers, for he radioed that "by an opportunity sent by the gods," he was about to engage American *fleet* carriers off the coast of Samar.

Kurita's sailors had been at battle stations for the better part of three days. Exhaustion was beginning to take its toll. Since the spotters on Kurita's ships reported Sprague's force as being Mitscher's fleet carrier force, Kurita ordered his gunnery officer to fire armor piercing rounds. The initial salvos caught the Americans off guard, but provided a literally colorful spectacle. *Yamato* carried dye markers in each shell so that her turret crews could distinguish from the color of the water spray each salvo created which geyser corresponded with which salvo, thereby allowing the gunners to adjust their aim accordingly.

The two forces were about twenty miles apart and well within range of *Yamato*'s eighteen-inch guns. Sprague's destroyers bravely charged the far superior force, while the few aircraft he had harassed the enemy by dropping fragmentation bombs, meant for close support of ground troops, on the decks of the battleships. But with victory in his grasp, Kurita decided to retire. Reinforced by aircraft from the other picket forces, Sprague's force was putting up a spirited defense. The bombardment of the carriers also seemed to be having little effect, largely because the armor-piercing shells penetrated the wooden decks of the escort carriers but failed to detonate, many continuing on through the thin hulls without exploding. This produced large holes in the American ships, but only one carrier was actually sunk. Kurita retired again through the San Bernadino Straits, terminating the engagement.

At nearly the same time that the two forces in the south were being reduced, Halsey's carriers caught up with Ozawa and his force. Meant from the beginning to be live bait for the aggressive Halsey, Ozawa had sent most of his aircraft to operate from shore facilities, and was unable to defend his carriers against the determined American attack. In the engagement, Ozawa lost four carriers and five other support vessels. The last carrier from the First Air Fleet, *Zuikaku,* joined her sister ships in a watery grave. The First Air Fleet in particular, and Japanese naval might in general, were destroyed in the battles of Leyte Gulf. Japanese naval power would never recover. The raw materials— even the iron ore necessary—were not available to rebuild the fleet.

Although none of the participants realized it until it was over, this was the greatest naval battle in history. No less than 282 ships were engaged, and nearly 190,000 sailors. The United States lost one light carrier, two escort carriers, two destroyers, and one destroyer escort, and about 200 aircraft, with a total of 2,800 battle deaths; the Japanese lost one fleet carrier, three light carriers, three battleships (including *Musashi*), six heavy cruisers, four light cruisers, and eleven destroyers, some 500 planes, and had suffered over 10,000 battle deaths.

From the American standpoint, the battle is very controversial. Sometimes called the "Battle of Bull's Run," naval historians have long debated whether "Bull" Halsey was justified in dashing northward, since he did exactly as the enemy anticipated. True, he sank four enemy carriers, but if Kurita had not lost his nerve at the crucial moment, Kinkaid would have had no effective defense against *Yamato* and her escorting ships. It was a calculated risk, but one that Kinkaid did not appreciate. Halsey was his usual impetuous self. Establishing behavior patterns in battle is potentially the worst sin a commander can commit. Halsey's impulsive behavior led him to do exactly as the enemy had anticipated. The Japanese did not take effective tactical advantage of it, so Halsey had the best of both worlds.

But obviously Kinkaid, and more importantly, Nimitz at Pearl Harbor did not approve of his actions. Their opinions count for more than all of the later comment that could be, and has been, made. Nimitz's inquiry to Halsey, "Where is Task Force Thirty-Four?," sent as Halsey was engaging Ozawa, reflected more than mere curiosity by Halsey's superior at Pearl. Nimitz obviously did not appreciate Halsey doing exactly as the enemy desired, if indeed he had left Leyte unprotected. Nimitz had never before sent such a seemingly routine inquiry over his own signature to Halsey, and that fact alone betrays Nimitz's judgment, at least at that moment, on the matter.

From the Japanese standpoint, victory at Leyte Gulf would have meant little. At best, it would have lowered American morale and postponed the invasion of the remainder of the Philippines. All the Japanese would have purchased would have been time—time in which the American fleet would have brought up reinforcements, time in which Yamashita could have consolidated his plans.

In the wake of the Leyte disaster came a Japanese plan to snatch victory from the jaws of defeat. The idea was that a fleet of thousands of aircraft would deliberately crash land into Allied warships. Theoretically, the plan could have resulted in the sinking of the entire active Allied battle navy. Known officially as the Special Attack Corps, the air fleet had been founded by Vice Admiral Takijiro Onishi just before the Battle of Leyte Gulf, and a very few of its units had participated in the last hours of the battle, sinking the escort carrier *St. Lo.* The unofficial name was *Kamikaze* ("Divine Wind") corps, the name deriving from a typhoon that had once saved the Japanese home islands from invasion from mainland Asia. (Another reading of the same Japanese characters is *"Shimpu,"* the corps' usual name in Japan during the conflict.)

After the organization became nationwide in Japan, virtually every civilian young man within the requisite age brackets volunteered. The phrase "one plane, one ship" became their motto. Theirs was a largely volunteer organization, but experienced naval aviators were needed as guides and as leavening for the green recruits, and on occasion aviators whose normal units were decimated were also ordered to join. And Admiral Toyoda sometimes *ordered* ordinary naval aviators to imitate the *Kamikazes.* But a volunteer, elite *esprit de corps* was their hallmark. Statistics vary, but it appears that well over 4,000 volunteers died; it is believed that about 330 American ships were damaged, or sunk, by these suicide missions.

The only branch of the *Kamikaze* corps that saw substantial action was its aviation wing. The Japanese later began to put together a naval surface suicide group. Husbanded largely for the expected Allied invasion of the main islands, these men were to be pilots of suicide boats, vessels of small construction that would ram Allied landing craft. A very few actually saw service in the Philippine campaign. In addition, the long-lance torpedo was equipped for guidance by a human *(Kaiten)*, and underwater suicide frogmen *(Fukuryu)* were also recruited.

The American Navy never could properly rationalize *Kamikaze* behavior. It was widely rumored, particularly among navy enlisted personnel, that *Kamikaze* pilots were riveted into their cockpits, hypnotized, drugged, chained, or promised immediate entry into heaven upon death. None of this, of course, was true. Young men were literally happy to offer their lives for their emperor. In Japan today it would probably be impossible. But in wartime Japan, a generation not dedicated to materialism were willing to give up their lives. The mystique was not at all difficult to grasp for the average Japanese youth, although some parents naturally regretted their children's decision.

Upon joining, the volunteer wrote out a will, and also a farewell letter to his family. Then he was given training on the ground and eventually posted to an air base. He then waited for a target to appear. When a target came within range, volunteers were called for, although if a trainee did not yet feel at peace with himself it was not necessarily a disgrace, in effect, to refuse the call. If time allowed, he had a farewell toast with his commanding officer, after which he embarked on his first and, hopefully, only suicide flight. An experienced pilot would guide his group to the target, and then he was on his own. If the target disappeared, he returned to the ground, although landing with a planeload of explosives set to detonate on contact was no easy matter.

If his target was a battleship, he crashed at the base of a turret; if a carrier, he aimed for one of the flight elevators. Some special pilots were actually instructed to land on an American carrier and hurl grenades at the gasoline supply lines, and a few did so. The *Kamikaze* corps never was an effective physical weapon, though they caused considerable damage at Okinawa, as will be seen. But psychologically, they made the enemy seem superhuman, ready to make sacrifices the average American warrior could not comprehend. The American Navy and Marine Corps could never successfully appreciate Japanese motives, much less successfully represent them to enlisted men, and the subject is one both services avoid to this day. Americans are too secular and rational to comprehend fully the motives of the young men who willingly gave their lives in the service of their country.

With the Japanese Navy now essentially out of the picture, the American Army was free to press its attacks on Leyte. Once again the Japanese had determined to make Leyte a decisive confrontation. Japanese troops on the island were minimal at the beginning of the campaign, but some 45,000 reinforcements were sent in an attempt to stem the advance of the American forces. The battle for the island lasted a full two months, with the Japanese surrendering ground only after inflicting heavy losses on the U.S. forces. By Christmas Day of 1944, the U.S. Army could declare the island secure, but "mopping up" operations continued well into the next year. MacArthur was in the habit of declaring an island secure before the enemy was entirely eliminated, a habit that was not appreciated by officers who had to write the family of enlisted men killed after the general's proclamation had been published in stateside newspapers.

General Yamashita had taken a substantial risk in committing so many of his soldiers to the fight on Leyte. He seriously depleted the number of troops that would be available to him for the defense of Luzon. By capturing Leyte, the Americans had cut the Japanese garrison on Mindanao off from the force on Luzon and could deal with the separate forces at their leisure.

MacArthur now prepared to retake from the Japanese the northernmost island of Luzon, with its capital city of Manila. Although he denied the fact, he chose to follow almost the exact same invasion route taken by Homma late in 1941. He would land troops in the north at Lingayen Gulf and push the Japanese to the south and east. He was also determined to make the men who had been responsible for his humiliation early in the war pay for their insolence. With no danger of Japanese naval intervention, the landings on Luzon were scheduled for January 2, 1945.

The Japanese still had a force of a quarter of a million men under the command of General Yamashita. Yamashita did not advocate following MacArthur's strategy of 1941—retreating to Bataan—because of American naval strength but instructed his field commanders to fall back and defend the airfields and then the mountains on the east coast. Yamashita himself withdrew to the Philippine summer capital, Baguio, situated on what amounted to a small mountaintop. Here he was in isolation in every sense of the word. Dispatch runners took an inordinately long time, or did not get through at all, because of guerrilla activities. And his radios worked perhaps one-fourth of the time, because of defective batteries, evidently weakened by the humidity. Yamashita was ill-informed concerning MacArthur's progress, and

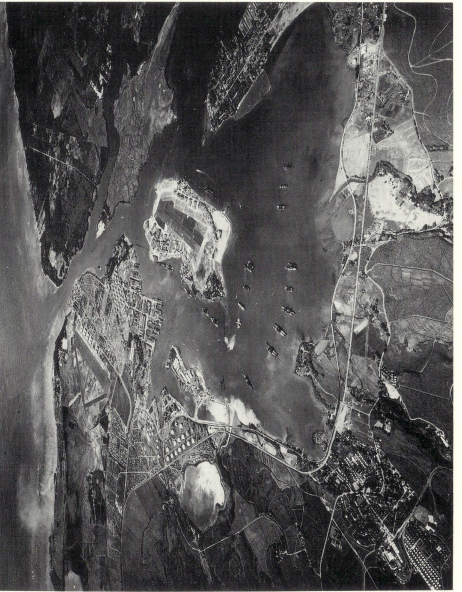

Pearl Harbor on a weekend morning in October 1941. In the center is Ford Island; just to its left is Battleship Row, which on this occasion included one aircraft carrier. *(National Archives)*

The Naval Air Station on Ford Island, Pearl Harbor, during the December 7, 1941, attack. *(U.S. Navy)*

A clock brought up from the battleship *Arizona,* showing the time of her destruction in the Pearl Harbor attack. *(U.S. Navy, courtesy of Mr. Michael Wenger)*

Japanese war dead on Guadalcanal, August 1942. *(National Archives)*

American war dead on Tarawa, November 1943. Photographs like this caused widespread shock and outrage in the United States. *(National Archives)*

From left to right, General MacArthur, President Roosevelt, Admiral Nimitz, and Admiral Leahy on board the cruiser *Baltimore,* July 26, 1944, in Pearl Harbor. *(U.S. Navy)*

Wartime humor, the Philippines, spring 1945. *(U.S. Army)*

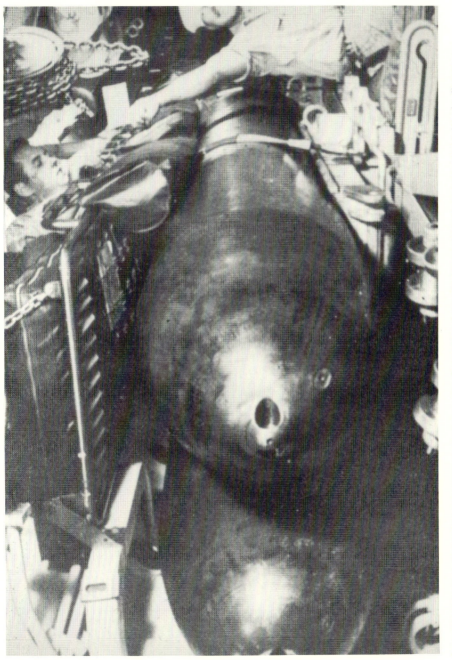

Crowded quarters aboard an American submarine; the *Gato*-class sub was approximately twenty-seven feet in diameter. *(U.S. Navy)*

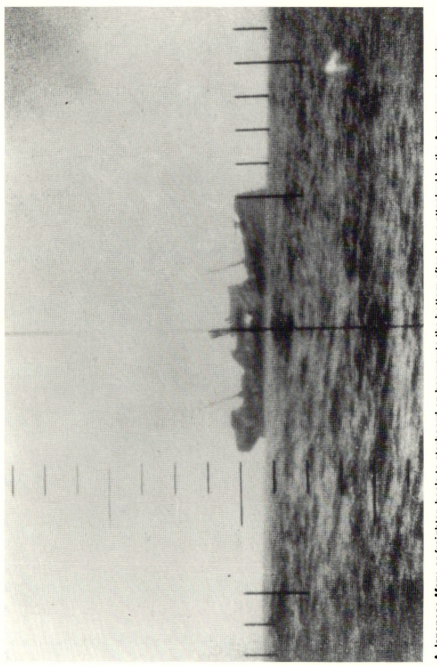

A Japanese *Maru*, or freighter, heels to starboard on her way to the bottom after being attacked by the American submarine *Guardship* on September 4, 1942. This photo was taken through a periscope. *(U.S. Navy)*

An Oakland, California, newsstand, February 27, 1942. *(American History Slide Collection, Instructional Resources Corporation)*

Americans of Japanese ancestry on their way to relocation camp. *(American History Slide Collection, Instructional Resources Corporation)*

Chiang Kai-shek, Madame Chiang, and General Stilwell, April 1942. *(U.S. Army)*

The Burma Road, early in the war. (*U.S. Army*)

A P–51 fighter takes off from Iwo Jima. *(American History Slide Collection, Instructional Resources Corporation)*

The American carrier *Franklin* receiving a *Kamikaze* hit in her masts, March 1945.
(U.S. Navy)

This "moonscape" is Osaka, Japan, after an American firebomb attack in late spring 1945. The craters are from high-explosive contact bombs that were used to make fire-fighting efforts more difficult. *(U.S. Army)*

B–29s at the Boeing plant in Seattle, Washington, spring 1945. *(U.S. Army)*

Signed at _TOKYO BAY, JAPAN_ at _0904 I_
on the _SECOND_ day of _SEPTEMBER_ , 1945.

重 光 葵

By Command and in behalf of the Emperor of Japan
and the Japanese Government.

梅 津 美 治 郎

By Command and in behalf of the Japanese
Imperial General Headquarters.

Accepted at _TOKYO BAY, JAPAN_ at _0908 I_
on the _SECOND_ day of _SEPTEMBER_ , 1945,
for the United States, Republic of China, United Kingdom and the
Union of Soviet Socialist Republics, and in the interests of the other
United Nations at war with Japan.

Supreme Commander for the Allied Powers.

United States Representative

Republic of China Representative

United Kingdom Representative

_Union of Soviet Socialist Republics
Representative_

Commonwealth of Australia Representative

Dominion of Canada Representative

_Provisional Government of the French
Republic Representative_

Kingdom of the Netherlands Representative

Dominion of New Zealand Representative

**The conclusion of Japan's formal Instrument of Surrender, signed September 2,
1945, on board the battleship _Missouri. (U.S. Army)_**

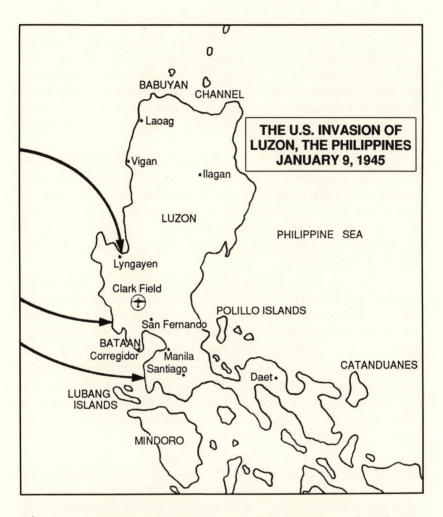

THE U.S. INVASION OF
LUZON, THE PHILIPPINES
JANUARY 9, 1945

few of his ordered countermeasures were implemented. Local commanders issued their own orders to oppose MacArthur's advance, or
they were not issued at all. Portions of Luzon fell to MacArthur largely
by default.

On January 9, 1945, Lt. General Walter Krueger landed in Lingayen
Gulf, almost without opposition. By January 23, he had reached the
vicinity of Clark Field. In late January and early February elements of
General Robert Eichelberger's Eighth Army made landings to both the
north and the south of Manila.

Yamashita promptly declared Manila an open city—a city that

would not be defended. Rear Admiral Mitsuji Iwafuchi decided nonetheless to contest the city, after a fashion. Using his 18,000 troops, largely Imperial Marines, he ravaged and pillaged the city for its last three days of Japanese occupation. The U.S. Thirty-Seventh Division and other elements of the Sixth Army approaching from the north, together with elements of the Eight Army approaching from the south, had the unenviable task of liberating the city, block by block, beginning on February 3, 1945.

The Japanese committed unspeakable atrocities. They entered hospitals, tied the patients to their beds, and set the beds afire, using gasoline where available. They gouged out children's eyes, raped and then killed women. The Imperial Marines alone were guilty; years later, witnesses and survivors recounted those last terrible days of Japanese occupation, and almost exclusively they named Iwafuchi's marines as the guilty parties.

On March 3, 1945, Manila was declared secure, but only after a month of bitter fighting, including the destruction of Intramuros, the old inner walled city, which was nearly impregnable in a prenuclear age. And Corregidor had been stubbornly defended as well, requiring a parachute drop on February 16 to help retake it. The fight was everywhere bitter, and civilian casualties appalling in a city with so high a population density. At least 20,000 Japanese died defending the city and environs. MacArthur then wisely used Manila as a port from which to pour in supplies and reinforcements for the liberation of the remainder of Luzon.

The liberation of Luzon and especially Manila meant the end of two and one-half years of Japanese oppression to the Filipinos and also the end of captivity for a large group of men who had been held in prison camps since very early in the war. There were several prominent POW camps near Manila; hence, General MacArthur had made a point of liberating Allied POWs as rapidly as possible. The men who were released from these camps rarely resembled the men who had entered them in 1942.

The code of *Bushido* does not allow for a soldier's captivity. Since they themselves would willingly die rather than become POWs, the Japanese thought that Western soldiers shared similar beliefs. It came as something of a shock when entire garrisons chose to give themselves up rather than risk being killed in a hopeless pitched battle. The Japanese first experienced a crisis with excessive numbers of prisoners at Singapore, when Percival surrendered his garrison of nearly 100,000 men. The Japanese were unprepared to deal with that large a number of enemy personnel. The resulting movement of troops to prison camps, under the most brutal conditions, cost the lives of many Allied soldiers. Japanese programs to exploit the prisoner populations later in the war would account for many more casualties.

The Americans who defended the Philippines in 1941 had suffered terribly at the hands of the Japanese. When Bataan fell in April of 1942, the Japanese had not anticipated having to deal with so large a prisoner population. Arrangements had been made for the transfer of troops from the front lines to camps prepared for them in the rear. The system collapsed when the materials necessary for the move were not available, and the imminent attack on Corregidor demanded Japanese full attention. The resulting trek from the tip of the peninsula to Camp O'Donnell became known as the Bataan Death March.

Adequate supplies of food and water were not available for the men, and their premarch condition was never taken into account. Many were forced to walk the entire sixty-two-mile trip without eating, and received water, if at all, from the Filipinos who happened to populate the route. During the march, the Americans and Filipinos were subjected to various forms of abuse, ranging from searches and theft to physical violence and outright murder. Stragglers were not tolerated; the slightest infraction of a Japanese command could mean instant execution. Most of the men were weakened from the five month struggle before the march began. Those who survived the ordeal found conditions at the various camps ultimately a worse ordeal than the march.

The diminished physical condition of the prisoners rendered them extremely susceptible to numerous diseases. Malaria, dysentery, beri beri, and other jungle infections, which ordinarily could be controlled with a healthy diet and proper medication, killed large numbers of men in all of the camps during the early stages of the Japanese occupation. The filthy living conditions and poor diets of the prisoners resulted in a death rate of nearly one in four for men in Japanese captivity.

On May 30, 1942, Prime Minister Tojo ordered that in order to receive food rations, prisoners would have to complete certain amounts of work related to the area in which they were being held. For some men this meant an opportunity to escape from the death which pervaded the camps, if only for a short time. For others it was certain death. Already malnourished, the men were put to work on building projects intended to strengthen Japan's hold on her empire. The most famous of these, the Thailand to Burma railroad, provided the setting for *The Bridge on the River Kwai,* a movie based on POW life under the Japanese. (In truth, however, the POWs who built the bridge were French, not British.)

By the end of 1942 the number of Americans held in Japanese POW camps was estimated at 20,200. The main body of these were located in the Philippine Islands. As the war began to progress to Japan's disadvantage, an effort was made to transport POWs to the home islands to serve as a work force in war industries. This project was not particularly successful because of the effectiveness of America's submarine campaign. Most of the enlisted prisoners remained in the Philippines, while senior officers were transported to camps in Manchuria and China.

When American soldiers liberated the POW camps in 1944–45, the men they found were scarcely recognizable. Physically they were shells of the men they had once been. Psychologically they had been forced to reconcile themselves to the idea of being prisoners and had become conscious of the value of their own lives to their Japanese captors. Often, they had survived by coincidence or luck, and had only good fortune to thank for not having become a casualty of the Japanese brutality. These men were rapidly repatriated and were welcomed home as heroes, but were incapable of playing any further role in the downfall of the nation that had held them in captivity since 1942.

There was an active underground force in the Philippines and some prisoners did escape and join its forces. Mindanao was the location of the greatest concentration of such an underground, because of the nature of the terrain, fierce hostility by the Filipinos, and the fact that the Japanese had a smaller force to patrol it than Luzon. Here the Filipino resistance forces operated in the hill country with little interference from the Japanese. However, men captured while serving with these groups or men caught attempting escape to serve with them were almost without exception executed. For the men in the POW camps of Luzon, the primary concern was simply living to see the next sunrise; ultimately, the hope of liberation was all that sustained them.

A combination of factors determined life or death in captivity: the attitude of the commanding officer, a prisoner's physical condition, mental attitude, and above all, whether or not a buddy system was established in the camp. Here, in the few instances when Americans were quartered with captured Britons, they learned from their allies. Otherwise, in an every-man-for-himself climate, few but the hardiest or most stoic of individuals survived. Those few men who remained together as cohesive units survived far better. One group of marines who were allowed to remain together during the Bataan death march emerged alive, almost to a man, at the end of the conflict. The average internee liberated by MacArthur had been through a nightmare, which he could not even begin to recount unless he had somehow managed to keep a diary. MacArthur could only apologize to the survivors. Many perished even after repatriation. Captivity rendered the prisoners sensitive to disease, both mental and physical, long after the end of the war.

The campaign for the Philippines must have seemed as long-lived to MacArthur as the captivity had seemed to the men he liberated. The Philippine archipelago contains some 7,000 islands, 5,000 of which are inhabited. Luzon itself is covered by much rugged terrain; indeed, Yamashita surrendered on his mountaintop headquarters only upon hearing the emperor's surrender broadcast on August 15, 1945. The actions on Luzon cost the United States nearly 8,000 dead, while Japanese battle deaths have recently been placed as high as 192,000. The Philippine underground had done a good deal to aid the liberation of the islands, as virtually any participating Filipino still alive today can recount. Everywhere the Filipino people rallied to MacArthur and rose up against the Japanese. No reliable estimate of Filipinos killed during the liberation has ever been made, but it was doubtless high.

MacArthur now violated the cardinal principle of island hopping. He went southward to attack Mindanao. His desire to do so is perhaps understandable. The island held POW camps, and two full Japanese divisions. The American Eighth Army made over fifty landings before even reaching Mindanao. Here, landing on April 17, 1945, they were greatly aided by the inhabitants, who in some instances rose up and literally hacked the local Japanese garrisons into pieces with bolo knives. About 50,000 Japanese perished, and perhaps 2,500 Americans. But MacArthur now went further yet. He instigated a basically Australian reconquest of portions of Borneo, using the Seventh Fleet and portions of the Army Air Corps under his command as well. Since he had recrossed the equator, he could also command Australian forces. Allegedly, he wanted to procure oil-rich regions, but he conquered real estate long since bypassed, and as far as Tokyo was concerned, isolated and useless. Again MacArthur, who would claim, inaccurately, to have originated the island-hopping strategy, violated its basic tenets.

The Japanese' greatly regretted the loss of the Philippines. For Tokyo it was a staggering blow. Japan's critical supply routes to the southern resource regions ran astride the Philippines, and these were now completely severed by the American submarine effort against the Japanese merchant marine. The populace in general was told that the Americans were being lured toward the home islands, where they would be destroyed in a decisive battle. But for the elite that ran the country, the Philippines held both physical and symbolic value. It was the logistical touchstone of the Japanese empire, and the Americans had conquered it. Life at home had in fact become a nightmare, thanks to the American submarine effort against Japan. That campaign must now be examined.

Suggestions for Further Reading

Philip Crowl, *Campaign in the Marianas* (Washington, DC: Army Historical Office, 1960), is the army's semi-official account. Stanley Karnow, *In Our Image: America's Empire in the Philippines* (New York: Ballantine, 1990), gives a novel insight into that area's wartime years but must be used with caution. Edwin Hoyt's *To the Marianas* (New York: Van Nostrand, 1980) and *The Battle of Leyte Gulf* (New York: Weybright and Talley, 1972) are acceptable, if superficial and undocumented. Probably the best account of the Leyte Gulf operation, although brief, remains James A. Field, Jr., *The Japanese at Leyte Gulf: The Sho Operation* (Princeton, NJ: Princeton University Press, 1947); but see also C. Vann Woodward, *The Battle for Leyte Gulf* (New York: Macmillan, 1947)—the author, renowned for his writings in another field of American history, was in naval intelligence during the conflict; Donald Mcintyre, *Leyte Gulf: Armada in the Pacific* (New York: Ballantine, 1970); Adrian Stewart, *The Battle of Leyte Gulf* (New York: Charles Scribner's Sons, 1979); and Stanley Falk, *Decision at Leyte* (New York: Norton, 1966). Timothy Maga's *Defending Paradise* (New York: Garland, 1987) contains interesting information on life in wartime Guam. Samuel Eliot Morison's volumes in his history of U.S. naval operations during the conflict are still quite worthwhile, especially *New Guinea and the Marianas, March 1944–August 1944* (Boston: Little, Brown, 1953) and *Leyte, June 1944–January 1945* (Boston: Little, Brown, 1958). The *Kamikaze* corps is best chronicled in Rikihei Inoguchi, Tadashi Nakajima, and Roger Pineau, *Divine Wind: Japan's Kamikaze Force in World War II* (Annapolis, MD: Naval Institute Press, 1959). For the POW experience, see Donald Knox, *Death March: The Survivors of Bataan* (New York: Harcourt Brace Jovanovich, 1981); E. Bartlett Kerr's *Surrender and Survival: The Experience of American POWs in the Pacific, 1941–1945*

(New York: William Morrow, 1985); Capt. Edwin Dyess, *The Dyess Story* (New York: Putnam, 1944); William E. Brougher, *South to Bataan, North to Mukden* (Athens: University of Georgia Press, 1971); and finally, Hank Nelson, " 'The Nips are Going for the Parker [pen]:' The Prisoners Face Freedom," *War and Society* 3 (September 1985): 127–43.

7. Submarines, Firebombs, and Survival

Submarine Warfare
Life in Japan
Life in Japan's Empire
Japan Prepares for Invasion
Japanese-Americans in the United States

The First World War proved the value of the submarine as a naval weapon, but on a relatively small scale. In the Second World War all of the major belligerents planned and executed submarine campaigns against their enemies, with varying results. The German effort in the Atlantic is popularly believed to be the most successful example of undersea conflict. This is not so; the Pacific theater provided a far larger arena of operations for the submariners. While slow to achieve effectiveness, the American effort in that ocean eventually, when taken within context, dwarfed that of Nazi Germany in the Atlantic in terms of the result it achieved against its intended target.

The Japanese and American submarine campaigns could scarcely show greater diversity. The Japanese possessed decided advantages at the outset. Specifically, their navy possessed the long-lance torpedo for submarine use. Because it was oxygen-driven, it did not leave a telltale stream of bubbles in the water. These torpedoes were among the deadliest of the war from the standpoint of low malfunction and non-explosion rates. Equipped with a reliable contact detonator when fired from a submarine, they would usually run true.

The Japanese delivery vehicle, the *I*-class submarine, was potentially just as fearsome. Displacing 2,200 tons, it was slightly larger than American submarines, had higher surface speeds, and, almost identically with them, had a safe diving depth of about 300 feet. Its usual complement was eighty officers and enlisted men. The average *I*-class submarine carried seventeen or eighteen torpedoes, but it could not be effectively rigged for silent running. And the *I* class had a cruising range of 10,000 to 17,000 miles, which was slightly greater than that of its American counterpart. Unfortunately for the Japanese, the Imperial Navy did not equip submarines with radar, whereas radar was routinely installed aboard American subs after late 1942.

Worse, Yamamoto evidently agreed with the naval general staff in Tokyo, which decreed that American warships were their submariners' targets of choice. This constituted a major error because it failed to take into account America's far longer supply lines in the Pacific. The American merchant marine would have been a vulnerable, tempting target indeed had the Japanese directed a major, sustained effort against it. The obvious choke points existed: from the Panama Canal, to San Diego, to the Hawaiian islands, Australia, and New Zealand. But the Japanese simply did not use them to attempt to disrupt Allied supply lines.

In the opening days of the war the Japanese effort was dogged by bad luck. During the attack on Pearl the midget subs had nearly given away the attack prematurely, while the fifteen *I*-class subs that ringed Hawaii had sunk nothing of consequence, if only because the air raid itself was so successful. At Midway, the submarines assigned to screening duties between Pearl and Midway arrived too late to warn Nagumo that American carriers were indeed headed toward his carrier force. The midgets further failed at Port Darwin during the Midway operation. They did manage, in a contemporary attack (May 30, 1942) at the harbor of Diego-Suarez on Madagascar, to damage a British battleship and sink a tanker. The British did not realize that the midgets operated from a mother craft. Fearing that the Japanese had a secret base somewhere in the vicinity, they seized the entire island, to no avail.

Yamamoto placed little faith in the midget subs, however. This was probably justified, as they automatically rose to the surface after discharging their torpedoes, which he regarded as too great a risk for the two-man crews. He also displayed little knowledge of wartime conditions in the United States. For the first year of the war he maintained a screen of at least three *I*-class subs off the West Coast, where they did indeed sink a few merchantmen. Some were equipped to carry not a midget sub, as they had to Pearl, but a small pontoon-equipped floatplane, which was used on several occasions to drop incendiary devices on the forests of the Pacific Northwest. This was their designated target, on the assumption that a forest fire would do the greatest possible material damage to the American war effort. Perhaps it did. But the effect of dropping the odd explosive device on, say, San Francisco, was evidently never even considered. What the effect would have been on the populous West Coast cities will, of course, forever remain a matter for speculation.

The Japanese did score a few glittering prizes with their torpedoes. The carriers *Yorktown* (June 1942), *Wasp* (September 1942), *Hornet* (October 1942), and later the cruiser *Indianapolis* (July 1945) were the greatest kills achieved by Japanese submariners. More American merchantmen were sunk. No really accurate count is available, but the totals were minuscule compared to the losses the U.S. merchant marine suffered in the Atlantic. As the Americans began their advance across the Pacific, the submariners were all too often asked to run supplies to garrisons bypassed and now isolated behind American lines. Indeed, the Imperial Army actually developed a small fleet arm in the guise of special garrison duty submarines. These were quietly sent to take supplies to isolated island posts. There can be no duty more fatal to a crew's morale than that of playing blockade runner for a beleaguered garrison. By 1945 the Japanese submarine service was a shadow of its former self, with roughly 130 of the Imperial Navy's subs having been lost at sea, out of a basic number of 170 that engaged in one or more wartime patrols.

The American submarine effort was far different. Roosevelt had asked the Congress that a state of war be declared against Japan as of the beginning of the attack against Pearl, on the chance that an American submarine might have torpedoed a Japanese vessel. None had. The first days of the American submarine effort were not glorious; Admiral Thomas Hart, in charge of the small Asiatic Fleet, discovered that many of his skippers were a bit too cautious, although the gold bullion of the Philippine government was successfully evacuated by submarine.

When Nimitz took command at Pearl, the submarine service underwent swift and positive changes. Although in many ways a submariner by temperament, Nimitz quickly gave the submarine command at Pearl to Vice Admiral Charles Lockwood. Lockwood soon split his submarines between Pearl Harbor and the base at Fremantle, near Perth, on the western coast of Australia. Fremantle was commanded by Rear Admiral Ralph Christie, who remained subordinate to Lockwood. Both men did not hesitate to cut deadwood out of the command structure. This was especially true after the battle of Midway. Lockwood, though brand new to the job, did not hesitate to retire those he found to be overly cautious. Nimitz had hoped the submariners would play a significant role in that encounter, but they did not.

Perhaps the most basic trouble was American torpedoes. On Pearl Harbor day, the U.S. Navy had seventy-three submarines in the Pacific; the Japanese had sixty. The standard American sub was *Gato* class. In the course of the conflict the United States operated a total of 250 submarines, of which fifty-two were lost, accounting for a total of 3,505 men killed. A *Gato*-class sub displaced about 1,500 tons, had a surface speed slightly over twenty knots, and carried a crew of seventy-seven men. Torpedo inventory, at exactly two dozen tin fish, was greater than that of the *I*-class sub, although the *Gato*'s effective cruising range was less, at about 10,000–12,000 miles. But from the first, American submariners complained that their torpedoes were defective.

Nonetheless, from the opening day of the war unescorted Japanese merchantmen fell prey to American submarines. But, unknown at the time, American steam-driven torpedoes ran at a greater than set depth, often as much as eight to ten feet deeper. Their magnetic detonators, which could theoretically break a ship's spine by exploding beneath the vessel's keelplates, usually failed to function at all. Further, their contact detonators were defective: torpedoes seemed to explode when transecting with the target at anything *but* a ninety-degree angle, which was supposedly the perfect, "textbook" shot. Given the number of torpedoes fired and ships sunk, it took over seven torpedoes to sink the average Japanese ship. This was obviously a high average.

In mid-1943 the turning point came for the submariners. They had already taken a significant toll, having sunk about 142 Japanese merchantmen by the end of 1942. The basic Japanese naval cipher for merchantmen—tankers included—was not broken by the Americans until early 1943, when its secrets fell victim to an American cipher team attached to the command structure at Pearl. The suffix *maru* is attached to all Japanese merchantmen, and the *maru* cipher was cracked at precisely the moment when the Japanese had begun convoying in an attempt to stem their merchantmen losses. Now the location of each convoy was laid bare to prying eyes at Pearl, and in a very precise manner: the exact coordinates for each convoy were given nearly every day, as well as names of individual ships, cargo carried, and what specific escort each convoy had for protection. Seldom has cryptography yielded such useful fruits.

American submarine captains henceforth found hunting very worthwhile indeed. The matter of the *maru* cipher was a very closely guarded secret during the conflict. Each submarine captain was required to sign an oath to the effect that he would not reveal its existence to anyone, including his officers or crew. Some captains did tell their second in command, and the ships' radio personnel knew as well, but the Japanese never suspected that the Americans had penetrated the code.

The only problem lay with the naval Bureau of Ordnance, which issued torpedoes. Its officers continued to insist with a stubbornness that must have been maddening that American torpedoes were *not* defective. Then on July 24, 1943, came the submarine *Tinosa* and her encounter with the 19,000-ton whaling factory *Tonan Maru III*. Targets this large were rare. *Tinosa*'s skipper put several torpedoes into her, none to fatal effect. He fired a total of fifteen torpedoes at his target, of which eleven were duds. Saving his final torpedo for the Bureau, he turned his prow back toward Pearl. The Bureau of Ordnance, however tacitly, admitted that something was wrong. Tests in the water and then on land—the torpedoes were dropped from a cherry picker—disclosed that a ninety-degree hit would crush the exploding pin before detonation could take place. By this time, the magnetic detonators had been deactivated, and the problem of running depth solved. A new torpedo, electricity-driven, was introduced and dubbed the Mark XVI. It was slower than the former steam driven torpedoes, but was otherwise an almost quantum leap improvement. The result would be disaster for the Japanese merchant marine.

Tankers were always priority targets since Japan had almost no oil resources of its own. By November 1943 the number of Japanese cargo vessels was smaller than on December 7, 1941. New Japanese ship construction was concentrated almost exclusively on oilers. The combined fleet, in order to lessen the load, moved its basic anchorage to Tawi Tawi, south of Mindanao, and then to Singapore itself by mid-1944. Of all the steel allocated in Japan for shipbuilding in 1944, only one-sixth went for new warships; the remainder was allocated for the merchant marine, and almost all of that was for tankers. Some commentators have contended that the U.S. Navy should have concentrated exclusively on sinking tankers. This argument ignores the fact that each convoy in turn was attacked; concentration exclusively on tankers would have revealed the Americans' penetration of the *maru* cipher.

When warships were encountered, Lockwood naturally ordered that carriers be regarded as the primary targets. Ten Japanese carriers ultimately slid beneath the waves as submarine victims. The most important of these was probably *Shinano*. Begun as a slightly larger version of *Yamato, Shinano* was the largest warship hull ever constructed to that date. Since time had proven the now deceased Yamamoto correct concerning the value of naval air power, the naval general staff decreed that *Shinano* be finished as a carrier. As such, she would have displaced close to 72,000 tons when fully loaded. With a flight deck of steel and concrete, she left Yokohama scarcely seaworthy. She was not yet ready for battle and had no aircraft aboard.

She was bound for Hiroshima on the Inland Sea, but the submarine *Archer Fish* found her well before that. In the early morning hours of November 29, 1944, *Archer Fish*'s skipper fired four torpedoes into *Shinano*. Her own captain, Toshio Abe, was at first not overly concerned. *Musashi*, after all, had taken no less than nineteen torpedoes at Leyte Gulf before sinking. But *Musashi* had been manned by a full complement of highly trained and experienced crew. *Shinano*, it turned out, had not been properly tested for watertight integrity, and the electric pumps for evacuating intruding sea water did not operate properly. By mid-morning she sunk, taking over 1,000 men with her.

One of the most prodigious submarine skippers of the war was Richard O'Kane, captain of the *Tang*. Until his ship was sunk and O'Kane became a prisoner of war, he sank twenty-four Japanese merchantmen for a total of 93,824 tons. In October 1944, during the Leyte Gulf action, O'Kane encountered several Japanese merchant convoys. He fell victim, ironically, to one of his own torpedoes, which, in a not-unknown malfunction, described a full circle and detonated against the hull of his own ship twenty seconds after firing. Manning his own conning tower, O'Kane was thrown into the water. He was captured by Japanese who had been aboard a ship he had just sent under, and was probably glad to be transported to an actual prisoner of war camp. In addition to the Congressional Medal of Honor, O'Kane received three Navy Crosses and an equal number of Silver Stars.

By the end of 1944, with the reconquest of the Philippines, American submarines began to venture into the Sea of Japan. This was no mere propaganda stunt. Something of a ''sub scare'' eventually ensued, as many fishermen refused to venture out of sight of shore—if even that far—in their sampans. By early 1945, American aircraft began attacking not only merchantmen but Japan's larger, seagoing sampans; the results for the diet of the civilian population were catastrophic. Japan has always had a basic diet of fish and rice; its fish catch was now reduced nearly 40 percent, while the rice crop for the last two years of the war was poor (the worst since the famine year 1931), largely because of climatic conditions. Despite an offensive in China that provided a direct land link with Indochina (except that ultimately the rice had to be shipped by sea from Korea to one of the home islands), little rice from southeast Asia reached Japan. Some farmers in Indochina had been forced to plant jute instead, while Chinese bandits plundered Japanese land supply lines with Indochina. As a result, malnutrition became widespread while resultant diseases, especially tuberculosis, were increasingly endemic.

Not long after Yamamoto's death in 1943, the Japanese began to organize convoys, although never to the extent that the American navy did in the Atlantic. American submarine forces responded by wolfpacking, or concentrating, their submarines, with catastrophic results for the Japanese. By the spring of 1945, thirty-five out of forty-seven regular Japanese convoy routes between Japan and its possessions south of the Philippines had been completely abandoned. By the end of the war, U.S. submarines would send no less than 1,113 Japanese merchantmen to the bottom. A somewhat smaller but quite significant number of freighters were also eliminated by airpower, and 201 Japanese warships of all types were sunk by submarine action as well.

While losses in the American submarine service were within acceptable limits, they were far from insignificant. Although only 2 percent of the navy's total manpower served in submarines, a staggering 22 percent of those 16,000 men perished. The sailors received combat pay, but little else, except the occasional decoration in return.

Life on an American submarine was not the glamorous life Hollywood has projected. Nature, human nature, and the enemy always posed obstacles for any submarine skipper. Even more than carrier aviators, submariners required recreational facilities on shore beyond the ordinary, and these were not always to be had, especially in Fremantle and its environs. Worse still, the navy developed Midway Atoll as a submarine base as the war progressed, and Midway possessed virtually no first-class shore facilities.

Life was cramped, noisy, difficult, and dangerous under the best of circumstances. Of the fifty-two U.S. submarines lost during the war, all but two perished in the Pacific. Any submariner could never be certain if he was going to constitute part of this number. The submarines operated out of Pearl (Midway was sometimes substituted as a home port for subs based out of Pearl) or Fremantle, or later, just at the end of the conflict as the Japanese empire contracted, Guam or Luzon. The later bases afforded fewer opportunities for recreation, but yielded in the long run fewer hours at sea and probably higher kill ratios. And, of course, in the tradition of the silent service, there was little in the way of public recognition. Life was not always pleasant, but the sacrifices probably seemed worthwhile.

Life in Japan by late 1943 was even more squalid, largely because the U.S. submarine campaign severed contact with the overseas empire. The Japanese may have conquered the Eldorado of the South, but they never enjoyed its fruits, since the American submarine effort isolated them from their newly acquired territories before they could begin proper exploitation of the areas. Serious, official rationing had begun as early as April 1941, six months before Pearl Harbor, when rice purchasing was restricted in many cities. Other commodities were added to the restricted list on an as needed basis, and the system spread from Japan's cities to embrace the entire nation. This in turn led to the inevitable black market operations, which became so blatant that in some provinces the authorities actually encouraged it, since the profiteers sometimes seemed to have access to commodities that the authorities had believed exhausted.

Dealing with the black market required finesse. Usually, payment was demanded not only in cash, but also in the form of family heirlooms, art objects, and the like. The Japanese who ran the black market were true professionals as such things go. They had their own law in the guise of territories controlled, standardized methods, even specific hours and places of operation. Dealing with them was not pleasant, but became a necessity for the majority of urban Japanese by the late summer of 1945.

The most serious military shortages were fuel oil and aluminum. The oil shortage was compensated for in part by whaling, which harvested a combustible fuel, and by pressing the roots of pine trees, which also yielded a useable fuel. But the results in both cases were meager. In fact, some gasoline destined for civilian use was reportedly diluted with sake. The very few Japanese who still operated automobiles found it necessary to push their automobiles to the tops of hills, then drift the vehicles downhill in first gear in order for the gasoline to spark. Some Japanese attempted to convert their cars to burn solid fuels, but this was not officially encouraged and met with little success in the long run. There was, however, no substitute for bauxite ore, and by early 1945 there was almost no aluminum left in Japan. In desperation, the Japanese manufactured planes out of magnesium, which has low combustion temperature that made this practice counterproductive from the pilot's point of view. In a desperate search for all metals, Japanese housewives were called on to turn in unneeded objects. The Japanese also ransacked their conquered empire, even commandeering coins to be smelted down for their brass content.

The most restricted civilian commodities were rice, coal, iron ore, salt, and virtually any eatable commodity one can think of. By the spring of 1945 only the army's secret police, the dreaded *Kempeitei,* very high-ranking civilians, and flag- or star-grade military officers were officially given gasoline for private or official automobiles, and then only in very small quantities. The Americans' restriction of two-and-a-half gallons per week would have seemed an incredible luxury to the Japanese.

Homes went without coal for heating, pneumonia became commonplace, pipes froze, and sanitation was difficult, particularly for city dwellers. Long lines at markets became common. Any neighbor with a close relative who owned a farm suddenly became the most popular person on the block—he or she was, in effect, a potential source of food. Even the silk industry was curtailed. Kimonos became scarce, and a national standard dress was introduced, reducing life to the truly shabby. Metal objects for civilian use were no longer manufactured. While the government still encouraged early marriage with many children, young couples had to wait and literally inherit a frying pan, much less a hibachi.

As early as March 1943 the government had tacitly admitted that all was not well when it proclaimed a national "smile week" to raise public morale. Worse, in February 1944 the press announced a fifteen-point program for the "simplification" of the standard of living. These measures included the conversion of consumer items factories to war goods production, the closing of geisha houses, the conservation of energy, fewer holidays, and increased employment of women in the civilian work force. School grounds were to be planted with vegetable gardens. Even afternoon newspapers were discouraged, a measure of desperation in what was surely the most widely read population of all the belligerents. Few complained, but Tojo, chief of the army general staff as well as premier and minister of the army, obviously did not endear himself to the working population, especially when the seven-day work week became common.

Women for the first time played an acknowledged role in the economy, if only because so many men of draft age had been called to the colors. The munitions industry in particular began employing them. Premier Tojo's wife shattered all precedent when she made public appearances in factories and urged women to increase worker productivity. She also made radio broadcasts to the same effect. The Japanese used their secret weapon—long hours and hard work—to produce what they could of the modern military necessities. Travel became a luxury. Pullman cars were discontinued on almost all train runs, or else they were restricted to military officers. Police permits were necessary for civilian train travel beyond routine commuting. Foreign nationals of neutral nations were increasingly harried by frequent nocturnal visits from the *Tokko,* the special police that usually monitored the activities of foreigners.

Amphetamines were distributed to civilian workers. Until their use was restricted to prescription distribution, (this occurred only in 1950), misuse was common, probably in part because of their appetite-reducing effect. The entire nation was on a nationalistic binge. Teaching of foreign languages was curtailed. In one sense wealth, property, or even social rank no longer mattered, for neighbors were now all equal: all of urban Japan joined or participated more intensively in required neighborhood societies, groups that became in effect a firewatch/bucket brigade for each block. Air raid practice became common, blackouts frequent. Entire rural districts were put on electric power rationing, with electricity generated only during the hours immediately after dark. Chemical fertilizer became rare, and Koreans living in Japan, who had long been regarded as second-class citizens, were pressed into farm labor forces.

Life, in short, was no fun. Many legitimate and film theaters were closed, and virtually the only movies shown were leftovers from the 1930s, which depicted the Chinese and Westerners in general as vicious beasts. Even book printing was curtailed. The only available literature was the current propaganda, which demonstrated how Japan was winning the conflict with the clever strategy of drawing the Americans close to the home islands before defeating them.

Just before the conflict broke out, a young lady from California arrived in Japan to visit a sick aunt. A graduate of UCLA with a degree in zoology, on Pearl Harbor day she became an enemy alien. Iva Ikuko Toguri avoided being sent to a detention camp by volunteering to do English-language propaganda broadcasts for the Japanese. At first she was identified simply as "Tokyo Ann," as in *ann*ouncer, and she frequently simply identified herself as "Orphan Annie, your favorite enemy," but her eventual favorite nickname became simply Tokyo Rose. She had a silky, bedroom-like voice and for a salary of $6.60 a month, she broadcast nightly.

The propaganda she disseminated was obvious. Indeed, she even panned her own material on occasion. The remainder of Tokyo's radio broadcasting personnel were not as effective but did include captured American Navy and Army officers who broadcast rather obnoxious propaganda to their colleagues still in the service of their country. Tokyo Rose alone, however, was widely listened to by American Navy and Marine personnel, in part because she always seemed to have an adequate supply of Glenn Miller recordings, probably obtained via one of the neutral embassies in Tokyo. Every evening a Japanese Army colonel, whose name is lost to history, spoke after her program was over. To the last day of the conflict he sought to disabuse his unseen American audience of the notion that the United States was winning the war.

To oversee the nation's radio grid, the *Kempeitei* set up a special monitoring facility in Tokyo. Every station in the country was monitored day and night, with the police ready to arrest any announcer who even hinted that all was not well. In truth, an arrest was never made, and the entire effort proved unnecessary in the end. A great majority of Japanese unquestioningly and dutifully believed the official government line. They were shocked when the emperor spoke over the radio in August 1945 and revealed the truth to his subjects.

Hard though it was, life in the home islands remained tolerable until the night of March 9–10, 1945. On that evening a flight of over 300 American B–29 bombers began the first and probably most successful fire bombing in the Asiatic theater of the conflict. (See chapter 9 for a discussion of American bombing strategy.) Major General Curtis LeMay's B–29 bombers, aided by gale-force winds at ground level, reduced the sixteen-square-mile *Shitamachi* district of Tokyo to ashes in a conflagration that burned for four days. Indeed, some of LeMay's pilots became physically sick from the stench of burning flesh, which rose to greet those who participated in the later phase of the raid. LeMay then began systematic fire bombing of other cities as well as of the remaining portions of the greater Tokyo-Yokohama area. Victims of the American bombing raids, were, in LeMay's words, "scorched and boiled and baked to death."

Japanese cities were unfortunately built to burn, and were far better incendiary targets than European urban centers. In the series of fire raids that ensued, the death rate was very high, and the social dislocation engendered was also disastrous. The Japanese attempted to implement a system in some major cities to identify the dead and the missing, but the records centers themselves were urban and burned to the ground together with their contents.

On Roosevelt's orders, the imperial palace was left untouched. But one night in May 1945, during a fire storm resulting from the bombs, flaming debris leapt the moat and razed a portion of the imperial residences within the 500 acres that comprise its grounds. Thereafter the royal family, at the insistence of the court officials, slept in special underground shelters. Legions of children were orphaned in Japan's cities, more rapidly than anyone could count them. By the late summer of 1945 they roamed the streets of what remained of Japan at will, preying upon the unwary by practicing cannibalism. Cities became depopulated. Police restrictions notwithstanding, the populace sought refuge when possible with relatives in the country.

The authorities evacuated children from cities in some instances. They were sent to farms or small country villages, but the rural population often failed to nourish them adequately, and many perished from tuberculosis. A fair number discovered that they were orphans only at the end of the war, when they returned home and discovered their families were dead.

By late summer of 1945 American aircraft flying from the northern Mariana Islands and from carriers roamed at will over Japanese cities. Life had become another species of living hell. Entire square miles of Japanese cities ceased to exist. Perhaps worst of all, anyone could die without suffering a visible burn. The fire storms left oxygen deprivation in their wake, and the elderly especially, whose vital capacity to absorb oxygen was diminished, would be found dead in the morning, sometimes many miles from the area of combustion. Yet, few visibly flinched.

If the sirens sounded and American bombers appeared, one left one's home at once and headed for the nearest stream or river, in which everyone immersed themselves. But if the fire was too close or too intense, the stream would probably boil, and anyone in it would die. The total number killed in the fire bombings is unknown, but the most recent count puts the number at over two million, which is much higher than the army authorities acknowledged at the time. And certainly many more citizens were left homeless as a result of the fires. The Imperial Army dismissed the raids as "routine" while they encouraged the neighborhood firewatch associations to greater efforts against American incendiary bombs. But since American incendiary devices contained napalm or, at the end, generated their own oxygen, normal fire-fighting procedures with water alone were unavailing, which the army would never publicly admit. The B–29s—nicknamed *B-sans* by most Japanese—became so dreaded that surviving crew members of the few that were downed were frequently killed by the normally law-obeying civilians.

Life for the emperor's conquered subjects in the empire outside of the home islands was another matter. The Great East Asia Co-Prosperity Sphere was quickly and quietly dubbed the Co-Poverty Sphere by the emperor's newly conquered subjects. Certainly, it quickly became just that. The Bank of Japan did not hesitate to print money on an "as needed" basis, and the result of this was chronic inflation. China in particular was never treated with even an outward semblance of decency. On the basis of Tojo's radio pronouncements in particular, it remains unclear if Tokyo ever considered China part of the Prosperity Sphere. Korea fared very poorly, receiving treatment unequalled among the conquered nations. Korean men were drafted into the Imperial Army and Navy to perform menial labor. Korean women were recruited to serve as the nucleus of Comfort Battalions, which "serviced" troops in the field in the sexual sense. After taking them prisoners, the Americans set these Comfort Battalions to work as practical nurses, a task at which they proved excellent.

Tokyo's Asian puppets felt increasingly ridiculous as the war progressed. Henry Pu-Yi, once the child emperor of China, ruled Manchuquo for the Japanese. He became increasingly subservient to the Japanese Kwantung Army, which administered his domains with an absolute hand, engaging in hideous atrocities against the Chinese populace on an open and unbelievably wide scale. Officers were known to rape Chinese women publicly, sometimes literally in the street. Young Chinese were occasionally used for live bayonet practice. Wang Ching-Wei, probably a Kuomingtang deserter who became ruler of a portion of the remainder of China in 1940, also found his authority greatly eroded by the army. He remained but a puppet, while his supposed subjects were brutalized by the army.

Even in Burma, the most cooperative of Japanese possessions, the originally tiny Burmese Independence Army, which fought for Burmese independence, swelled in size as Japanese oppression increased. The Japanese, who had promised almost immediate independence to the Burmese, increasingly treated Premier Ba Maw, a fervent collaborationist, as an inferior. Before long the Japanese had to extend their occupation to the entire country; the northern portion of the country initially had been relatively free of Japanese occupation troops.

Indonesia, which had also at first welcomed the Japanese, was oppressed by the army as early as March 1942, when the right of political protest was severely curtailed through a series of crudely worded military proclamations. Nationalists like Achmed Sukarno were put under police surveillance. The Japanese Army divided the nation into three occupation zones, and study of the Japanese language, even the singing of the Japanese national anthem, became mandatory. None of this endeared the Japanese to the Indonesians. As in all the other Japanese possessions, there was a relatively small but highly effective civilian resistance movement in operation long before 1945.

By the summer of 1945 the Japanese braced themselves for the first invasion wave of Americans, which they expected momentarily. All prepared for what would be the supreme test of Japanese morale: resistance to the Allies. The Japanese organized a national guard-like force of 27 million civilians, most of whom were armed with the basic weapons for members of this force—sharpened bamboo spears. Men and women alike were issued rifles when possible, and children were shown diagrams of American tanks and instructed where to place (and hold) a grenade in order to destroy it. Trenches were dug around each maritime or coastal village. The ministries of War and Navy were partially evacuated from Tokyo to rural areas. The many caves that are spread throughout Japan's four home islands were stockpiled with provisions and made into improvised fortresses. It was in two such cave complexes that the sections of the two ministries removed from Tokyo were relocated.

Civilians were prepared for the worst. One extremist even proposed that elderly people, women, and children be eliminated in advance to conserve the remaining food supplies, but the army rejected as over-zealous this suggestion, which came from one of its own. When one civilian reportedly asked the military what they would do if the Americans did not invade the country but simply left the Japanese to starve and burn, he drew the interesting reply, "We'll really be in a fix then." The slogan "One hundred million die together" became the new national wartime slogan by midsummer 1945. This betrayed the Japanese official "belief" that 100 million people now inhabited the home islands; this was, however, only a target figure. As far as we know, the home islands comprised seventy-nine million inhabitants.

The *Kamikaze* corps (see the previous chapter) prepared for its most heroic effort. Virtually every young man of eligible age in the nation had his name inscribed on a basic recruitment roster. The Japanese had prepared *Kamikaze* planes with portions of their fuselages manufactured of silk, to conserve metal. Planes and fields, with supplies of gasoline secured nearby, were later found during the American occupation that had been completely unknown at the time to the Allies. The *Kamikaze* boat squadrons also prepared for their first substantial action. The same was true for the suicide torpedoes *(Kaiten)*: long-lance torpedoes were adopted to be driven into their targets by a human operator. And underwater frogmen *(Fukuryu)* were recruited for suicide missions against American vessels, especially landing craft.

Finally, the Japanese attempted to intensify an effort already underway to bring the war to the North American mainland. *Operation Flying Elephant* had begun on November 3, 1944 (the emperor Meiji's birthday), reportedly from the slopes of Mount Fuji. *Flying Elephant* was meant to avenge Doolittle's unexpected bombing of Tokyo in April of 1942. Large hydrogen-filled balloons, thirty-two feet in diameter, were put into the air, with the hope that they would drift eastward in the jet stream. They carried both incendiary and antipersonnel charges. They were, for their day, sophisticated weapons. There was some talk in Japan of using them to carry pathogenic bacteria to the North American continent, but this was never done. Conversely, the worst fear in the United States seems to have been that they would be used to carry a saboteur to this country, particularly if the Japanese developed larger prototypes. The balloons were released, roughly, along the fortieth degree of northern latitude, and were meant for the American Pacific Northwest, where it was reasoned that they would come to earth before encountering the Rocky Mountains. They would take two days to reach North America. Some 9,300 balloons were so released, the last in early August 1945. Civilians were pressed into service to construct the paper balloons in theaters no longer open to the public because of the war.

No one was sure of the results achieved. The facilities that had manufactured the balloons had been largely burned down by late spring of 1945, but many were in storage and had survived. The results in America were mixed. Some brush fires were undoubtedly started. A total of 285 balloons were found in the United States, or otherwise known to have arrived. The actual number will never be known. Balloons were found as far north as Alaska, as far south as Mexico, and two as far east as Michigan. Six people were killed by one explosion in Oregon. The American atomic bomb project was briefly interrupted when one of the balloons caused a power outage at the atomic energy plant at Hanford, Washington. As late as the 1960s an unexploded balloon was found in Alaska. A 1973 U.S. government pamphlet warns that hundreds are probably still to be discovered and remain dangerous.

Operation Sunset was the essential American response. A series of special radar stations were established to detect incoming balloons. In addition, the Army Air Corps from the Aleutians to Los Angeles was kept busy searching for and destroying the devices. The results achieved by the balloons were obviously poor, but the Japanese did not know until the 1970s when a U.S. government pamphlet described their effort, that they had been moderately successful in some respects.

In the far reaches of what remained of the empire, Japanese subjects were safe from fire-bombing attacks, but local populations fell under increasing exploitation and outright brutality as the end of the conflict obviously approached. What was in effect slave labor began, and the army everywhere enrolled so-called volunteers to build emplacements and fortifications. Japanese promises of independence now seemed ridiculous. (A general grant of independence had been given to almost the entire empire in mid-1943.) The closer the Allies came to a particular conquered area, the more brutal the Japanese Army, the almost exclusive occupation authority, became.

Even by its own standards, the army practiced brutality on its enlisted personnel. Corporal punishment was common. Striking of enlisted men was actually encouraged in the course of maintaining routine discipline. The number of deaths in basic training, usually held in Manchuria, grew, and as the army found itself frustrated by defeat, it literally devoured its own. In the Philippines, garrisons on bypassed islands, reduced to starvation, sometimes resorted to cannibalism of the least fit garrison soldiers. The worst examples of Japanese brutality, however, probably occurred in China.

The Japanese Kwantung Army became a replica of the local Chinese war lords whom it had never quite managed to exterminate. Chinese laborers were maltreated to such an extent that they survived only a very few days. One notorious facility, Camp 731, located north of Mukden at Pingfan, engaged in large-scale medical experiments, sometimes on American personnel. Tests were performed to establish human endurance levels to such extremes as cold, frostbite, and blood loss. Surgical experiments were conducted to study human resistance to severe trauma and resultant infection. And inevitably, since American POWs were involved, there were tests made to compare Caucasian and Asiatic reactions to extremes of disease and climate.

Worse, the camp authorities under Lt. General Shiro Ishii for most of the conflict, engaged in chemical and bacteriological warfare against the Chinese, spreading bubonic plague behind Chiang Kai-shek's lines. Ishii and his colleagues also experimented with anthrax, typhoid, typhus, and other diseases as methods of warfare. The Chungking regime complained of Japanese biological warfare to both Washington and London, but Chiang's claims went unbelieved at the time. After the conflict, however, American authorities carefully debriefed some of Camp 731's personnel, and verified the nature of their experiments and work. Small wonder that the Japanese made efforts at the end of the war to eradicate Camp 731 physically. These attempts were unsuccessful. Like the Germans, the Japanese discovered that death camps could not readily be made to disappear without trace.

When the Soviets entered the war in August 1945 and promptly invaded Manchuria, the Japanese officers of the Kwantung Army fled in cowardice and terror. Ranking officers commandeered trains, which left enlisted men to the unenviable fate of becoming Soviet prisoners of war. Everywhere the army left hordes of executed civilians as defeat approached. The Imperial Army betrayed its own honor. After the

surrender, the only factor preventing local war crime trials from enact-
ing a greater number of indictments was the fact that Japanese troops
were needed to preserve order until legitimate governments could be
reestablished.

In the end, survival became the solitary goal of the inhabitants of
Japan's empire, both on the home islands and elsewhere. From the
euphoria of the first six months of the conflict, Japan was now on
the verge of an Allied invasion. Fittingly, had the Japanese known
it, the Pentagon plan for the invasion was code-named *Downfall.* It
envisioned a conflict that would last at least until the fall of 1946,
and might entail as many as a million *Allied* (not solely American)
combat deaths. This does not seem an unreasonable estimate. Invasion of the home islands would have been a slaughter unprecedented
in all of human history. The civilian population as well as the military would have resisted to the last, using the caves that honeycomb
the home islands. Little of Japanese society would have survived,
and the Japanese battle deaths and civilian casualties would have
been enormous. The army's slogan, "One hundred million die together," suggests the Japanese mind-set in the late summer of
1945. It seemed that only a miracle could prevent the invasion from
taking place. Washington named Douglas MacArthur to command
it. Had he done so, his reputation in postwar Japan would certainly
not have been as positive as it turned out to be.

Early in the conflict the American military and civilian establishment had been eager to gain Russian participation in the eventual
invasion of the home islands. The Soviets were notorious for their lack
of concern about casualties, and American planners were at first anx-
ious that Russian troops help conquer the home islands. President Roosevelt obtained a definite pledge in February 1945 at Yalta that the
Soviet Union would enter the war several months after Germany surrendered, in return for which he promised the Kremlin numerous Japanese possessions, from the northern portion of Korea, to the Kurile
islands, to the Japanese portion of Sakhalin. Critics have contended
that this was unnecessary *largesse,* in part because the atomic bomb
would soon render the Japanese defenseless, and partly because the
Soviets would probably have desired to participate in the war against
the Japanese in any event, once Germany was defeated.

There is a degree of truth in these arguments, but it is the logic of
twenty-twenty hindsight that motivates Roosevelt's critics. No one

could have been sure that the atomic bomb would function, since it had not yet been tested when Roosevelt made the promise. Further, a test date had not yet even been projected. And, as will be seen, when the atomic devices *were* used, they did *not* compel Japanese surrender. Doubtless the Soviets would have participated in the conflict, but one may argue that Roosevelt simply wished to codify or formalize their gains. The Russians were not promised any portion of the home islands themselves, and, finally, Soviet participation in the conflict did compel the prompt surrender of the Japanese, and this did save many American lives.

Invasion would have meant an incalculable number of Japanese deaths. It would have entailed house-to-house fighting, with tremendous civilian casualties. The effect on the American personnel participating in such a conquest would have been severe. There were even those in Washington who urged that chemical weapons be used against the population of the home islands, but there is no evidence that such suggestions were seriously considered.

Americans of Japanese ancestry living in the United States fared far better than the Japanese in Japan, but life was not what it might have been for many of them. Though long accustomed to being treated as second-rate citizens, and though they endured nothing compared with their ancestors in Japan as the war neared its end, life had quickly turned unpleasant after Pearl Harbor. There had been much talk on the West Coast, and even in Hawaii, the most tolerant of American possessions, of a Japanese "fifth column" that was waiting to betray the United States and open the country—particularly the coastal portions of the west—to a supposed Japanese invasion.

On Pearl Harbor day, 127,000 Americans of Japanese ancestry lived in mainland America, over 112,000 in the Pacific seaboard states: California, Washington, and Oregon. Soon after Pearl Harbor, rumor had it that many *Issei* (first-generation Japanese) had purposely settled near vital defense installations, especially in California. Feelings ran so high that many Chinese-Americans literally put makeshift cardboard signs around their necks proclaiming their nationality, to protect themselves against open racial discrimination and even beatings. And in Hawaii, Buddhist temples and Shinto shrines were closed for the duration of the conflict.

Canada, together with Mexico and many other of America's friends south of the border, promptly gave in to pressure from the U.S. State Department to relocate their Japanese populations. It is hard to imagine what danger the two Japanese living in Paraguay posed to that nation's vital interests, but they were nonetheless promptly interned. The one nation that might have had something of a case against the Japanese, Chile, where the Japanese ambassador bullied the government during the first six months of the war, intimating that a Japanese fleet was just over the horizon—did nothing against their minuscule Japanese population.

Several of America's Latin neighbors literally sent their entire Japanese populations to the United States; Peru was especially craven in this respect. In the United States itself, and particularly in California, pressure was intense to intern Japanese. Some of the concern was doubtless sincere, such as that of Earl Warren, then California's attorney general, who evidently believed that some Americans of Japanese ancestry posed a danger to the national interest. Others, including local commerce groups, made their case so vehemently and with such unction that their greed for the land owned by Americans of Japanese ancestry was glaringly evident.

In the spring and summer of 1942 the Japanese roundup and internment program began. A War Relocation Authority was established, headed for its first three months by Milton Eisenhower, brother of the future president. Approximately 110,000 Americans of Japanese ancestry, about 70,000 of whom were American citizens *by virtue of birth in this country* (naturalization of Japanese had not been permitted since 1790), were relocated by this authority. In general, the victims of the authority had two weeks to sell their belongings, since they were allowed to take with them only what they could carry. Selling of land and possessions was not compulsory (one could simply "abandon" them), but many did sell land to speculators. Those who did not usually had friends who promised to look after their property. Nonetheless, many of those who did not sell returned home after the war to discover that their property had been vandalized.

The people to be relocated were tagged like cattle, after someone spread the stereotype that all Orientals looked alike. The internees were moved into tar-paper barracks, without individual sanitary facilities. There were ten official relocation centers, the furthest as far east as Arkansas, in addition to numerous temporary assembly centers. The smallest relocation or internment center housed 7,000, the largest

20,000. A few internees became so embittered that they asked to be repatriated to Japan. Some, including college students, were able to leave the centers on "indefinite leave" status. Others would be temporarily released to harvest farm crops. All were held in overcrowded conditions, however, that were several times worse than was permitted by law in federal penitentiaries.

Compared to the treatment meted out to American POWs and civilians in Japan, the Japanese-Americans made out fairly well. But the United States was a democracy, and American law should have prevented the internment in the first place. There was talk as well of interning aliens of German and Italian ancestry. This would have entailed the internment of quite a large number of citizens indeed.

In Japan, the general population was well aware of America's internment policy. The Japanese people were then and are now probably the most prolific newspaper readers in the world. Their press frequently reprinted excerpts from neutral papers, that told of the internment. The Japanese government protested via neutral governments—particularly those of Spain and Switzerland—to no avail. It was particularly incensed when the entire Japanese population of Panama was arrested on Pearl Harbor day and treated in a very inhuman manner.

Worse was the Tule Lake episode. In Tule Lake, in northernmost California, a camp was established for what became the most recalcitrant internees. Among them were those who had stated they would like to be repatriated to Japan. The camp was a 2,900-acre truck farming operation that provided produce for the U.S. military. The local population learned only by rumor of what was happening within the camp. They were quite naturally disturbed about having such a facility in the area. After some serious disturbances in November 1943, the army was moved in, doubtless an overreaction. For a week or two newspapers on the West Coast wrote of Tule Lake more than of the war in either theater of conflict.

News quickly reached Tokyo. The State Department had been in communication with the Japanese government, largely via the Spanish government, concerning the exchange of 6,000 sick or disabled American POWs in Japan for Japanese who wished to return to their homeland. There had been two prior successful exchanges involving several thousand civilians. Negotiations for a third, to consist largely of POWs, stalled after the army arrived at Tule Lake, were never successfully resumed. Perhaps they would never have succeeded. But the Japanese, who scarcely needed any incitement to mistreat POWs, reacted to the American Army's arrival at Tule Lake by further abusing American prisoners, sometimes telling their victims that their torture was in response to the doings at that internment camp.

The last of the internment camps was not closed until the end of 1946. Remarkably, a few very elderly Japanese did not want to leave the camps and actually had to be removed by force! Japanese internees had also been held at other facilities, nationwide, including even Ellis Island in New York harbor. So far as is known, all were released by the end of 1946.

Civil liberties are frequently curtailed in wartime, but not until 1988 did Congress and the White House apologize for this breach of civil liberties and make payment of $20,000 to each surviving internee. And, again, however cold the comfort, it was likely better than the treatment Americans of Japanese ancestry would have received had they been returned to Japan. Still, the entire internment procedure was part of an interracial war, and as such, comprises one of the most regrettable episodes of the entire conflict.

The average Japanese knew nothing of the mistreatment of American POWs during the war, nor of the atrocities committed in China, until the late 1970s when the Japanese press aired such subjects for the first time. During the conflict the Japanese faithfully accepted whatever the official propaganda line was. But no words could allay the fear that gripped the population of the home islands by the summer of 1945. An American invasion was expected imminently. Indeed, a fear gripped the Japanese such as was felt probably only by the Carthaginians at the approach of the Roman army. All Japan prepared for the worst as the summer of 1945 waned.

Suggestions for Further Reading

Clay Blair, *Silent Victory* (New York: Lippincott, 1975), is the best account so far of the American submarine effort against Japan, but it must be supplemented by Ronald Lewin, *The American Magic: Codes, Ciphers and the Defeat of Japan* (New York: Farrar Straus Giroux, 1982). Richard O'Kane's story is best told in his own book, *Clear the Bridge! The War Patrols of the U.S.S. Tang* (Novato, CA: Presidio Press, 1989). The most useful account of the Japanese submarine effort, outdated but not supplanted, is Mochitsura Hashimoto, *Sunk! The Story of the Japanese Submarine Fleet, 1941–1945* (New York: Holt, 1954); an individual

Japanese account is provided by Zenji Orita, *I-Boat Captain* (Canoga Park, CA: Major Books, 1976). A first-rate reference book for both American and Japanese submarines is Erminio Bagnasco, *Submarines of World War Two* (Annapolis, MD: Naval Institute Press, 1977). Joseph Enright, *Shinano!* (New York: St. Martin's Press, 1987) recounts well the sinking of that ship. Information pertaining to life in wartime Japan may be found in Thomas Havens, *Valley of Darkness: The Japanese People and World War Two* (New York: Norton, 1978); Saburo Ienega, *The Pacific War, 1931–1945* (New York: Pantheon Books, 1978); Hoito Edoin, *The Night Tokyo Burned: The Incendiary Campaign against Japan, March–August 1945* (New York: St. Martins Press, 1987); and Tessa Morris-Suzuki, *Showa: An Inside History of Hirohito's Japan* (New York: Schocken Books, 1985). By far the best study dealing with the interracial nature of the conflict is John Dower's seminal work, *War without Mercy: Race and Power in the Pacific War* (New York: Pantheon Books, 1986). *Japan's Greater East Asia Co-Prosperity Sphere in World War Two: Selected Readings and Documents,* ed. by Joyce V. Lebra (New York: Oxford University Press, 1975), provides some positive information on the topic. The only biographical study of Tokyo Rose in English is Masayo Duus, *Tokyo Rose: Orphan of the Pacific* (New York: Kodansha, 1978). Ryuji Nagatsuka, *I Was a Kamakaze* (London: Schuman, 1972), has some interesting comments on the subject. The materials on *Operation Flying Elephant* are drawn primarily from Robert C. Mikesh, *Japan's World War II Balloon Bomb Attacks on North America* (Washington, DC: Smithsonian Institution Press, 1973), but see also Bert Webber, *Retaliation: Japanese Attacks and Allied Countermeasures on the Pacific Coast in World War II* (Corvallis, OR: Oregon State University Press, 1975). The latest work on Japanese chemical and biological warfare is Peter Williams and David Wallace, *Unit 731: Japan's Secret Biological Warfare in World War Two* (New York: Macmillan, 1989). The most informative studies of Japanese internment in this country during the war include U.S. Commission on Wartime Relocation and Internment of Civilians, *Personal Justice Denied* (Washington, DC: Government Printing Office, 1982); Dillon S. Meyer, *Uprooted Americans* (Tucson: University of Arizona Press, 1971); Morton Grodzins, *Americans Betrayed* (Chicago: University of Chicago Press, 1949); and Michi Weglyn, *Years of Infamy* (New York: William Morrow, 1976), although the last must be used with some caution. Scott P. Corbett, *Quiet Passages: The Exchange of Civilians between the United States and Japan during the Second World War* (Kent, OH: Kent State University Press, 1987), details a little-known facet of the conflict.

8. The CBI Theater

China
Burma
India and Indonesia
The Significance of the CBI War

China, Burma, and India constituted what was known as the CBI theater of the conflict. It was under a unified Allied command for most of the war. Allied veterans who participated in campaigns there consider that they have long been ignored. In truth, their real complaint may be that the fighting in the CBI theater was not decisive in defeating the Japanese. The theater was at the end of the longest supply line in the world. It was constantly undersupplied in comparison with every other theater of the conflict. And it never received its fair share of publicity or attention in either the American or the British press. The CBI theater was the backwater area of Allied operations and was to the main area of conflict in the Pacific what the Italian campaign was to the Allied effort against Germany—an interesting but ultimately indecisive sideshow.

But secondary though the CBI theater may have been, it possessed its own intrinsic importance. The areas involved were vast. Many were very densely populated. And the political makeup of the region today largely derives, as will be seen, from the Japanese conquest and its political consequences.

President Roosevelt took a special interest in the China theater, as did the Luce publications, *Time* and *Life*. Henry Luce, editor in chief of these two magazines, had been born in China of missionary parents. He therefore displayed a natural interest in things Chinese. In FDR's case, the interest stemmed from familial connections with that nation. His mother's family, the Delanos, had made their fortune during the nineteenth century in the China trade, including, so it appears, opium. Roosevelt in particular hoped that China would be a great democratic power, or at least presence, in the postwar world. In this he would encounter considerable opposition from the British. In fact, Prime Minister Winston Churchill had an opposite view, believing that China would not be a power for many decades to come; indeed Churchill held a decidedly nineteenth-century Victorian view of the matter, and thought the Chinese would not be capable of effective self-government without, at the very least, substantial advice from the Occidental powers until long after the conflict.

China had been ruled by the Manchu dynasty until 1911, when a republican revolution forced the abdication of the last emperor, the boy Henry Pu-yi. Dr. Sun Yat-sen, widely regarded as the father of the revolution, was not in China when the revolution toppled Pu-yi from his throne. Traveling in the United States to raise money for the revolutionary cause in the various Chinatown areas on the West Coast, Sun was caught by surprise in Denver when the revolution occurred. After hurrying home, he was soon elected president of the Chinese republic, but there were always those who contested his claim to power. Indeed, he never headed a regime in the capital of China, Peking, which would almost certainly have brought him diplomatic recognition as head of government by the Western powers. And Sun himself seemed to oscillate between periods of dreamy idealism and ones of hard-headed political realism. His party was the *Kuomintang,* the Nationalist party, which aimed at modernizing China.

Sun died suddenly of cancer in March 1925. His heir apparent was Chiang Kai-shek, who had been working with the Soviets to reform the Chinese military, although Chiang himself never embraced Marxist ideology. He had founded the Whampoa Military Academy, China's first substantial attempt to emulate West Point. Chiang, a man of humble origins, was adept at accumulating personal power. He did not hesitate to employ his cadets and academy graduates to strengthen his political position. Everywhere he consolidated his power, even marrying to further his ambitions. In 1927 he wed the wealthy Mei-ling Soong, who belonged to a Shanghai family that had converted to Christianity. Chiang's own conversion to that religion, which was basically sincere, increased his standing as a reputable head of state in the eyes of the Western powers.

Mei-ling, one of three quite ambitious sisters, had gone to both high school and college in the United States. Some Westerners in Shanghai, within the international settlement in that city, referred to her contemptuously as a "banana," a Chinese who was Westernized, that is, still yellow in skin tone but white inside. This was unfair. Mei-ling was a patriotic Chinese, although on occasion she did not hesitate to put her

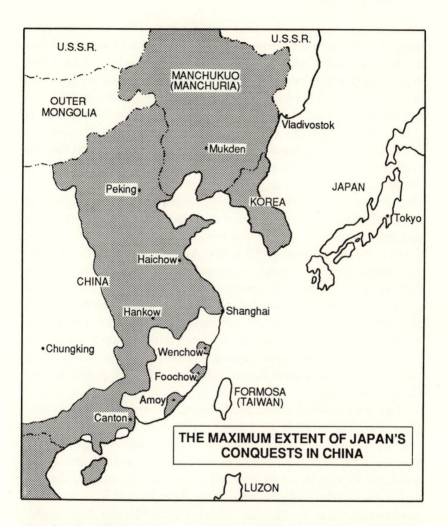

THE MAXIMUM EXTENT OF JAPAN'S CONQUESTS IN CHINA

own fortunes first and those of China a distant second. She was perfectly fluent in English, was widely idealized in the American press, and appeared on the cover of *Time* magazine several times in the 1930s and 1940s.

Chiang married her for her wealth as well as her Christianity. He had been married twice before Mei-ling. His two sons were products of these prior unions. Madame Chiang could not bear her husband another child, a fact that, she claimed, ultimately led to an all-but-open dissolution of their marriage by late 1944.

Chiang never had a proper chance to implement his plans for reform. In 1931 he was confronted with the loss of his wealthiest province, Manchuria, to the Japanese, a blow from which China would not recover until after 1945. In 1937, after the Marco Polo Bridge incident, Chiang was even more openly at war with the Japanese as they invaded additional portions of his country. Chiang was forced to borrow money abroad, although he did not hesitate to manipulate the exchange rate of the Chinese currency to enrich his family's coffers.

Chiang's second greatest problem, after the Japanese, was the Chinese Communist party, under Mao Tse-tung. At first the Communists' power base had been in the south. But in the famous "Long March" Mao started out in November of 1934 for north China. He began with 35,000 followers. His own brother died during the march, and he had abandoned two of his own infants before it began. In the course of 235 days he moved his men 6,600 miles. Averaging seventeen miles per day, crossing eighteen mountain ranges and twenty-four major rivers, the Communists marched across eleven Chinese provinces, almost every inch of the way contested, all on foot! Mao established himself near the relatively (by Chinese standards) prosperous northern town of Yennan, within Shensi province, although only about 5,000 men survived the march. Mao then began a vigorous campaign effort for recruits to the Communist cause, spreading his own brand of rural Communist ideology.

Chiang was ever Mao's bitterest enemy, although Mao and his guerrillas proved a burden to the Japanese as well. On very rare occasions Chinese troops actually cooperated with the Japanese when Mao was their common enemy. As Mao's power increased and the area of Japanese rule expanded, rural China fell more and more into the hands of war lords or bandit chiefs, who everywhere formed a local, second government. Even within the international settlement in Shanghai, gangs terrorized Chinese merchants at night, forcing them to pay tribute or protection money. Chiang himself even took to collecting taxes years in advance, evidently to help finance his campaigns against the bandits, Communists, and Japanese. Thus by 1941 Chiang had his hands full. He was understandably relieved when he learned of the Japanese attack on Pearl Harbor.

On Pearl Harbor day Chiang realized that America would indeed eventually defeat the Japanese. He determined to make no further substantial effort to oust the Japanese from his country. Everywhere the various local Chinese military commanders were ordered to cease all but the most minimal resistance to the Japanese. In effect, something of an unofficial truce with the Japanese was cemented in some areas. The Japanese in particular did not hesitate to violate these truces around harvest time, when they would engage in "rice raids" to pillage the local rice crops. They were therefore able to gain foodstuffs for their own army, while denying it to the Chinese. Nonetheless for two years there was almost no formal fighting between Chinese and Japanese troops in China.

This obviously disturbed the United States. China received Lend Lease supplies after Pearl Harbor, as well as numerous loans. Roosevelt determined to see that the material and money sent to China were not squandered, although he enjoyed almost no knowledge of conditions in China, either political or military. Consequently, in March 1942 General Joseph Stilwell arrived in Chiang's capital, Chungking, to serve as chief of staff of the Chinese Army. In effect he was second in command, second only to Generalissimo Chiang himself. Stilwell was fluent in Chinese, having had prior military service in China.

Not only did Stilwell know China well, he was on very good terms with Chief of Staff George Marshall in Washington; he was reputedly the only officer who regularly addressed Marshall by his first name. So far, so good. But Stilwell had a sarcastic nature, which was evident well before his advent in China. Indeed he had long been known by the nickname "Vinegar Joe," and he evidently relished his reputation as a cynic. An energetic worker, he was impatient of lassitude, corruption, or simple complacency in high places, which meant that he was inevitably bound to become a fervent critic of Chiang. After several weeks at his new assignment, Stilwell had already undertaken some very basic, sorely needed reforms of the Chinese Army, which were to win him the almost universal respect of its officers and enlisted men alike. But Stilwell soon engaged in his penchant for sarcasm: he code-named Chiang "peanut," and Chiang almost surely knew about this. On one or two very impatient occasions, in a tasteless parody of President Roosevelt's infirmity (the president was confined to a wheelchair), Stilwell referred to his commander in chief as "Rubberlegs." Stilwell had scarcely arrived when Chiang began a campaign to have him relieved, working partially through his ambassador in Washington. But largely because of the support of General Marshall, Stilwell remained, for the moment, at his post.

Chiang had an ally in his attempts to relieve Stilwell in the person of

Major General Claire Chennault, a rather maverick Army Air Corps general who had arrived long before Pearl Harbor to command the Chinese Air Force. Even then Chennault had mainly American flyers under his command. Chennault was a tactical genius. The first American general to see the Japanese Zero fighter plane in action during the year 1940, he wrote Washington of its potential and enclosed something like blueprints for construction of an aircraft to combat it effectively but was unfortunately ignored. General Marshall in particular had little use for Chennault, and not without some justification. Marshall frequently, and quite correctly, referred to Chennault as nothing but a "paid agent" of Chiang. Chennault accepted very large sums either as pay or as outright gifts from Chiang. Further, when Chennault's Americans actually entered into combat against the Japanese after Pearl, they required very large pay incentives, sometimes even to take to the air. Money seemed to be the cement that held Chennault's group of flyers together.

To be sure, there was precious little else to attract American flyers to China, except the promise of adventure itself. In the mid-1930s, the Italians had been in charge of the Chinese Air Force. Chennault had taken over after they left and inherited many problems created by the Italians. First, they had graduated as pilots almost every candidate who applied for flight school, regardless of vision, aptitude, and the like. Second, when the Italians left, they took all the aerial maps of China with them. Thus, Chennault had to begin at square one by establishing a basic cartography operation, which, given China's vastness, was not always as successful as Chennault and his flyers would have liked.

Chennault's flyers adopted the name "Flying Tigers" and they were greatly romanticized in the American press. Chennault was naturally a firm believer in air power. Although virtually blind in one eye, he became an ace; eventually he accounted for no small number of downed Japanese aircraft. His importance became all the greater after February 1942, when the Burma road from Lashio in Burma to Kunming in China, the only supply route left into China, was permanently closed because of the Japanese conquest of Burma. Supplies now had to be flown from north*western* India into China. Because of a Japanese air base at Myitkyina in northern Burma, this air route went over the eastern Himalayan Mountains, from India to Kunming in southern China, at an altitude of 21,000 feet. Known as "flying the hump," it was dangerous work indeed; anyone lost over the mountains could not be rescued.

Chennault's American airmen, who were allowed to down Japanese aircraft only after the attack on Pearl, suffered a major setback early in 1942, when they officially became part of the Army Air Corps as the Fourteenth Air Force. Put on normal combat pay and evidently denied further incentive pay, almost all of the original pilots quit as of July 4, 1942. (One who left for future adventures in the Solomon theater was Gregory Boyington, hero of a future television series.) Chennault had the unenviable task of having to train replacements rapidly. But Stilwell now demanded that greater emphasis be given the Tenth Air Force, under Brigadier General Clayton Bissell, which had charge of bringing in supplies from India. Stilwell asked Bissell to devote a greater percentage of supplies flown over the hump to materials for the Chinese Army, while Chennault, perhaps understandably, wished to transport, almost exclusively, supplies for his own aviation effort against the Japanese.

In response, Chennault, with Chiang's blessing and encouragement, began deluging Washington with position papers and, when possible, personal letters stating that air power alone could defeat the Japanese, at least in the Chinese theater of the conflict. This led to bitter disagreement between Chennault and Stilwell, the latter maintaining that Chennault's argument was put forward in part to ingratiate himself with Chiang. Stilwell also contended that Chennault carried not only supplies but contraband in his aircraft, a charge that doubtless carried substantial truth, since bribery was then the mainstay of bureaucratic existence in China. Anyone who wished to work effectively with Chiang's government often found it useful, if not absolutely necessary. Stilwell was one of the very few Westerners in China who probably did not resort to it.

Stilwell and Chennault spent their time in China locked in internecine conflict. Stilwell undoubtedly had by far the better grasp of the military realities of the situation, and he alone was fluent in Chinese. But Chiang sided automatically with Chennault, and from the first Chennault did everything humanly possible to have Stilwell relieved. To say the very least, their situation was not American military cooperation at its best, but it was probably inherent in the circumstances in China, with its blatant, rampant corruption.

Chiang closeted himself in his chosen capital of Chungking and in effect began husbanding supplies for the civil war with the Communists, which he correctly predicted would begin the day the Japanese surrendered to the Americans. Washington, understandably, took a dim view of his attitude. American leadership also never accepted Chennault's contention that air power alone could defeat the Japanese. But every morning that Madame Chiang was in China, she sent a lengthy epistle to General Stilwell, filled with her husband's supposedly sage military advice, espousing the virtues of "deep column tactics" as opposed to the "adventures" in which Stilwell hoped to engage against the Japanese. Stilwell did what he could with the 300-division Chinese Army and organized the first effective medical service in that army's history.

The Japanese put a price on Stilwell's head. This Stilwell actually found advantageous. Whenever he ordered a front-line general in the Chinese Army to advance and the order was disobeyed, Stilwell would simply appear at the recalcitrant general's headquarters. This would attract much Japanese sniper and patrol attention, evidently in the hope that they could literally cash in on the reward posted for his head. In turn the Chinese general would usually be moved to some minimal military action, if only to get Stilwell out of his command area. It was a negative command method, but it did ensure some resistance to the Japanese, who otherwise moved more or less at will throughout the Chinese countryside.

Eighty-five percent of China's people lived in rural areas. The average amount of land farmed by each family was only one and one-seventh acres or possibly even less. These peasants probably did not care who governed the nation, except that they opposed the Japanese occupation when their areas were affected. Stilwell perhaps understood their sentiments better than any of the leaders in Chungking. Whenever possible, he took care not to allow his military operations, maneuvers, and inspections to interfere with the peasants' crops, and there is some evidence that he knew how susceptible many of the peasants would be to Mao's particular brand of peasant Communism.

Stilwell managed to piece together several divisions that could operate with artillery support (usually referred to as the Y force, although this designation was not consistently used in Washington). But he never managed to engage the Japanese seriously, which was always Washington's advice. Chiang Kai-shek kept his embassy busy in Washington with complaints against Stilwell; only Marshall's unstinting support kept him in China.

Chiang remained aloof in Chungking, ignorant of the state of his armies. Stilwell routinely sent him reports on military matters, but these evidently went unread. On one occasion, when informed of one of his general's incompetence, Chiang turned his cane on the offending officer, apparently believing that a good public thrashing would restore competence. Chiang evidently had a shortsighted view of his ultimate command responsibilities and was not infrequently unaware of conditions even *inside* his own capital.

Madame Chiang, as the American press usually dubbed her, visited the United States from November 1942 through May 1943, in part for medical treatment. She was greeted by an astonishing outpouring of public approbation and addressed capacity crowds in the Hollywood Bowl and Madison Square Garden. Behind the scenes, ensconced on the second floor of the White House, she behaved like spoiled, petulant royalty. As might have been expected, she sang Chennault's praises and castigated Stilwell. The joint chiefs were particularly alarmed by her visit, for she made no secret that she thought America's "Europe-first" decision an error that she intended to have corrected. Probably the highlight of the visit was her address to a joint session of Congress, but she made no headway in reversing the Europe-first decision. Almost everyone in Washington breathed a sigh of relief when she departed.

Roosevelt kept an open attitude toward Chiang himself until the First Cairo Conference, held in late November 1943. For the first time, Chiang was questioned personally about the state of his army, his plans concerning the Japanese, and his possible aid in ousting the Japanese from Burma, which had once been a Chinese tributary province. Chiang had been sent in advance numerous position papers, studies, and war plans by his allies, but if he actually received them, he did not read them. To Chiang, future military planning consisted, perhaps understandably, of ways and means to contain and defeat the Communist menace within his own country.

At Cairo, much to Churchill's annoyance, Roosevelt insisted that China be the first topic discussed by the participants. It was Chiang's curtain call, although he did not know this. When quizzed by the commander in chief for the Far East, British Admiral Louis Mountbatten, about the state of his own armed forces, Chiang could not answer the most basic questions, much less give a detailed summary of his planned operations against the Japanese, since he in fact had none. Stilwell fielded most of Mountbatten's questions while Chiang watched with growing anger. Then Chiang revealed the depth of his own ignorance. The Allied leaders began a discussion of *Buccaneer*, a planned amphibious operation against Burma, later canceled partly for lack of landing craft. Someone made mention of the monsoon season. Madame Chiang Kai-shek, who had insisted on acting as her husband's interpreter, suddenly began a heated discussion in Chinese with him. After a decent interval, Mountbatten interrupted to ask what the discussion concerned. Madame Chiang informed Mountbatten that Chiang had never heard of the monsoon season and evidently refused to believe it really existed. There could have been no greater demonstration of Chiang's military ineptitude. He could not describe military conditions in his own army, much less anticipate what those conditions might be elsewhere.

Everyone left Cairo disillusioned with Chiang, who alone thought he had given a passable performance. Roosevelt reputedly wondered aloud if his government might not find a substitute for Chiang, although if he did have such thoughts, no action was taken, even though it was known in Washington that Madame Chiang's ambitious and very wealthy brother, T.V. Soong, wanted to replace Chiang. Thereafter Roosevelt was more susceptible to the views of his secretary of the treasury, Henry Morgenthau, who had previously warned the president that every loan in cash made to China ended up in Chiang's own foreign bank accounts or in that of his wife's family.

The Chinese continued to press for financial aid, arguing in what amounted to both financial, diplomatic, and military blackmail, that if China dropped out of the war, a million more Japanese troops would be free to fight the American troops engaged in the Pacific. Roosevelt and Morgenthau were evidently moved by this logic. They continued to pour money into the coffers of Chinese officialdom. The Luce publications in this country continued to extol Chiang and his wife as the saviors of China, but behind the scenes the federal government in Washington now had only contempt for a man who practiced blackmail upon them. All told, Chiang received over one and one-half billion dollars in American aid. If recently revealed FBI files are correct, over a billion dollars of that amount was routed into personal bank accounts. Further, while China, including Manchukuo (as Manchuria had been renamed), contained a million Japanese troops, many were raw recruits in training or were otherwise surprisingly inept. Witness that when the Soviets invaded Manchukuo in August 1945, they experienced only the most token opposition. Had Washington known the true quality of the Japanese military on the Asian mainland after Pearl Harbor, the United States might have been less inclined to tolerate Chiang's blackmail.

In October 1944, Roosevelt caved in to pressure applied by Chiang and announced General Stilwell's recall. As a sop to Stilwell, Roosevelt pointedly remarked to the press that a personality clash was involved and that basic military competence was not in question. Stilwell's successor, Major General Albert Wedemeyer, did not have Stilwell's China background, but he was able to concentrate exclusively on China itself, without having to devote undue attention to the Burma problem that had long plagued Stilwell. But the Chinese Army had been at its peak under Stilwell. His loss was a blow from which it did not recover.

At almost the same moment as Stilwell's recall, a new American ambassador arrived in Chungking: General Patrick Hurley, blundered into the post without prior knowledge of the Orient. Soon code-named "albatross" by the Office of Strategic Services (OSS), Hurley addressed Chiang as "Mr. Shek." On occasion he gave out Oklahoma Indian war whoops, which in one instance evidently temporarily convinced the generalissimo that Hurley was unbalanced. Hurley visited Mao Tse-tung and his lieutenant Chou En-lai at Yennan, and promptly urged Chiang to allow Communists to participate in his government. Chiang's reaction to this proposal can well be imagined! Chiang had little use for the ambassador; on one occasion, as Hurley was leaving his residence, Chiang loudly ordered that the windows be opened right away to let the smell of the foreigner dissipate.

In Washington Roosevelt was now preoccupied with the Russians and the fate of postwar Europe. He paid the Chinese problem less attention as each month passed. Perhaps it was just as well. In May 1944, the Japanese exploded the myth that they could not move at will in China when they launched an offensive in southern China to gain a land route for transporting the Indochinese rice crop to Japan and also to seize some of Chennault's key air fields. It was their largest offensive in China since 1938. It cost them few casualties, at least from Chinese fire. Since an all-land route to Indochina was ultimately impossible for Japan, the offensive gained them little, except for the air fields, which were of marginal value.

When Harry Truman became president in April 1945 after

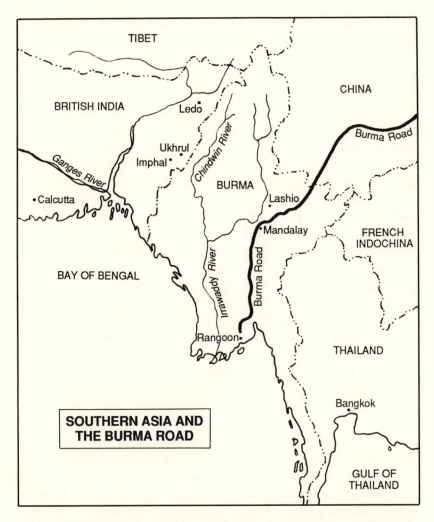

TIBET

BRITISH INDIA   Ledo

CHINA

Burma Road

Ukhrul
Imphal

Chindwin River

BURMA

Ganges River

Calcutta

Lashio

Mandalay

FRENCH
INDOCHINA

BAY OF BENGAL

Irrawaddy River

Burma Road

Rangoon

THAILAND

Bangkok

**SOUTHERN ASIA AND
THE BURMA ROAD**

GULF OF
THAILAND

Roosevelt's death, he encouraged Chiang to think of the wisdom of a coalition government that would include Communist party members, on the ground that this was the only realistic solution to the China problem. Such an agreement was eventually reached, but it was never executed.

For the Americans in part of Stilwell's or Chennault's command, serving in China was doubtless the experience of a lifetime, despite the poverty-stricken, wartime conditions. Stilwell's predictions concerning the Chinese leadership held true. Chiang's government would fall of its own weight, and he and his clique became exiles in 1949. He lost power because of his lack of knowledge of his own people, in whose fate he had often seemed so disinterested.

In the CBI theater the only real Allied military successes were in Burma. There the British were desperate to regain the initiative against the Japanese. They had lost Burma in early 1942, thereby giving the Japanese empire a border on India, the brightest jewel in Britain's own imperial crown.

The Japanese victory in Burma had been so rapid and well executed that it appeared that the Japanese were capable of driving on to India with little delay. British political power in Burma was completely displaced by mid-May of 1942. The Japanese chose to consolidate their power in a receptive Burma, waiting for the rainy season to pass before even considering launching any further advances in south central Asia. With the demise of British military strength in Burma and the failure of any Allied naval units to challenge Japanese control of the seas, this delay did not seem unreasonable. The victories that had already been achieved had placed the Japanese forces well ahead of schedule, and for the army there seemed time enough to conquer India later, if they so desired. Domestic unrest in that country had already begun to work in favor of the Japanese. Still, the Indian subcontinent remained surprisingly calm, despite the evident threat of Japanese invasion. Indeed, about two million Indians volunteered for service with the Indian armed forces, which came to constitute one of the greatest volunteer forces in the history of warfare.

To give at least the illusion of being on the offensive and lend credence to its claim that Burma would again be under British rule after the conflict, the British high command initiated a series of limited offensives against occupied Burma. Thus came into being the "Chindits," the Seventy-Seventh Indian Brigade, under Brigadier General Orde Wingate. Wingate conceived of the nuisance raid. He proposed to penetrate Japanese lines, relying on air drops for supplies The Chindits first entered service in February 1943, when they set out to sever two railways in Burma. One was cut, but the damage was quickly repaired. Wingate's forces were scattered and returned to India in small groups, some taking months to make the journey. The raid was a military failure, but this was not the view taken by the English-language press in India, who hailed it as a military coup.

The next move came from Stilwell. Frustrated by his growing inability to command troops in China, since Chiang almost always managed to countermand his orders, Stilwell determined to lead a Chinese army into Burma. His ultimate goal was to reopen the Burma road. In this he would not succeed, although he did liberate a portion of northern Burma. Stilwell's Thirty-Eighth and Twenty-Second Chinese divisions kicked off in October 1943, pushing southward into Burma from India through the Hukawng Valley. He was supplied by air. Meanwhile, work on a bypass of the Burma portion of the supply route had begun, pushing east from Ledo.

Also in October Vice Admiral Louis Mountbatten became Supreme Allied Commander of the Southeast Asia Command. At first he operated out of Delhi but later he moved his headquarters to the cooler city of Kandy, in central Ceylon (now Sri Lanka). Mountbatten had as his area commander in Burma Lt. General William Slim, who proved excellent in training men for jungle duty.

In 1944 the American provisional infantry regiment known to history as "Merrill's Marauders," under the command of Major General Frank Merrill, arrived in Burma. Their efforts inflicted serious losses on the Japanese, but were not as successful as had been anticipated.

A second Chindit expedition was prepared, again under Wingate. In early March 1944, employing gliders, it landed behind Japanese lines but could not disrupt the Japanese offensive against India, which had just begun. Wingate was killed on March 25, 1944, when his aircraft crashed into a mountain in the jungle. He was replaced by Major General W. D. Lentaigne.

The Japanese meanwhile had reorganized their forces in Burma. As with all of the Japanese forces holding conquered lands in 1944, the army in Burma was forced to deal with new realities. The empire was no longer capable of properly sustaining all of its far-flung forces. Area commanders were increasingly instructed to stand and fight with the resources they had, enjoying little hope of future assistance. The Japanese Army in Burma now found itself facing this situation. Any offensive measure had to be successful because every loss was irreplaceable. The British had recovered well enough to make a substantial commitment to the defense of India and the reconquest of Burma on land; the Japanese Navy could no longer sortie into the Indian Ocean. In all, it appeared that the time had passed for the Japanese to consider expanding their empire.

The senior command of the Japanese Burma Army was now under

Lt. General Shozo Kawabe. His immediate superior was Field Marshall Count Terauchi, headquartered in Saigon. The Burma Army contained six divisions. Two were in southwest Burma, under Kawabe's command; the other four, in the north, were under Lt. General Renya Mutaguchi. Kawabe had asked General Mutaguchi to prepare for an offensive against eastern India. Mutaguchi's force would consist of three divisions that had been reinforced to almost 100,000 men, all veteran combat troops accustomed to jungle life. Mutaguchi had a dual objective: first, to seize the fortress town of Imphal, just across the border and also the key to domination of the Imphal-Kohima plain of Manipur, which would be the base of any British attempt to reconquer central Burma; second, to sever the railway line into Assam, which passed through Manipur and carried many supplies to the southern terminus of the Hump. Strategically significant, however, was that in order to accomplish these goals, Mutaguchi would have to cross the vast mountain ranges of eastern India.

On March 6, 1944, Mutaguchi began his invasion of India from central Burma when he crossed the Chindwin River. One division was dispatched toward Kohima, two toward Imphal. The British had been expecting the offensive, possibly (the materials are still classified) aided in advance by cryptography. But they had no idea of its size. The British managed only at the last moment to reinforce Imphal. On April 4, the Japanese invested Imphal, and began its siege. Three British divisions defended it. General Slim organized an airlift for Imphal and Kohima as well and began a relief campaign from India, which reached Kohima on April 20.

The Japanese besieged Imphal with a stubbornness unusual even for the Imperial Army. Slim continued to aid the besieged garrison via airlift. But the Japanese, who had counted on capturing British supplies, did not take equal measures to sustain their troops and began to suffer from attrition. They encountered stiff resistance, and the revolt in India they had hoped for did not materialize. Then the monsoon rains began, making further resupply efforts by the Japanese almost impossible. They had delayed too long—they should have begun the offensive several weeks sooner. After eighty-eight days, the siege of Imphal was broken on June 22, 1944. But the Japanese retreated relatively intact and slowly. They had lost 65,000 men, the majority to disease, malnutrition, and drowning. Slim pursued them, inflicting further losses.

The Japanese brought in General Hoyotaro Kimura to replace Kawabe. During the summer monsoon rains, when the temperatures can remain high and the humidity can make one yearn for the return of the dry summer heat, Kimura reorganized his army. He received reinforcements, reaching a battle strength of 250,000 men. His strategy was realistic. He would slowly yield ground to the enemy, allowing them to conquer portions of central Burma. Gradually his own supply lines would contract, while the Allied lines would lengthen.

What Kimura did not appreciate was Allied air power—not so much combat air power, as logistical strength, which allowed all manner of supplies to be dropped to the British, something the Japanese never imagined. Parachutes were used for supplies that might break; otherwise, supplies were "free dropped," without chutes.

By early 1945 four major Allied armies were busy reconquering Burma: the British XV corps were pushing toward Akyab on the Bay of Bengal; Slim was advancing on a broad front; a Chinese force was moving toward Burma from the north; and Lt. General Daniel Sultan was approaching the old Burma road from the west. The Japanese resisted, but General Kimura deliberately let the enemy penetrate central Burma.

Merrill's Marauders were attempting an end-run maneuver of the Japanese Army, hoping to cut them off and crush them against the mass of Allied soldiers approaching from the north. Kimura realized what was happening, since it was a favorite tactic of the Japanese themselves. He turned his full attention to Merrill, leaving only enough soldiers in the north to prevent the Allies from pouring through on his flank. He then attacked Merrill's comparatively smaller force in strength and nearly crushed it, managing to escape the trap planned for his troops. Kimura was forced to withdraw the main body of his surviving forces into Thailand. There he had little respite, for that nation, like the other Japanese conquests, had mounted a resistance movement against the Japanese conqueror.

Slim conducted a brilliant campaign in the north, and his training methods paid off. Aided by some native tribesmen, who revolted behind enemy lines, he was able to make rapid gains against the weakened Japanese force. Following these campaigns, the Japanese force in Burma was reduced to little more than a nuisance.

In the early spring of 1945 the British extension to replace the Burmese portion of the Burma road was completed. If it had been operative when originally planned, six to twelve months earlier, it might have enabled the Chinese Army to mount at least a limited offensive against the Japanese. Opened as the Ledo road, after its new Indian terminus, it was soon renamed the Stilwell road. It had a pipeline running its entire length, which allowed a greater amount of supplies than ever before to reach China.

By mid-spring, the British realized they could seize Rangoon, the capital city and a major port, before the May monsoon rains began. Thus, the interservice race for the city began on April 1, 1945. On May 1, an amphibious landing was made at the mouth of the Rangoon river, in a display of an *"I will get there first"* attitude, which in the long run was not helpful. The British too suffered from interservice rivalry.

On May 1, 1945, the Japanese evacuated Rangoon, but the British did not know this. The next day, however, a British plane overflying the city reported that there were no Japanese in the city, at least none in uniform. The pilot landed, helped the local population release prisoners of war, and then paddled down the river to tell the army that the Royal Air Force had liberated the capital!

At this point the British had succeeded in routing a Japanese Army that was hardly its equal. The Japanese in Burma were suffering all of the effects of the successful Allied submarine effort and were incapable of retaining the fighting capability they once possessed. As soon as the siege of Imphal was broken, the Japanese commanders were forced to commit the remainder of their reserves to a doomed withdrawal effort. The focus shifted from increasing the empire to merely sustaining the existing forces. The campaign became only a sideshow to the main attraction that was taking place in the waters surrounding the home islands of Japan.

There was no further substantial action in Burma after May, since the monsoon rains began and the Japanese forces began a slow withdrawal to Thailand. Mountbatten began planning for a major amphibious operation against Singapore in 1946. Had this come about, he would probably have had considerable success, for the Japanese Army in Malaya had its hands full with a growing resistance movement.

The remaining theater under Mountbatten's command, India itself, witnessed conflict, but not of the overt military nature seen in Burma. Instead India was on the very brink of civil revolt, which would undoubtedly have been followed by a religious civil war between Hindu and Muslim. This civil war smoldered just below the surface throughout the greater portion of World War II.

Roosevelt had hoped at first that the British might make substantial concessions toward Indian self-rule. He raised the matter with Churchill but only once, at least in person. Churchill's reaction was frosty, and Roosevelt let it drop, although for more than a year after Pearl Harbor the American liberal press continued to raise the subject from time to time.

The Indians themselves did not neglect the matter, however. The two greatest Indian political figures were Mohandas Gandhi, the leader of the Congress party, and Muhammad Ali Jinnah, the Muslim leader. Gandhi had organized a campaign of "individual civil disobedience" to British rule and on occasion stated that he would prefer Japanese rule to that of Britain, if that were India's *immediate* two choices. By May 1941 some 15,000 Indians had been jailed for civil disobedience. Britain eventually promised independence but only after the conflict, which satisfied no one. Gandhi thereupon asked that the British "Quit India" at once, in which case he promised to resist the Japanese. When the British authorities tacitly refused, Gandhi's followers engaged in more active resistance to British rule. Several thousand were arrested. Gandhi himself was put under a form of house arrest, during which his wife died. India was fortunate to have a new viceroy in the person of Archibald Wavell. He handled a terrible growing food crisis (more than 1.5 million people died of starvation in the Bengal) quite adeptly and calmed some of the anti-British sentiment in the nation as well. The Congress party grew less restive. Jinnah, however, remained free throughout the crisis and frequently stated that Japanese rule would be preferable to British, although he may have made these statements out of simple political expediency.

Churchill refused to consider independence during the world war. He argued that even after the war, independence would mean a religious civil war, which in fact later occurred. Probably the key to retaining India, even for a few years, had been the successful British campaign in Burma, which impressed many Indians with British determination, while demonstrating that the Japanese could be defeated even in an area that had initially welcomed them as liberators.

In Indochina, the Japanese had been in control longer than in any other of the Southern Resource Areas. Here a rebel known as Ho Chi

Minh opposed the Japanese occupation. He and his guerrilla forces, a combination of nationalists and Communists, known as the Viet Minh, had received aid and supplies from America, and some also from Chiang Kai-shek, who supported them because they were anticolonialist. By the time Japan surrendered, almost all of northern Indochina had been liberated. When on September 2, 1945, Ho Chi Minh proclaimed Indochina independent, an American adviser was standing on the platform with him.

The CBI theater was obviously of life-and-death importance to the men who fought there, and the individual acts of bravery by soldiers on both sides of the conflict are too numerous to recount. The war, however, was neither won by the Allies nor lost by the Japanese in this theater of the conflict.

But despite its peripheral importance to the outcome of the conflict as a whole, the CBI struggle was of vast importance to the millions who inhabited those nations. It helped lead to a civil war in China, which eventuated in the establishment of a Communist regime. It led in India, soon after the war, to a British promise of Indian independence and Commonwealth status. It also gave the Burmese something of a taste of independence and paved the way for the British loss of Burma as well. Similarly, the resistance movement in Malaya would eventually turn on the returning British overlords. As a few Americans (including Pearl Buck) had warned the White House from the first, the average Asian, at least in theory, would prefer Japanese domination rather than domination by the white man, and, at least in the first instance, this was true. Britain and the other colonial powers might try to reestablish their empires, but in the long run they would not succeed. The fact that in many areas the surrendering Japanese forces had to be given back their weapons to keep order until the European colonial powers' forces could arrive in strength did not help white prestige in Asian eyes. Everywhere, Japanese conquest paved the way for the independent nations in southeast Asia that exist today.

Suggestions for Further Reading

The best English-language studies dealing with wartime China are biographies of the major figures involved: see especially Barbara Tuchman, *Stilwell and the American Experience in China, 1911–1945* (New York: Macmillan, 1970); Martha Byrd, *Chennault: Giving Wings to the Tiger* (Tuscaloosa: University of Alabama Press, 1987); Sterling Seagrave, *The Soong Dynasty* (New York: Harper and Row, 1985); and William Slim, *Defeat into Victory* (London: Weidenfield & Nicholson, 1960). The best military studies on China during its civil war period are Peter W. Kozumplik, "The Chinese Civil War," in the West Point Military History Series, *The Arab-Israel Wars, the Chinese Civil War and the Korean War* (Wayne, NJ: Avery Publishing, 1987); F.F. Liu, *A Military History of Modern China, 1924–1949* (Princeton, NJ: Princeton University Press, 1956); and the more general but quite valuable work by James Sheridan, *China in Disintegration: The Republican Era in Chinese History, 1912–1949* (New York: The Free Press, 1975). Unfortunately, much of the available material on the campaigns in southern Asia is often romanticized and tends to lack objectivity. Until the mainland Chinese can devote attention to this turbulent period of their history, the best basic source for the era remains The Asia Society, *Encyclopedia of Asian History*, 4 vols. (New York: Charles Scribner's Sons, 1988), which contains a wide range of articles on many political and military topics, all of considerable perceptiveness.

9. The Final Campaigns

Iwo Jima
Okinawa
The B–29
LeMay and Firebombing
Operation Downfall and the Atomic Bomb

Iwo Jima is part of a small island group very aptly named the Volcano Islands. A geologist's paradise, Iwo is eight miles square, experiences frequent earth tremors, and lacks any vegetation. It has steaming sulphur pits, an abundance of volcanic rock formations, and on rare occasions, hot lava flows. The air reeks of sulphur, since ocean breezes are rare. Almost exactly 750 miles south of the Japanese capital, the island was ruled as part of Tokyo Prefecture itself. It was regarded as an integral part of the Japanese home islands, at least for administrative purposes.

The Allies would almost certainly have overlooked this island but for its strategic function: the Japanese had transformed it into a sophisticated observation platform, which included more than one radar installation. It functioned as their forward air raid warning station, advising of approaching American bombers from the Mariana Islands long before they reached Japan. In addition, the Japanese obviously intended to use the island as a forward fighter base to interdict American air strikes against the home islands. If the island were conquered, the Americans could reverse this role, and use Iwo Jima for fighters to cover raids against Japan. More importantly, an air strip on the island, if of sufficient length, could be used to land crippled B–29 bombers returning from raids on the home islands.

As early as July 1944, after the loss of Saipan, the Japanese garrison on Iwo, under Lt. General Tadamichi Kuribayashi, began preparing to meet the Americans, on the assumption that the Allies might bypass the Philippines and head directly for Iwo. The Japanese decided to defend the high ground at either end of the island. Iwo Jima was topographically dominated by Mount Suribachi, nicknamed ''Hot Rocks'' by the Americans even before the invasion. The island's volcanic ash combined with concrete to form a substance far harder than even the Japanese had at first hoped. They honeycombed the island with bunkers, emplacements, and machine gun nests, all well camouflaged. Many of the Japanese emplacements where impenetrable even to direct naval gunfire. Iwo's defenders had no less than three air fields from which the island might be contested, with a garrison of about 22,000 men to defend it.

The U.S. Navy did what it could for the Marines scheduled to seize the island. It unleashed an intense three-day naval bombardment, including fire by no less than six battleships. But Iwo's fortifications remained largely intact. At dawn on February 19, 1945, Major General Harry Schmidt's Fifth Amphibious Corps, comprised of elements of the Third, Fourth, and Fifth Marine Divisions—well over 30,000 men—landed on its beaches. They were surprised, just past the water line, to find themselves ankle deep in ash. The first day's casualties were more than 2,000 marines killed.

It took a full forty days to conquer the island, although on February 23 the American flag was raised on Mount Suribachi by five brave marines, a scene immortalized in what became the most reproduced photograph of the war. American battle deaths were 6,800; the Japanese lost all of their garrison, with the exception of 212 who were taken prisoner. To this day, geological expeditions to the island uncover caves with Japanese bodies sealed in them. The marines wondered aloud whether it had been worth it. The Army Air Corps had no doubt. On the day the island was declared secure, March 16, 1945, sixteen B–29s returning from bombing the Japanese home islands made emergency landings there. By the war's end, 2,251 other B–29 pilots did the same, saving the lives of 24,761 air crew. Iwo Jima became a small but vital cog in the American war effort against Japan.

This left one last island before Japan itself: Okinawa, the key island in the Ryukyu chain, which was needed as a staging area for the invasion of the home islands. Here was a direct preview of what the conquest of Japan itself would be like. Okinawa was considered by many Japanese to constitute a fifth, if unofficial, home island, even though its inhabitants were culturally perhaps as much Chinese as they were Japanese. Japan had officially annexed Okinawa in 1879. Although the Okinawans considered themselves to be loyal Japanese, the Japanese did not arm civilians on the island (in contrast to what they would attempt in the home islands themselves to prepare for an Allied invasion). Okinawa is sixty-seven miles long and from three to twenty miles wide; the average width is eight miles.

The Okinawa campaign is the first true *Allied* effort in the Pacific. For the first time, British warships participated in an island-hopping campaign. On the direct orders of Prime Minister Winston Churchill, the British Admiralty had begun transferring capital ships from the Atlantic to the Pacific as of late November 1944 to fulfill Churchill's pledge that the moment the German Navy was essentially defeated, he would begin shifting British naval might to the Pacific.

The American Navy, proud of its rapid expansion since Pearl Harbor, did not relish British aid, even though the British carrier *Victorious* had previously served in the Pacific from March to August 1943, when she was sorely needed (after the loss of the *Wasp* and the *Hornet*). The specter of a species of international naval rivalry raised its head and it might have taken a serious form had the Allies invaded the home islands. In Washington, Admiral King, who had never approved of the Europe-first decision, was especially chary of accepting British aid. Indeed, the further one was from the actual battle scene, the more opposition to British participation one seemed to find in the American naval establishment.

But practical considerations slowly overcame all objections. First, Churchill had made the promise of British aid at American insistence early in the conflict. Indeed, at one point the prime minister had offered to incorporate the promise into a formal treaty, but Roosevelt said that he accepted Churchill's word on the matter. The only real drawback to actual British participation turned out to be the lesser fuel capacities of the Royal Navy's ships, which gave them a shorter operating range; they were also somewhat slower than their American counterparts. British carrier decks were constructed of steel, whereas American flattop decks were made of American teakwood, which allowed for a softer landing if a crippled aircraft came in. But the British decks were soon to prove as *Kamikaze*-proof as anything yet devised by the Allies.

No fewer than five British flattops, each about 25,500 tons, would help in the operation. These included HMS *Formidable, Illustrious, Indefatigable, Indomitable,* and *Victorious.* All but the second of these suffered direct *Kamikaze* hits during the operation. All sustained, relatively speaking, less damage than the American carriers in the area similarly afflicted. British battleships and cruisers aided as well.

The U.S. Navy code-named the Okinawan conquest *Operation Iceberg,* which seems inappropriate for an island devoid of snowfall but that is often literally muddied by an annual rainfall of over 120 inches. Ashore, the Japanese Thirty-Second Army, under Lt. General Mitsuru Ushijima, prepared his 130,000 men, mostly Manchurian veterans, to meet the Americans. He also conducted extensive propaganda among the island's nearly half-million civilian inhabitants. He assured them that they would die if they fell into American hands. His officers actually informed the Okinawans that American soldiers, and marines in particular, brought with them gorillas to tear apart civilians as part of the American marines idea of a sporting event. As farfetched as the claim was, no small number of Okinawans believed it. If questioned, the Japanese Army solemnly gave assurances that in order to join the Marine Corps in the first place, a recruit was required to shoot one of his parents in the presence of a recruiter! Such are the myths an interracial war breeds.

On March 14 American carriers under Mitscher and British flattops under Vice Admiral Sir Bernard Rawlings began the isolation of Okinawa by bombing nearby islands, especially those that had air strips or operational military harbors. Here for the first time *Kamikazes* began their intended role on a large scale. A very rare photograph shows the carrier *Franklin* receiving a hit, her deck crew gazing in both wonderment and fear and just beginning to react physically, as a Japanese pilot crashes his plane high above, into her masts. The *Franklin* was so badly mauled that, while officially "saved," she was never operational again. The new carriers *Yorktown* and *Wasp,* namesakes of the prior carriers of the same name, were also hit. Special fire-fighting apparatus designed by the New York Fire Department extinguished the fires aboard all three flattops, but 825 crew members perished. And in between jazz recordings, Japanese radio propaganda broadcasters gave nightly assurances that this was a mere prelude to future horrors.

The American Tenth Army under Lt. General Simon Bolivar Buckner, an army officer, led the conquest of the island. He initially commanded four army and two marine divisions. This was the first time an army general commanded a major assault on a Pacific island. The marines were hesitant to accept his leadership but had no choice after Nimitz agreed to the arrangement. Later some marines and naval officers lodged bitter complaints against Buckner's leadership, but a certain amount of negative comment may have been inevitable given the formidable task the Americans faced on Okinawa. And, of course, interservice rivalry, which had been a problem ever since the days immediately after Pearl Harbor when each service had unofficially tried to place principle blame on the other for the attack, played a role in motivating the complaints; the rivalry now reached its wartime zenith, with each side expressing reservations about the arrangement. No one knew then that Okinawa would be the last conquest of the war, or that it would also be the bloodiest.

On March 23, 1945, the Allied naval force began both the bombardment and aerial strafing of the island. On a nearby island, about 350 suicide boats were captured before they could receive their crews. Each was to have been operated by two or three men and carry something like an underwater bomb attached to a pole for ramming purposes as well as hand grenades to pitch into American landing craft. On the morning of April 1, 1945—Easter Sunday—the American task force, using the relatively new amphtrac or tractor-like landing craft, reached the beaches of Okinawa. The Japanese had decided *not* to contest the island at the waterline, in part because it had served as a prewar artillery school. The Japanese garrison therefore knew every topographical feature and contour of most inland areas, meter by meter. Japanese artillery fire would be coordinated, accurate, and deadly as never before. This fact was evidently unknown to the Allied high command structure beforehand.

The marines and army troops literally walked ashore in some areas, as initially only a very few snipers fired at them. General Buckner ordered some of his forces to turn north. Indeed, the northern portion of the island fell with relatively little resistance compared to what was to ensue elsewhere. When the American troops turned south, they promptly encountered the Machinato Line, part of an interlocking system of fortifications that extended south almost to the very end of the island. Artillery was skillfully hidden in cave mouths, which made even sighting it almost impossible for the Americans. Buckner's forces, well over 100,000 men strong, promptly engaged the Japanese in intense fighting, sometimes hand to hand. It was to be their worst trial of the war. Soldiers or marines frequently took temporary refuge in lyre-shaped burial vaults (Okinawans bury their dead above ground in concrete and stone tombs), especially during Japanese artillery barrages. Flamethrowers were used on an unprecedented scale, and Okinawa witnessed the first military use of the helicopter, albeit in a very

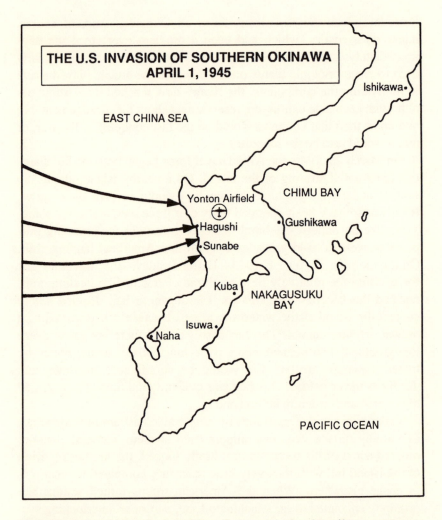

THE U.S. INVASION OF SOUTHERN OKINAWA
APRIL 1, 1945

EAST CHINA SEA

Ishikawa•

Yonton Airfield

CHIMU BAY

•Hagushi

•Gushikawa

•Sunabe

Kuba

NAKAGUSUKU
BAY

Isuwa •

Naha

PACIFIC OCEAN

limited and experimental fashion (it was used primarily to evacuate wounded).

The Japanese high command in Tokyo decided on a desperate effort to stay Okinawa's fate. On April 6 the battleship *Yamato,* escorted by one light cruiser and eight destroyers, left for Okinawa, with her fuel tanks only 63 percent full. This was by any definition an obvious suicide mission. Her training cadets were compelled to leave the ship before she sailed. And she was without benefit of air cover. *Yamato's* supposed task was to destroy American landing craft and engage the Allied fleet. Admiral Spruance, warned by U.S. submarines of her mission, sent Mitscher's carriers after her. The next day his aviators located her, definitely placing seven torpedoes into her hull and possibly several more as well. At 4:23 PM she went under, as did her accompanying cruiser and four of the destroyers. It was the last sortie of the Japanese Navy. There was now no conventional naval strength of any consequence left in Japanese home waters.

The *Kamikazes* now began what was to be their greatest attempt of the war to sink American warships. Their effort at Okinawa was named the *Ten-Go* operation, the Heavenly Air Offensive. It was divided, roughly, into ten separate series or waves of attacks against the Allied fleet. Over 3,000 sorties were flown, and twenty-one American ships were sunk. Naval casualties included the fleet carrier *Hancock,* damaged with seventy-two deaths, and the battleship *Maryland,* a Pearl Harbor survivor, damaged with sixteen killed. It was a terrifying experience. Hospital bays were soon filled to capacity, mainly with burn victims. On some vessels navy corpsmen literally exhausted their supply of morphine attempting to quell the cries of the injured. More than one officer wondered what sort of effort the Japanese might make to defend the "sacred soil" of their four home islands. They may have been motivated to ponder so by Tokyo Rose, who assured anyone listening that the *Kamikaze* effort at Okinawa was just a pale preview of efforts to come. In all, 330 Allied naval vessels required repairs, or were permanently out of action, in addition to those that had been sunk outright. Marines who returned to ships at the end of the campaign, and saw sailors writhing under bandages from burns inflicted by the *Kamikazes,* resolved never to criticize shipboard personnel ("bluejackets") again.

Buckner continued to experience trouble in pushing south, but the problem was evidently now isolated and was most evident on his right flank. There the Twenty-Seventh Army Division, whose performance had been weak on Saipan, gave a poor showing once again. It was soon relieved by Marines. The Machinato Line was pierced on April 24, although the Americans promptly encountered a second line, the Shuri, two days later.

Buckner was now faced with an obvious choice; he had absolute control of the sea, with the exception of the *Kamikazes.* He could have attempted a landing on southernmost Okinawa, thereby bypassing the fortifications, or he could use direct frontal assaults to reduce the Japanese positions. Many of the marines under his command, veterans of prior campaigns, fervently hoped he would choose a second landing. Instead Buckner decided to implement something of a compromise: a direct frontal assault but with a double envelopment, which would push forward on both his right and left flanks at the same time. Given the casualties engendered, it would probably have been wiser to attempt a landing on southern Okinawa. Only on May 11 was the double envelopment offensive launched, and on May 31 both the Japanese right and left flanks were pierced but with appalling losses to the attackers.

On June 1 the final offensive to penetrate the last Japanese fortification line on southern Okinawa began. Buckner did not live to see his task concluded. A bursting Japanese artillery shell claimed his life on June 18, 1945. Four days later General Ushijima, having been promoted by Tokyo to full general in recognition of the price he had made the Americans pay for the island, took his own life as enemy troops approached the cave in which he had his headquarters. A few days later the island was essentially secure, except that many Japanese survived in caves. Some emerged days, weeks, and even months later to engage in their own one-man *Banzai* charges.

The casualties were the heaviest that any single island had cost the American forces. About 7,400 Americans died outright on the island, but the navy had lost perhaps 5,000 more men who were killed while offshore, mostly from *Kamikazes*. Japanese losses can only be estimated. About 107,000 were killed outright, while an additional 20,000 were sealed in caves to die of starvation, suffocation, or cremation if gasoline had been poured in after them. About 4,000 Japanese planes were lost, while the number of U.S. naval aircraft lost was 763, with no fewer than 458 falling in combat with Japanese aircraft. The Japanese had well-camouflaged airfields on the islands adjoining Okinawa, and numerous planes had gotten in the air to engage Allied aircraft in dogfights. The air battle was a greater contest than the Marianas Turkey Shoot, but it has received little attention from historians, and American authorities suppressed news of it at the time. It seemed a spectral preview of the air battles to come once the United States attempted to invade Japan's home islands.

Conditions on Okinawa had been extraordinarily grim. Civilians had frequently been caught up in the fighting. Here, at least, they had not to any appreciable extent openly aided the Japanese Army, although no small number took their own life rather than be captured by the Americans. About 75,000 civilians perished during the campaign. Many, however, were prevented from suicide by Americans of Japanese ancestry who, for the first time, were employed on Okinawa as translators and were equipped with bullhorns to advise the local population that death would not be their fate if they peaceably surrendered.

The frequent rains—on occasion so heavy men literally could not see their hands in front of their faces—had sometimes made hand-to-hand fighting almost like mud wrestling. In some cases Americans and Japanese had literally strangled each other to death. Excavations on the island to this day occasionally disclose skeletons with their hands locked around each other's throats. American physicians logged 14,077 cases of battle fatigue or neuropsychiatric casualties among the troops who participated in conquering the island. Thus, the equivalent of a full division had to be relieved, some of course only temporarily, for reasons other than wounds or physical illness. And this on an island where civilians had not to any measurable degree participated in the struggle. The heavy artillery bombardments accounted for no small number of these cases, as did the very extensive use of flamethrowers, which were sometimes accidently used on civilians. It was hard to tell, in combat conditions, whether Japanese soldiers or Okinawan civilians occupied a particular cave. While the costs of an invasion of the four home islands can only be conjectured, of course, many of the American soldiers and marines who had participated in the Okinawa campaign later wept unashamedly out of relief when they learned of Japan's surrender.

As early as January 1944, Major General Henry "Hap" Arnold, head of the Army Air Corps, had informed the White House that an invasion of the home islands might not be necessary. He cited the new B–29 bomber as promising an alternative. Arnold was immensely proud of the American nation's new air weapon and seriously concerned that it would be misused. Indeed, he always reserved decisions concerning its strategic use to himself. He was probably motivated in part by the disappointing record of the B–17 in sinking ships.

Although described earlier, the B–29 Superfortress merits further comment for the unique role it was to play in the bombardment of the Japanese home islands. The B–29 was capable of carrying up to 20,000 lbs. of bombs, including the first nuclear weapons, while the earlier B–17 Flying Fortress would usually carry only 6,000 lbs. of bombs on a mission and lacked the ability to carry the new weapon. The Superfortress could also cruise at a higher speed than the B–17: 290 miles per hour for the former and 182 for the latter. The range of the B–29 also greatly outdistanced that of the B–17: the B–29 could carry the war to the heart of the enemy at a round trip range of 3,250 statute miles, while the B–17 was restricted by its limited range of 1,100 miles round trip. The B–29 came equipped with pressurized crew stations for comfort at high altitudes, ground-mapping radar, and remote-controlled gun turrets. The number of aircrew on board fluctuated between ten and fourteen, depending upon the mission requirements. (Almost always fourteen went on every combat mission, even when not strictly necessary, for there were always ground crew personnel who would go along as ''observers,'' space permitting.)

Ordered into production in January 1942, the B–29s flew their first operational mission on June 5, 1944. The B–29 had the heaviest airframe constructed by any nation to that date. Fully loaded, it could carry over 100 percent of its own weight in the air, gasoline included.

Small wonder, then, that Arnold did not want his B–29s under the command of General MacArthur. He was also leery of a navy commander, especially Nimitz, giving his airmen orders. The B–29 had first been used in the China-Burma-India theater of the conflict but with mediocre results. Beginning in early June 1944, flying from air fields in the vicinity of Cheng-tu in China, the B–29s were used in attempted raids against the Japanese home islands. But aviation gasoline was scarce in China, and the bombers had bugs that were still to be worked out. Also, their production had not yet been standardized. Further, bomber command in China did not seem to grasp fully the new bomber's potential. And their bases were technically vulnerable to Japanese attack as well as to raids by local war lords, who were always in search of booty.

As a result, after the Marianas were secured in July 1944, the B–29s were husbanded there. In December 1944 the B–29s in China were withdrawn and stationed there as well. Arnold's B–29 commander in the Marianas was Major General Heywood Hansell, who headed the Twenty-First Bomber command. Hansell basically decided to emulate the European theater of the conflict, ordering the daylight strategic bombardment from high altitudes, of aircraft factories in Japan.

Thus on November 24 more than one hundred B–29s attempted a raid against an aircraft factory in the greater Tokyo area. This inaugurated a series of over one hundred bomber raids, at about five-day intervals. The aircraft loss rate became about 6 percent, as opposed to the 5 percent that had been considered the greatest acceptable loss figure. Further, bombing from an altitude of 30,000 feet frequently placed the bombers in or near the jet stream, which greatly affected their accuracy, fuel consumption, and navigation, often interposing a heavy cloud cover between the aircraft and their target.

Aircraft factories remained the priority targets. Results on the ground, however, were disappointing, as reconnaissance photographs clearly disclosed. Frequently the factories that were hit were only slightly damaged, or on occasion the bombers missed altogether, releasing their payloads into the countryside. Nonetheless, as the year 1944 ended, Hirohito specifically warned his service chiefs that weather and altitude alone could not protect Japan against American bombers. His warning evidently made little impression on the Japanese military.

On January 19, 1945, the first truly successful raid was conducted. Some sixty bombers smashed an aircraft plant near the town of Akashi on the Inland Sea, reducing its production by about 90 percent. Meanwhile, Hansell also began experimentation with incendiary bombs against Japanese targets, evidently on Washington's suggestion. But Arnold was now clearly impatient. Hansell's days in command of the B–29 bomber force were clearly numbered.

Thus the stage was set for Major General Curtis LeMay, who was to become the patron saint of those who wished to see Japan bombed into oblivion. LeMay had won his spurs as an airman in Europe, where he was an advocate of daylight precision bombardment. He had then briefly taken a bomber command in India. Finally, on January 20, 1945, he assumed command of the Twenty-First Bomber Command on the Marianas, which comprised the B–29 bomber force. At first he did little different from his predecessor, with the same disappointing results. Then, on February 19, Arnold suggested that LeMay try incendiary strikes. On February 25 LeMay launched a 231-plane raid on aircraft plants in the Tokyo area. The raid proved the value of fire-bombing against virtually any Japanese target, however—a fact that was scarcely lost on LeMay.

LeMay now carefully studied his options. He believed, evidently, that Japanese antiaircraft shells could not be fused to explode below

10,000 feet; doubtless he was also aware of the lack of fuel remaining for the remnants of the Japanese Air Force. Reportedly after learning of the results obtained against a mock Japanese city constructed in Utah and subject to firebombing, he chose his strategy. Not specifically informing Washington in advance, he decided to risk all on a gigantic fire raid on Tokyo. He deliberately selected a flimsy, low-income district of the Japanese capital for extinction. LeMay ordered the bombers almost completely disarmed (only their tail guns remained in most instances), for he would send them in at night when Japanese fighter opposition, which had no radar direction, would be at a minimum. This partial disarmament would allow an even heavier bomb load than usual. LeMay ordered his planes to approach the target at several altitudes, varying from 5,000 to 8,000 feet, safely below the jet stream, thereby greatly increasing the accuracy of the planes' bombsights. He also ordered his airmen to bomb in an X pattern, allowing fires to start that would burn toward their center.

The majority of the 334 B–29s that left the Marianas that day, March 9, 1945, dropped their bomb loads over Tokyo. Their payload was napalm firebombs that spread fire on the roofs of many dwellings in the target area. While the raid progressed, LeMay paced the floor of his headquarters, fully aware that his reputation was almost certainly at stake, since General Arnold had become visibly impatient with him. The attack lasted three hours. Gale force winds were blowing on the ground, guaranteeing the spread of any fires that were started. Supposedly executed to support the Allied operation against Okinawa, the raid was instead a test of LeMay's hope that he could kill Japanese civilians in so great a number and so rapidly that the conflict would be brought to a swift conclusion.

At least 150,000 civilians perished in the course of the raid. Indeed, the resulting fires burned for four days. Japanese records reveal that 267,171 buildings were destroyed. The actual number was probably higher, although that total alone represents almost one-quarter of the buildings in the Tokyo city area itself (as opposed to the greater Tokyo-Yokohama area, for which no records are available).

The firebombing raids that followed were a great success from a military standpoint. Japanese cities, constructed principally of wood and paper, were built to burn, especially when population density is also taken into account. The fire torch was applied not only to Tokyo again but also to Nagoya, Osaka, Kobe, Kawasaki, and Yawata.

LeMay showed great personal interest in the raids, sometimes personally debriefing pilots and crew. He was particularly impressed when a thermite magnesium bomb became available, for such a bomb could under the proper conditions burn through steel.

On June 16 LeMay began rotating targets, switching temporarily to medium-sized urban centers. The few reconnaissance photographs released to the press were on rare occasions published in the United States. LeMay had obviously adopted the technique the British used in Europe—simple terror bombing, the exact opposite of precision daylight bombardment. Earlier Washington had vehemently opposed the use of terror bombing against Germany. Few seemed to notice or care. There were those who raised their voice in protest against the indiscriminate taking of civilian life, although doubtless one had to be on the ground to know just how effective the bombing was. The clerical and liberal press in America raised occasional questions about the morality of mass civilian bombing and frequently cited President Roosevelt's request, made in 1939 at the outbreak of the war in Europe, that all belligerents refrain from bombing purely civilian targets.

But after Pearl Harbor and Bataan most Americans came to accept that slaughter of the enemy, whether in uniform or civilian dress, was the quickest way to end the conflict. Further, LeMay genuinely believed that Japanese industry was in part handicraft industry and that Japanese workers took home part of their work to be completed after their hours in the factory were done. There was undoubtedly some truth in this assertion, although not so much as LeMay thought. Workers in the silk industry, especially women, had traditionally engaged in such work. It also held true for a few other segments of production as well. But it was the exception, not the rule, a fact LeMay should have certainly realized.

Time magazine in particular supported LeMay, which was understandable since its owner, Henry Luce, was a devoted Sinophile. *Time* frequently told its readers that LeMay would bring a speedy end to the conflict, thereby saving American lives, and gave its readers the impression that LeMay had embarked on nothing less than a holy crusade against the barbarous Japanese. Other American magazines duplicated *Time*'s copy, although debate about the efficacy and ethics of such bombings continued, even occasionally in the *New York Times*. Some went even further, advocating the use of poison gas against the Japanese for good measure. One scheme bruited about in Washington was to spray the Japanese rice crop with the pesticide DDT; nothing came of it.

The Japanese had no way to deal with the rain of death from the skies, except superstition. Rumor had it that Hiroshima had not been touched because, however implausibly, President Truman's mother lived in the near vicinity. One prominent religious couple survived a fire raid but found their goldfish dead. Believing that their fish had somehow died for them, they put them in their shrine, and the practice caught on. Possession of goldfish became the goal of the more religious, superstitious, or frightened. When the supply of live goldfish was exhausted, porcelain ones were manufactured as substitutes. The social dislocation caused by the bombings, as described in chapter 8, was great. LeMay almost certainly believed he was shortening the conflict; in actual fact, he did not do so, as will be seen, but many in Washington, as well as London, believed otherwise at the time.

From July 10, 1945, onward, as the Japanese prepared for invasion, they also suffered from carrier raids against their home islands. Mitscher's task force, under Admiral Halsey, roamed the seas around Japan more or less at will. It was accompanied by British carriers, which used Ulithi as their staging area. More than 3,000 Japanese aircraft, the majority of them *Kamikaze,* were destroyed on the ground. Japanese who lived in coastal villages on the Pacific were now subject to direct Allied attack. American aircraft strafed whole towns, as well as bombing strategic targets. The total number of aircraft involved included more than 1,000 American and nearly 250 British.

It seemed that the next phase would be invasion. *Operation Downfall,* the invasion plan, placed MacArthur in charge of the land forces with Nimitz in charge of landing all troops. The first of MacArthur's forces were scheduled to land on the home island of Kyushu on November 1, 1945. Honshu was scheduled for invasion on March 1, 1946, the objective being nothing less than the seizure of the greater Tokyo-Yokohama area itself. With total Allied casualties (including those incurred by Soviet forces participating in the attack) projected as high as one million before all resistance in Japan ceased, most soldiers and marines were understandably lacking in enthusiasm for the forthcoming campaign. And for the more zealous or inexperienced, Japanese propaganda broadcasters gladly provided a nightly recital of the likely horrors to come if the home islands were invaded.

For a few privileged insiders there seemed to be an alternative: a newly developed weapon, which, if it functioned as planned, promised to end the war quickly. The atomic bomb, America's most secret project during the war, was in large part made possible by Hitler's racial bigotry.

Individual American physicists had undertaken nuclear research in the 1930s, but their efforts were uncoordinated and sometimes overlapped, and work progressed slowly. Many of the scientists who would eventually spark the bomb project had been residents of Nazi Germany. A fair number left in the late 1930s when it became evident that Hitler would indeed implement the racial policies he had outlined earlier in his autobiography, *Mein Kampf*. Most at first settled in Great Britain.

The refugees in question may have been scientists of international repute, but Britain's most urgent scientific project at the time was radar. Hence, the German scientists found university teaching positions, although they continued their nuclear research, concentrating on the theoretical aspects of atomic fission. Then Professor Frederick Lindemann (knighted as Lord Cherwell), Churchill's only scientific adviser during the war, organized the scientists into the world's first truly workable atomic bomb project. But Britain was bankrupt and work did not progress beyond the theoretical stage. Further, there was no place in the United Kingdom that could not be bombed by the German Air Force. Lindemann had given the project the code-name *Tube Alloys*.

The British offered the project to the American government. Roosevelt readily accepted. The American *Manhattan Project* was born in the early fall of 1942, when the refugee scientists arrived and joined forces with their American colleagues.

Major General Leslie Groves, a West Point graduate with an interest in higher mathematics, headed the program. His qualifications proved limited, however. Grove's idea of security was simplistic. On one occasion, for example, he had the Selective Service draft illiterates to serve as janitorial help. At another juncture he wanted to draft the entire scientific staff into the army so that he could enjoy the luxury of giving them orders. Still, he did cooperate with the scientific staff to complete a bomb that might prove to be a dud. And expenditures for the project reached the two-billion-dollar mark before the first bomb was even test-fired. No one privy to the matter doubted that nuclear fission would release an incredible amount of heat and light; but some held that it would be a relatively slow process, which would mean in effect that the new weapon would have no explosive power per se.

The base project was established in a former boys' school in the town of Los Alamos, New Mexico. Work progressed simultaneously in other centers, but Los Alamos remained home base for the undertaking. Progress was uneven, although this was probably inevitable given the complexity of the task and the large number of researchers involved. The necessary uranium, fortunately, proved easy to obtain, which was a decided plus for the scientists.

Many of the scientists working on the project were virtually professional pacifists; they labored to construct the world's first atomic weapon, at least in part, because Nazi Germany was known to have a similar project underway. Evidently no one knew that the Japanese also had such a project, although it was foiled by a lack of uranium. In late 1944 the U.S. government learned that Nazi Germany had more or less abandoned its atomic bomb project, but this did not deter work, since it was now widely assumed among those in the know that an atomic device would force the Japanese to surrender.

On the evening of July 16, 1945, the desert floor trembled as the first atomic device was successfully detonated in New Mexico. The decision was then made by President Truman to use such a device on the Japanese, although not before considerable thought and reflection, something he would later downplay. (A recently discovered letter to his daughter Margaret reveals that the president did indeed agonize over the decision.) In the end Truman decided that dropping the bomb would compel early Japanese surrender and thus, basically, save Japanese as well as American lives. LeMay was ordered to remove certain Japanese cities from his target list so that they could serve as testing grounds for the new weapon.

Some critics have contended that the Japanese should have been invited to a demonstration of the new weapon. This is at best a questionable suggestion. A nation with a *Kamikaze* corps, a civilian defense force of 27 million, and professional Samurai warriors would be unlikely to send a representative. To do so would have meant, in a sense, fraternization with the enemy, which is not encouraged by the Japanese military ethic. Others have suggested that an atomic device should have been detonated at high altitude over a Japanese city. But if this had occurred, the Japanese Army would probably have written it off as "routine," which was in fact their precise response to the Hiroshima bomb. And such a high-altitude detonation would have released radiation, which later precipitation would have conveyed to earth, possibly inflicting in the long run far more damage over a wider area than explosion of the device at a conventional altitude.

The more interesting question is why the bomb was employed. Doubtless Truman thought he was shortening the war, although, as will be seen, the bomb did not do this. Then too, he probably wished to impress the Russians with its might and possibly repay the Japanese for the atrocities visited on American service personnel. Finally the scientists themselves confessed to a certain curiosity—albeit, at least in retrospect, perhaps a morbid curiosity—as to the effect the bomb would have on human beings. Thus, on August 6, 1945, the world's first atomic device was exploded over Hiroshima, and three days later the world entered the nuclear age when a plutonium device was detonated over Nagasaki. Japan would soon surrender, but not because of the devices exploded over those two cities. And so now it is to the surrender saga itself that we must turn.

Suggestions for Further Reading:

For Iwo Jima, Whitman Bartley, *Iwo Jima* (Washington, DC: Government Printing Office, 1948) is a semiofficial Marine Corps narrative of the island campaign; the U.S. Navy has provided a similar, brief narrative in its *Analysis of Air Operations: Iwo Jima, February-March 1945 and SOWESPAC Activity* (San Francisco: Pacific Fleet, 1945); Richard Newcomb, *Iwo Jima* (New York: Holt, Rinehart and Winston, 1965) is an early oral history study of the conquest of that island; there are three eyewitness accounts: Richard Wheeler, *Iwo* (New York: Lippincott and Crowell, 1980); Gallant T. Grady, *The Friendly Dead* (Garden City, NY: Doubleday 1964); and Robert Leckie, *The Battle for Iwo Jima* (New York: Random House, 1967); and Donald McKinnon, M.D., "Battalion Surgeon on Iwo Jima," *Marine Corps Gazette 66* (February 1982): 28–37, gives a rare but very professional glimpse of the medical problems corpsmen and doctors faced on that island, and by inference on many other islands as well. The semiofficial account of the Okinawa conquest is Roy Appleman, James MacGregor Burns, Russel Gugler, and John Stevens, *Okinawa: The Last Battle* (Washington, DC: Department of the Army, 1948); James H. Belote and William M. Belote, *Typhoon of Steel: The Battle for Okinawa* (New York: Harper and Row, 1969) is a workable account of the war's final campaign, but see also Ian Gow, *Okinawa 1945: Gateway to Japan* (New York: Barnes & Noble, 1988). A memoir account of the Okinawa campaign and Marine Corps Pacific island warfare in general is William Manchester, *Goodbye Darkness: A Memoir of the Pacific War* (Boston: Little, Brown, 1979). John H. Bradley's *The Second World War: Asia and the Pacific* (Wayne, NJ: Avery, 1984) is a well-done overall survey that forms part of the

West Point series of textbooks on American warfare; although sometimes more factual than interpretive, its sections dealing with Iwo Jima and Okinawa are particularly useful. A seminal history of Anglo-American relations during the conflict is provided by Christopher Thorne in his *Allies of a Kind: The U.S., Britain and the War against Japan, 1941–1945* (New York: Oxford University Press, 1978). Rikihei Inoguchi, Tadashi Nakajima, and Roger Pineau, *The Divine Wind* (Annapolis: Naval Institute Press, 1959), is a workable history of the *Kamikaze Corps;* an account including several interesting photos of the Japanese air and sea suicide efforts has been written by A.J. Barker under the title *Suicide Weapon* (New York: Ballantine Books, 1971); the latest title on the subject is Nahuso Naito, *Thunder Gods* (New York: Kodansha, 1989). No really comprehensive work on the firebombings exists, but see Martin Caidin, *A Torch to the Enemy: The Fire Raid on Tokyo* (New York: Ballantine, 1960); Hoito Edoin, *The Night Tokyo Burned: The Incendiary Campaign against Japan, March-August 1945* (New York: St. Martin's Press, 1987); the United States Strategic Bombing Survey, *The Effects of Strategic Bombing on Japanese Morale* (Washington, DC: Government Printing Office, 1947); and Robert Guillain, *I Saw Tokyo Burning* (New York: Doubleday, 1981). The standard work on the Manhattan Project is Richard Rhodes, *The Making of the Atomic Bomb* (New York: Simon & Schuster, 1986), which is better on the physics and personalities than on the politics involved. Any student of nuclear politics during and after the conflict should consult Martin Sherwin's *A World Destroyed: The Atomic Bomb and the Grand Alliance* (New York: Knopf, 1975). Laura Fermi in *Illustrious Immigrants: The Intellectual Migration from Europe, 1930–1940* (Chicago: University of Chicago Press, 1968) gives an idea of the debt Americans owe the British and the European community in general for the Manhattan Project; see also Margaret Gowing, *Britain and Atomic Energy* (London: St. Martin's, 1964) and Leslie Grove's published memoirs, under the title *Now It Can Be Told* (New York: Harper & Row, 1962). The latest work on the effects of the bomb is edited by Kyoko and Mark Selden under the title *The Atomic Bomb: Voices from Hiroshima and Nagasaki* (Armonk, NY: M. E. Sharpe, 1989); but see also Ronald W. Clark, *The Birth of the Bomb* (New York: Horizon Press, 1961) and Ferenc M. Szasz, *The Day the Sun Rose Twice* (Albuquerque: University of New Mexico Press, 1984). Finally Robert K. Wilcox, *Japan's Secret War: Japan's Race against Time to Build Its Own Atomic Bomb* (New York: William Morrow, 1985) is innovative and useful but should be used with great caution.

10. Japan Surrenders

The saga of Japanese surrender both begins and ends with the attitude and influence of the emperor, which must be explored in order to comprehend the surrender decision. Since the time of Meiji, the first constitutional monarch, the emperor of Japan has technically been only a ceremonial figure, who reigned but did not rule. Constitutionally and by common practice the monarch's chief functional role was diplomatic and ceremonial. He was head of state but not head of government. He received (or did not receive) diplomats more or less as he pleased. But in actual fact the powers of the monarch became popularly intertwined with the respect accorded him. Hence his position as defined by Shintoism, the state religion, made him the spiritual leader of the nation.

The emperor commanded total respect. Children were taught that he was half-human, half-descended from the sun goddess. Prior to 1945 teachers taught their students that they would be struck blind if they looked him in the face. When he left the palace on ceremonial occasions, the upper portion of all buildings along his route had to be cleared lest someone look *down* on him. Further, the emperor Hirohito in particular had a reputation for being fairly strong-minded concerning personal matters: witness that Hirohito had insisted on selecting his own wife, and chose a noble lady not on the list drawn up by the imperial household officials, much to their distress.

Of course, the military could also rationalize disobedience of the throne under the doctrine of *gekokujo,* which meant in effect that if they thought the emperor was being badly advised, military leaders could disobey the imperial will in order to serve the true needs of the empire. Therefore the emperor could easily find himself in what Americans now would call a catch–22 situation.

The reader will recall that Hirohito read a poem to his ministers and armed services chiefs several months before Pearl Harbor:

> If all men are brothers,
> Why are the winds and waves of the world so troubled,
> Why cannot all men live in peace?

The emperor clearly had substantial reservations about the war from the very beginning. Then, only three days after Pearl Harbor, while the military situation was still fluid, at least in the emperor's mind, Hirohito asked his ministers at a cabinet meeting about exploring the possibilities of a negotiated peace. No record of a discussion by the cabinet exists. But that Hirohito still entertained reservations about the wisdom of the conflict cannot be doubted.

During January 1942 Foreign Minister Togo told the Diet that he was ready to negotiate peace. His statement aroused a storm of protest from the more militant deputies. As each new victory became known, Premier Tojo received generic phone calls at his private residence, all of the *Banzai* variety. The fall of Singapore on February 15, 1942, convinced the emperor that Japan had a good chance of winning the war, for its forces had succeeded against all the odds in the book, and for that matter, ahead of schedule in every instance. By the end of March 1942 Hirohito was convinced that Japan had won. In the spring of 1942 the throne announced that the conflict was over. The defeat at Midway in June was at first unknown to the emperor, for Tojo, who intensely disliked the navy, gave out the following statement concerning the Midway encounter: "The navy anticipated that hegemony in the Pacific would be decided in one great battle, and indeed it has been." Thus, many Japanese believed that Japan had won the fateful naval confrontation.

Just four days after the defeat at Midway on June 4, 1942, the former Japanese ambassador to Great Britain, Shigeru Yoshida (who later became premier during the occupation) called on Privy Seal Kido in his office within the palace. He proposed sending former premier Konoye to Switzerland, the most neutral nation of Europe, where he could have no specific mission but would keep in touch with everyone he could and try to determine if there were any rumors of peace proposals that would be to Japan's advantage. Nothing came of the suggestion, but it does show that there were important people in Japan who desired an end to the conflict.

After the defeat at Guadalcanal in early 1943, Prince Konoye began meeting with other senior statesmen and former premiers at the Dai

Ichi building in Tokyo. They discussed means of removing Tojo from office or, conversely, how to place someone in the cabinet who would oppose continuation of the war. They decided that the relatively moderate Admiral Mitsumasa Yonai should assume the post of Minister of the Navy. The plan did not succeed, but the meetings demonstrate that some among the civilian ruling elite hoped to terminate the war soon. And Hirohito could scarcely have been unaware of their doings. One must therefore assume that he approved, however tacitly.

In January 1943 the American and British leadership had met at Casablanca. During an informal luncheon conversation, Roosevelt remarked to Churchill that he was going to issue an "unconditional surrender" statement that would rally the Allied forces. Churchill agreed, opining that it would make the Axis leaders "squirm." Thus did Franklin Roosevelt issue his famous unconditional surrender formula, which dismayed all of the Axis powers. But probably dismayed least was Japan, where a *Samurai* code that embodied a "no surrender" philosophy already held sway. Then on December 1, 1943, at the First Cairo Conference, the unconditional surrender policy was confirmed, while Roosevelt inspired a declaration that assured that all territories taken by Japan since 1895 by "violence and greed" would be restored to their rightful owners—this in part to placate the Chinese. What the reaction was in Japan is not known, but the Japanese leadership could not have been pleased.

The emperor observed the New Year's Day festivities of January 1944 with greater than usual solemnity. The Imperial Army in general and Premier Tojo in particular had now become *the* power in the land. Tojo had managed to accrue such power, in part because he was also Minister of the Army, that everyone envied him. No previous premier had exercised such prerogatives. Then in February 1944 he also temporarily assumed the duties of chief of the army general staff. And his wife joined him in his unpopularity. In an era long before women's rights were given consideration in Japan, she shocked the nation by appearing in factories and urging women to work harder. Public reaction to her radio addresses was even greater. People began calling Tojo's home and inquiring, "Why hasn't Tojo committed suicide yet?" As his wife sadly observed, these were probably the same people who telephoned Pearl Harbor morning to cry "*Banzai*" into the receiver. Tojo had nearly fallen from power in June 1944, when two cabinet ministers resigned over his conduct of the war. A month later, when Saipan fell to the Americans, the end was in sight.

Tojo had held power for a record time, since October 1941. Kido, among others, expressed displeasure, and Tojo was faced with near-open revolt by several of his ministers. Everyone knew Kido spoke for the emperor. Clearly, Tojo's days in power were numbered. He was even ridiculed within the army hierarchy, where he was known as the "superior private," a rank directly above that of private first class. On July 18, 1944, after much bitter debate and rancor, Tojo resigned.

The ensuing cabinet crisis was the last occasion on which the emperor expressed hope that the war might still be won. Kido and members of the *jushin,* the council of former premiers, were well aware of the problem of interservice rivalry in the imperial forces; it was worse than in any of the Allied military establishments, and they determined that it was one of the primary causes for Japan's military decline. As a possible solution they discussed a co-premiership utilizing an army general and a navy admiral, although the army general would clearly have greater power. Admiral Yonai was their choice as the navy candidate if the position materialized. But the navy man in particular would be in some danger from the army's secret police, the dreaded *Kempeitei,* which had been behind several actual assassinations as well as a host of unsuccessful ones.

The result was a compromise. The candidate chosen as premier was Kuniaki Koiso, a general. He was known to be studious and religious but suffered from poor health. Known as the "tiger of Korea," from his last post as governor general of Korea (like all Japanese military governors of Korea, Koiso had ruled with an iron hand), when Koiso arrived in Tokyo he was summoned directly to the palace. Word had evidently leaked to him, for he had already contacted several politicians and military figures and inquired concerning their willingness to serve in a cabinet. Koiso agreed to form a government, and Admiral Yonai accepted the posts of navy minister and deputy premier.

The emperor received them simultaneously to invest them officially with seals and authority of office; he urged both of them toward greater cooperation between the Imperial Army and Navy. He also advised that they do nothing to disturb normal relations with the Soviet Union.

From the first Koiso's strong-mindedness and independence were evident. However, the new premier did attempt to cooperate with the navy to a greater degree than had any of his immediate predecessors.

Koiso also implemented a replacement for the old Liaison Conference in the guise of the "Big Six" body, comprised of himself, the foreign minister, the ministers of war and navy, and chiefs of the army and navy general staffs. The Big Six was unofficial, and its findings had to be ratified by the cabinet, but it did represent a genuine start at something like a greater measure of interservice cooperation.

Koiso had scarcely assumed office when the conduct of the Soviet ambassador in Tokyo grew ambiguous. In the Kremlin Stalin himself had made several public pronouncements as well as private remarks to neutral members of the diplomatic corps in Moscow that explicitly classified Japan as a fascist state, suddenly treating the Japanese as if they were little better than Nazi Germany. This represented a departure from the usual Soviet propaganda line and greatly upset the Japanese. Tokyo's neutrality pact with the Soviet Union was still in force, but Kido opined to the emperor that if Russia triumphed over Germany— and it was well on the way to doing so—the Soviet Union might decide and/or the Allies might persuade it to enter the war against Japan. Both Kido and Hirohito viewed such a prospect as the greatest calamity that could befall Japan. They both believed Japan could and would survive an American occupation, but the Soviets, once entrenched on the home islands, would destroy Japan's national polity and cultural essence, for they would never willingly withdraw their troops.

By New Year's Day 1945 the emperor was reasonably certain that 1945 would be the last year of the war. Early in the new year he decided to consult with his *jushin*. There were six former premiers still alive with whom he could talk, including Tojo and Konoye. The emperor had them come separately to the palace that January, lest the *Kempeitei* be alarmed.

The advice the emperor would value the most was that of Konoye, who had been virtually his only wartime friend and political confidant, except for Kido. Konoye prepared his remarks in advance, for obviously Kido had told him that the monarch was seeking his opinion on the conduct and consequences of the war. Faithfully reconstructed by the historian Robert Butow, Konoye's remarks are illuminating. Hirohito must have found them sobering indeed.

Konoye told Hirohito that unconditional surrender was, in effect, something Japan would simply have to accept. The United States and Great Britain, he evidently reasoned, would respect Japan's culture and ultimately its sovereignty. Konoye then mentioned one of his greatest fears, a possible Communist revolution if the war were not terminated quickly. He urged Hirohito to seize the initiative and end the conflict soon. Konoye intimated that only the emperor's power could compel the military to accept surrender. The Imperial Army was *the* power in the land, and only Hirohito might persuade it of the wisdom of surrender. The emperor and Konoye might well desire peace, but unless the Japanese Army concurred, nothing could be done effectively to implement a surrender policy. A few of the civilian ruling elite might desire peace, but until the army could be moved to accept the concept of surrender, the elite's opinion simply did not matter.

Before anything of further consequence happened in Japan itself, on Easter Sunday, April 1, 1945, the Allies invaded Okinawa. The repercussions were immediate. The general feeling throughout the civilian and, more importantly, the military elite was that the Koiso regime was bankrupt. Koiso tried to rally support, but even the emperor remained neutral. Kido then indicated imperial displeasure with the current regime. On April 5 Koiso returned the seals of office. Another cabinet crisis was at hand. On that same day word reached Tokyo that the Soviet Union would not renew its neutrality pact with the Japanese. This meant that the agreement would expire on April 13, 1946, and was disturbing news indeed. It greatly colored the politics of the ensuing cabinet crisis.

Some historians have argued that the Russian notification of non-renewal of the neutrality pact meant little, since the Soviets assured the Japanese that they would abide by its terms until its actual expiration. But this argument belies common sense. Why had Stalin refused to renew it? And Soviet promises had meant little in the past. There was no reason to believe that the Stalin regime had suddenly turned over a new leaf.

The emperor was determined that this would be the last cabinet crisis of the war, and so was Kido. The difficulty now would be to find someone who would work to end the war while publicly declaring that he intended to prosecute the conflict to a successful conclusion. The specter of Russian participation in the conflict and also in the eventual Allied occupation of the nation was chilling indeed. But the Imperial Army remained unmoved. Hence the intention to surrender had to remain a secret, lest the *Kempeitei* assassinate the next premier.

Kido quickly conducted a search for a suitable replacement for Koiso. He hit upon retired Admiral Kantaro Suzuki, who commanded almost universal respect throughout the ruling bureaucracy. Suzuki stated that he would be willing to play *haragei* or "the stomach game," as he termed it: He would declare openly for continuation of the conflict, while his gut feeling, in the pit of his stomach, told him that the war was lost and peace was desirable. Suzuki fully realized that if he was not convincing in his role as military leader of the country anticipating victory, the *Kempeitei* would probably threaten or kill him. He would have to pretend outwardly to support the war, while quietly and discretely laboring for peace. It was a situation that would be both difficult and potentially fatal, should his intent leak to the army.

Suzuki made his job all the more difficult by insisting that former foreign minister Shigenori Togo return to office to help him in any eventual bargaining with the Americans. Suzuki evidently believed, rightly or wrongly, that Togo was a skilled negotiator who would be trusted by the Americans. Togo was perceived as something of a dove by the military. Hence his appointment as foreign minister might betray the true intent of the Suzuki government. Togo had gone into a self-imposed retirement in late 1942, after a disagreement over the handling of the new empire. He only agreed to return to office after he learned the actual intent of the Suzuki government. Togo too would have to play the stomach game to avoid arousing suspicion.

The first crisis the Suzuki government had to face was the surrender of its ally, Germany, to the Allied powers in early May 1945. The subsequent division of Germany by the Allies forewarned the Japanese of what they could expect in the event of a full-dress Allied invasion and conquest of the home islands (some warning of this division had been transmitted by Ambassador Hiroshi Oshima earlier, for the Germans themselves were privy to it before they surrendered). Hirohito was appalled by the division of Germany among the victorious powers. He correctly predicted that once Soviet troops were in occupation of German soil, German unity would be but a memory for many decades to come. Thus, the emperor informed Kido that Japan must avoid a similar fate at all costs. In a remarkably prophetic statement, the emperor also remarked to Kido that he feared Germany would never again be a united nation during their lifetimes.

Meanwhile Japanese diplomats in several foreign capitals had jumped the gun by approaching American envoys to inquire concerning possible terms of surrender. In Switzerland, Japanese diplomats sought out Allen Dulles, an OSS operative, with questions about what terms the Allies would be willing to accept in return for a Japanese capitulation. The same "peace feelers" were reported by the American embassy in Stockholm, Sweden. In no case, however, were the overtures made officially. The U.S. State Department, under Acting Secretary of State Joseph Grew, was uncertain how to interpret these reports. Grew was, however, sympathetic to the Japanese, having served as ambassador in Tokyo from 1932 to Pearl Harbor.

As usual, Washington leaked. News of these unofficial statements soon reached the press corps. Grew, substituting for Secretary of State Edward Stettinius (Cordell Hull had retired in 1944), then felt it incumbent to issue a statement concerning the matter. As much as he wished that the Japanese overtures represented the will of the Imperial Army, he nonetheless issued a press release that recognized that the military were the power in the land and still intended to fight to the last. His statement read in part:

> We have received no peace offer from the Japanese Government, either through official or unofficial channels. Conversations relating to peace have been reported to the Department from various parts of the world, but in no case has an approach been made to this Government, directly or indirectly, by a person who could establish his authority to speak for the Japanese Government, and in no case has an offer to surrender been made. In no case has this Government been presented with a statement purporting to define the basis upon which the Japanese Government would be prepared to conclude peace. . . .
>
> The nature of the purported "peace feelers" must be clear to everyone. They are the usual moves in the conduct of psychological warfare by a defeated enemy. No thinking American, recalling Pearl Harbor, Wake, Manila, [and] Japanese ruthless aggression elsewhere, will give them credence.
>
> Japanese militarism must and will be crushed. . . . The policy of this Government has been, is, and will continue to be unconditional surrender. . . .

Notice of this statement should help banish the claim made by some that Washington believed the Japanese *military*—and remember that surrender was impossible without its consent—were willing to surrender the nation to the Allies. No less a friend of the Japanese than Grew told the public that the Japanese military could not be trusted and probably did not desire peace in the first place.

The military in Japan were privy, at least at the highest level, to the next ploy the Japanese leaders used. They decided to turn to their greatest potential enemy, the Soviet Union, evidently as much to determine Russian intentions as to ask that they mediate with the Allies for peace. Soviet Ambassador Jacob Malik in Tokyo was approached by former premier Koki Hirota. Their first meeting took place on June 24. Malik proved unhelpful. Finally on July 7, 1945, the emperor decided to dispatch an envoy directly to the Soviet Union to deal with the Soviets. His choice for this unenviable task was Konoye. On July 12 Konoye appeared at the palace, accepting the emperor's mandate but stating in effect that he desired carte blanche to negotiate as he saw fit. Hirohito agreed, informing Konoye that the mission would be dangerous and that he would be risking his life. Konoye waved these considerations aside. This gladdened the emperor, who believed that for once Konoye would abandon sloth and faithfully prosecute his mission to the last.

In the Soviet Union Foreign Minister Vyacheslav Molotov and Premier Joseph Stalin were busy preparing for the upcoming Allied conference to be held at Potsdam, a suburb of Berlin, during the last two weeks of July 1945. Thus, the Kremlin postponed replying to the Japanese request that Stalin receive Konoye as a special envoy of the emperor.

At the Potsdam Conference, July 2–August 17, 1945, the Allies met for their third and last full-dress wartime summit. In a casual way President Truman, who had assumed office in April 1945 after Roosevelt's death, informed Stalin that the United States now possessed a weapon of unusual destructive power. The Soviet premier already knew of the Manhattan Project via several spies working on the bomb. Stalin replied simply that he hoped "good use" would be made of the new weapon against the Japanese. On July 26, 1945, the Allied leaders issued a proclamation to the Japanese, warning them that they faced "complete and utter destruction" if they did not promptly surrender. Stalin did tell President Truman of the Japanese desire to dispatch Konoye to the Kremlin on a peace mission. Truman already knew of these overtures via *Magic* decrypts of the relevant telegrams, but feigned ignorance when Stalin broached the subject. Stalin stated that he would "lull the Japanese to sleep" and not make a definite reply, intimating that Konoye would never come to Moscow. He proved as good as his word.

Stalin also indicated that Russia would definitely enter the conflict against Japan three months after the date of German surrender. Since the Germans had surrendered to the USSR on May 8, 1945, this meant that Stalin would have to deliver a declaration of war to the Japanese government by August 8. Here too he would honor his word. There was indeed no reason why the Soviet Union should not have participated in the conflict against Japan. Before his death President Roosevelt had already promised Stalin several Japanese possessions if he participated in the war against Japan. Thus, Stalin's reaffirmation of a definite date for Soviet entry into the Pacific conflict was normal, natural, and in a sense quite routine.

When the Japanese learned of the Potsdam Conference and the Allied proclamation concerning possible Japanese surrender, they realized they would have to respond. Premier Suzuki in particular could not ignore it. Suzuki unknowingly played into the military's hands. He used the word *mokusatsu* to describe his feelings toward the Potsdam proclamation. He literally meant to state that he wished to "kill with silence" the ultimatum. Perhaps the English phrase "no comment" comes closest to Suzuki's intended message. Newspapers received instructions simply to reproduce the premier's literal text with no comment of their own. But several prominent Japanese papers did editorialize, opining that Suzuki believed the Potsdam document was laughable or "beneath contempt." Thus, the Allies became convinced that Suzuki was far from ready to consider surrender. Even the *New York Times* told its readers that this was Suzuki's intent or meaning. This was true as far as the Japanese military were concerned, but it did not convey the true feelings of the civilian ruling elite.

Consequently Japan was condemned to atomic attack. As mentioned in the previous chapter, Truman decided that fission weapons should be used against the Japanese and it was widely anticipated that the bomb would compel surrender and thus save both American and Japanese lives. The first bomb was detonated above Hiroshima on August 6 at 8:15 AM. It took a full day for word of the catastrophe and its possible cause to become known in Tokyo. Only on the morning of the August 9 did Minister of the Army General Korechika Anami definitely learn that a single bomb had destroyed the city. Just before had come news of a proclamation by President Truman, monitored by Japanese radio, stating that it was indeed an atomic device, which had cost America two billion dollars to develop. No one in Tokyo was sure it was really an atomic explosion, so the head of Japan's own atomic bomb project, Dr. Yoshio Nishina (later a Nobel Prize winner), was dispatched to the city. He surveyed it from the air and then inspected the damage on the ground. Nishina promptly concluded that only a uranium bomb could have caused such damage.

In the early morning hours of August 9 (August 8 in Europe) Stalin kept his pledge, and Soviet troops invaded Manchuria. The declaration of war against Japan was issued via radio. The same radio monitors who had heard Truman's proclamation of a nuclear age for mankind also learned of Russia's declaration of war. Later that same morning came news of the Nagasaki bomb. But contemporary members of the cabinet and Kido affirmed that the essential impression was made by Russian intervention. The British official history of the war, *The War against Japan,* states that Russian participation in the Pacific conflict brought home to the Japanese government that "the last hope of negotiated peace had gone and there was no alternative but to accept the Allied terms sooner or later." Suzuki himself told General Anami:

> If we don't act now, the Russians will penetrate not only Manchuria and Korea but northern Japan as well. If that happens, our country is finished. We must act now, while our chief adversary is still the United States.

The emperor was impressed with the military potential of the bomb, as well as with the peacetime uses of atomic energy. This would perhaps provide part of the motivation to name it in the documents pertaining to surrender. But the emperor later confided to Kido that his basic reason for surrender was the threat of Soviet occupation. America, he believed, would eventually withdraw from the country, but the Soviets would never leave. This may seem to betray extraordinary foresight on the part of the Japanese, and in a sense it does; but all Japanese governments since the Meiji restoration have thought in terms of years, decades, and even centuries when making decisions, and Hirohito was merely following this tradition. The military dismissed the new American weapon as something like a magnesium "flashlight" device. Even when among themselves the military chiefs acknowledged its true nature, they claimed that if civilians were properly clothed in white garments they would not be harmed. In the end they issued several official pronouncements on the bomb, dismissing it as "routine." They *may* not have seriously meant this, but at the very least the word indicates the *Samurai* code and the mindset that it engendered.

Sometime early on the morning of August 9, *before* the world's first true nuclear device exploded over Nagasaki, the emperor and Kido decided that this was the day to implement a surrender policy. The most influential body in the land was the semiofficial Big Six, whose members then included Premier Suzuki, Foreign Minister Togo, Minister of the Army Anami, Minister of the Navy Yonai, Chief of the Army General Staff Yoshijiro Umezu, and Chief of the Naval General Staff Soemu Toyoda. As in cabinet meetings, Kido and one or two others sat in as unofficial, nonvoting members. And meetings were held in the presence of the emperor, who listened but, following tradition, refrained from speaking.

Normally Hirohito was the servant of the Big Six. Now he decided that the time had come to break precedent and demand that Japan surrender. Kido sent a young secretary of the prime minister to acquire the signatures of all the members so that an extraordinary meeting could be called, at an unspecified later date. Anami warned the lad that this had better not be one of Kido's tricks to implement a surrender policy, or he would kill the first man to mention surrender. The excuse was given that this was the only way to ensure, in the event of an emergency that might prevent some or all of the members from being reachable, that a meeting of this influential body could be called within the hour.

Upon receipt of the document, Kido immediately called a meeting and instructed the members of the body to come to the imperial palace. They gathered in the underground *obunko* complex, a small area used to house some of the emperor's books, a little before midnight on August 9, the meeting having been delayed by several false air raid alerts. The weather was hot and oppressive, and the meeting was held in this underground complex partly for comfort's sake. At ten minutes before midnight the emperor arrived. The meeting was called to order. The final chapter of the war was about to be enacted.

Anami, Umezu, and Toyoda took the line that the atomic bomb could be successfully defended against, if the proper antiaircraft measures were taken. No other mention was made of the device. The military agreed that the situation was desperate but maintained that they could still win. Their logic is difficult to grasp. After two hours of discussion, which indicated that the group was evenly divided on the question of surrender, Suzuki deemed it time to play his trump card. The premier had foreseen this development. By prearrangement, knowing that Anami, Umezu, and Toyoda, all ardent hawks, would deadlock the proceedings if it came to an actual vote, the emperor had agreed to speak. He had prepared a brief unwritten statement for the occasion. At this juncture, Suzuki called on the throne to express an opinion, since the body was deadlocked. Due to a hearing impediment, Suzuki failed to hear the emperor's initial response and asked a second time. All sat silent as Hirohito rose to address them as never before.

The emperor motioned for Suzuki to sit down. He then began his address. In a high-pitched, emotional voice he told the group: "I have given serious thought to the situation at home and abroad and determined that my people must suffer no longer." The emperor went on to compare the situation to that experienced by Japan during the Triple Intervention of 1895, when France, Germany, and Russia prevented Japan from gaining Korea, which it had won from China. He told those assembled that once again Japan would be forced to bear the unbearable, and that his ministers and his people had better prepare "to drink their own tears." The fact that his subjects were willing to die for him had not escaped his perception, but he could not require such a sacrifice. The very survival of Japan as a nation was at stake. Immediate surrender was the only means to assure that Japan would live on as a unified nation after the conflict.

When the emperor finished speaking, the decision had been made. Many of those assembled left in tears. The official decision to surrender had to be approved by a meeting of the entire cabinet. It met that same morning, and quickly approved the surrender policy. Virtually the entire government and military elite silently agreed, as if by instinct, that in only one sense could Japan's surrender be less than unconditional: the emperor must retain his throne. A proviso was therefore added to the surrender decision to this effect. Had the Allies rejected this condition outright, all agreed that Japan would continue the struggle to the bitter end.

That same morning, just after the cabinet meeting, Anami was evidently so moved by the Soviet entrance into the conflict that he issued a statement that contended that the unity of Japan was so important that a "Holy War" should be waged against the Soviet Union. He would later claim that this message was sent out by accident. This may have been the case, but it made Kido and Togo quite angry nonetheless.

The next task for Togo and Kido was to inform the Allies of Japan's willingness to surrender. Unfortunately the normal civilian radio stations were being both monitored and censored by the army, and no one could be sure that a militant officer might not invoke the doctrine of *gekokujo* to block the broadcast. That evening the message was sent out via the Domei news agency in Morse code, which somehow was not subject to censorship. It was in that manner that the Allies learned of the Japanese decision.

Popular opinion in the Allied nations favored trying the emperor as a war criminal, probably because of a lack of understanding of his true role in Japanese politics. Truman himself appears to have had no strong convictions on the matter. He offered no objection when American Secretary of State James Byrnes (appointed April 1945) told the American nation that "the ultimate form of government of Japan" would be determined "by the freely expressed will of the Japanese people," as had been envisioned at the Potsdam Conference. This message was then dispatched via the Swiss government to Japan. The Japanese had already learned of this policy in the early morning hours of August 12 via an English-language radio broadcast.

In Japan Foreign Minister Togo and several legal experts in his ministry somehow determined that the phrase "the government of Japan" did *not* include reference to the emperor. Hirohito himself stated that he accepted the proclamation. He did not fear that his people would vote against retaining him as monarch if the Allies put the question to the test in a plebiscite during the forthcoming occupation. The Allied military continued its campaign of bombing and strafing Japanese cities after these announcements were made. The rumor was even spread—no one knew its origin—that Tokyo itself would receive an atomic bomb attack on August 15.

Generals Umezu and Anami refused to accept Togo's opinion that the American reply did not include the emperor. Anami in particular began to back out of his silent acquiescence to the surrender decision. He argued that it would be better to wait until the Allies attempted an invasion. Once an initial landing had been thrown back into the sea, he reasoned that Japan would have greater bargaining power. In fact, Admiral Onishi, founder of the *Kamikaze* corps, opined that if 20 million lives were sacrificed in a special suicide mission, Japan could yet win the war. He did not, however, reveal what sort of special *Kamikaze* attack(s) he had in mind. On the morning of August the Americans precipitated matters by dropping leaflets on Japan, stating that the Japanese government had agreed to surrender and giving the essential terms of Byrnes's reply.

At a little before noon on August 14, 1945, the emperor convened the Big Six and the cabinet as one body. Hirohito stated simply but very firmly that all present had already agreed to a surrender decision; it displeased him that a second meeting was necessary to enforce the decision. As soon as the meeting terminated, Togo rushed to the Foreign Ministry and dispatched plaintext, uncoded messages to his ambassadors in Bern and Stockholm, stating that the Japanese government accepted the Allied terms of surrender. As Togo doubtless had anticipated, they were read by prying eyes before delivery at their destinations. Wire services the world over soon carried flash stories to the effect that Japan had capitulated. The world's costliest war was over.

Here the story should end, but it does not. Some of the younger Japanese Army officers viewed Russian entrance into the conflict as more of a challenge than a threat. This was especially true of some of the lower-grade staff officers in Tokyo. The emperor realized that this might be the case. He took necessary precautions. His brothers had spent several days assuring the military that the emperor desired surrender, and certain war heroes—Fuchida included—had devoted their energies to similar ends. Still the effect proved unavailing in one sense: troops on far-off islands could not be reached, and staff officers in Tokyo still busied themselves in preparing for disobedience.

Thus, on August 14 the emperor decided to broadcast a surrender rescript to the nation. Since every conflict was ended by an explanation by the throne, this one could be no exception. But the emperor would read it himself. Then, later in the day, Hirohito decided he did not trust his emotions. He asked Kido to arrange for him to record his message. This the lord privy seal proceeded to do with dispatch. Technicians from station NHK were sent for, came to the palace, and set up recording equipment. They did so in the Imperial Household Ministry, within the 500 acres that comprise the palace grounds. This was the natural place for the recording, since the military might attempt to stop the talk.

These precautions were not in vain. Indeed one staff officer in Tokyo had spent the last several days in plotting the undoing of the emperor's surrender policy. General Anami's son-in-law, one Major Kemji Hatanaka, was privy to the emperor's commands via Anami. He determined to stop the surrender himself. Hatanaka was without official transportation, and spent a lot of time on his bicycle garnering support among other officers for a palace revolt. Anami sympathized with his son-in-law's efforts but refused to support him. On the other hand he also did nothing to stop him, which as a superior officer he could have done with one word of command.

At 11:15 PM on August 14 Hirohito arrived at the Imperial Household Ministry to make the recording. He had never before spoken on the radio. Only once, in 1928, had the imperial voice been broadcast, and that was an accident. Hirohito came with the rescript in hand. It took less than twenty minutes to read. Placed in a room with a microphone, he became nervous. He spoke in a high-pitched voice, virtually shouting, evidently under the impression that the louder he spoke, the greater the number of his subjects who would be able to hear him.

Thus the first recording was not a good performance. A second was necessary. The emperor was told he could use his usual speaking voice, which he did. But now he was hoarse, and he skipped several syllables. Kido managed to signal the technicians that a third attempt was out of the question. The second recording was labeled "original" and the first "copy." The ten-inch disks were taken back to the residential portion of the palace grounds for safekeeping. They were to be played to the nation the next day, August 15, 1945, at noon.

Major Hatanaka knew that a surrender recording had been made, but he did not know the details. At 11:00 PM on the evening of August 14 he called on Lt. General Takeshi Mori, commander of the Imperial Guards Division. Mori evidently sensed that his interlocutor was up to no good, for he immediately launched into a monologue on his philosophy of life. Hatanaka listened with rising impatience. At 1:30 AM he drew his pistol and shot General Mori dead. Hatanaka then appropriated the general's seal and forged an order placing himself in temporary charge of the entire Imperial Guards Division.

Hatanaka proceeded to the palace, where he blundered into a portion of the imperial residence itself. He demanded to know the location of the surrender recordings but was unable to find them. Kido, however, became so nervous that instead of sleeping, he spent the night destroying documents that he feared Hatanaka might find and somehow use. At dawn Hatanaka's little drama ended, in part because an unsympathetic general arrived and ordered Hatanaka's men to disperse. Hatanaka seconded the order, leaving the imperial residence. After making an attempt at NHK to stop the playing of the recording, Hatanaka took his own life.

At 7:21 AM NHK announced to the nation that the emperor would address his subjects at noon. The rescript was written in official court Japanese, which was a mixture of Japanese and Chinese characters. It was generally unintelligible to the masses, especially if read without an accompanying printed text. The people would be forced to determine the emperor's meaning from the tone of his voice and such portions of the rescript as they could comprehend. Add to this the distortion inherent in cutting a ten-inch Bakelite recording at 78 rpm, and it seems doubtful indeed that his actual words were fully understood.

When the emperor's broadcast began, many expected to hear that the Allies had begun the invasion of the home islands and that they were to resist to the last. Only such an important message would require the emperor himself to address the nation. Never before had the general population of Japan heard Hirohito's voice. When Hirohito's recording began, the people were surprised by the high-pitched quality of the emperor's voice, but his tone betrayed the content of the message. Instead of aiding in the repulsion of an invasion, they were to suffer an even less enviable fate: surrender. Many wept. Now Japan would be forced to endure a conqueror's rule for the first time in her history.

The imperial surrender rescript is worth reproducing in full, for it not only implements the surrender policy but provides a recipe for the future, one which in effect the Japanese are still implementing to this day:

> To Our good and loyal subjects: After pondering deeply the general trends of the world and the actual conditions existing in Our empire today, we have decided to effect a settlement of the present situation by resorting to an extraordinary measure.
>
> We have ordered Our government to communicate to the governments of the United States, Great Britain, China, and the Soviet Union

that Our empire accepts the provisions of their joint [Potsdam] declaration.

To strive for the common prosperity and happiness of all nations, as well as the security and well-being of Our subjects, is the solemn obligation which has been handed down by Our imperial ancestors and which we keep close to Our heart. Indeed, we declared war on America and Britain out of Our sincere desire to insure Japan's self-preservation and the stabilization of East Asia, it being far from Our thought either to infringe upon the sovereignty of other nations or to embark upon territorial aggrandizement. But now the war has lasted for nearly four years.

Despite the best that has been done by everyone—the gallant fighting of the military and naval forces, the diligence of Our state servants and the devoted service of Our hundred million subjects—the war situation has developed not necessarily to Japan's advantage, while the general trends of the world have all turned against her. Moreover, the enemy has begun to employ a new and most cruel bomb, the power of which to do damage is indeed incalculable, taking the toll of many innocent lives. Should we continue to fight, it would not only result in the ultimate collapse and obliteration of the Japanese nation, but also would lead to the extinction of civilization. How are we to save Our subjects? By accepting the joint [Potsdam] declaration of the powers.

We cannot but express deep regret to Our East Asian allies who have cooperated with us. The thought of those officers and men as well as civilians who died in the battles or air raids pains us day and night. We have suffered unspeakably, and we hope you will accept Our imperial apology for all of this. We can only hope that future generations will enjoy peace. Having thus safeguarded and maintained the Japanese nation, we feel at one with Our people. Do not engage in outbursts of emotion which might have international significance, or in any internecine contention and strife, which might cause us to lose the confidence of the world. Let the entire nation continue as one family from generation to generation, ever firm in its faith that Japan will always exist, and mindful of the many trials and tribulations ahead.

Unite your total strength to construct the future. Cultivate the ways of rectitude; foster nobility of spirit; and work with resolution so as to enhance Japan's glory and *keep pace with the progress of the world.* [Emphasis added]

Perhaps the myths began as soon as the rescript was published in the evening paper, and people were able to study it fully. Kido's testimony as well as that of several cabinet members makes it clear that the Japanese surrender came in response to the Russian entry into the war and the fear of a Soviet occupation of the home islands. But Hirohito had not mentioned this in the rescript, for fear that any such reference might encourage the vengeful Allies to allow Russia to participate in the postwar control of Japan. Also the new American weapon provided a convenient, face-saving excuse for capitulation.

The importance of the atomic weapons' role in terminating the conflict vanishes when one considers the lengths to which the Japanese had gone in preparing for the Allied invasion of the home islands, as well as the zeal they had displayed during the final months of actual fighting. The fanatical resistance that had characterized Japanese determination on Iwo Jima and Okinawa demonstrated that the Japanese still had a lot of fight in them. The organization of a *Kamikaze* corps designed to destroy the American Navy at a tremendous cost in lives shows the lengths to which the Japanese had already gone to prevent defeat. A national guard of 27 million had been organized and armed with primitive weapons to drive the American invasion of the home islands back into the sea.

Since March 1945 the home islands had been subjected to the most murderous bombing campaign mankind had yet witnessed. Nearly 500,000 civilian lives had been lost monthly since March of 1945. Japan had failed to disrupt significantly any of the aerial bombardments undertaken by the Allies. Japan's willingness to absorb horrendous losses had already been established. The introduction of a more efficient weapon, even the atomic bomb, was not significant enough to bring about Japanese capitulation. Only the military intervention of the Soviet Union had moved the Japanese military to consider the unthinkable—surrender. And witness that even then, Hirohito had to command his generals *twice* to lay down the sword before the decision became actual Japanese policy.

Further an American Army intelligence study conducted after the termination of the conflict reinforces and verifies these conclusions. As summarized in the *New York Times* (August 3, 1989), the 1946 report concluded that the bombing of Hiroshima and Nagasaki provided a "pretext" for surrender, "seized upon by all [Japanese] leaders as the reason for ending the war," but that Japan's motivation to surrender came in the form of the Russian participation in the conflict, which the report described as "the disastrous event which the Japanese leaders regarded as [an] utter catastrophe and which they had energetically sought to prevent at any cost—Russia declared war and began moving her forces into Manchuria." How widely known this report was at the time remains unclear; but a section of the Pentagon bureaucracy evidently realized that Russia, which had compelled Japan to modernize in the 1860s, had similarly compelled her surrender in 1945. Only the threat of communism and Russian domination, the fear that Japan would suffer a Soviet occupation while losing both her unity and national identity in the process, was enough to overcome the Samurai mindset.

On August 27 General MacArthur arrived at a *Kamikaze* air base, Atsugi Field, located near Tokyo. His entourage was small, in part because he wanted to demonstrate his trust in the Japanese people. He established his office in the Dai Ichi building in downtown Tokyo, and his actual living quarters in the American embassy. His office faced the imperial palace and also a square where a radio propaganda broadcaster had once assured her listeners that MacArthur would be hung.

The official surrender ceremony took place aboard the battleship *Missouri* on September 2, 1945, in Tokyo Bay. Hirohito had to ask the Japanese delegates personally not to commit suicide, lest their taking their own lives seem to the Americans to invalidate their signatures on the surrender document. As the delegates came aboard, they were horrified to see rising suns painted on gun turrets, evidently denoting aircraft downed by *Missouri*'s antiaircraft guns, although it is also possible that they had been painted on simply for effect. MacArthur conducted the ceremony. He and Admiral Chester Nimitz signed for the United States. Representatives of the other major Allied, now United Nations' powers, also signed. There was considerable resentment among America's allies, however, because MacArthur had ruled that prisoners of war not liberated in the course of hostilities had to await the formal signing on that day before being freed from POW camps. There are many Australians in particular who to this day do not forgive MacArthur for this decision.

The cost to the various belligerents was awesome. The Japanese suffered one and a-half million battle deaths, and well over three million civilian deaths from the air raids, including the bombings of Hiroshima and Nagasaki. Total American casualties, killed and wounded in the Pacific, was later placed at 296,148. British, Australian, and other empire/Commonwealth forces suffered 185,000 battle deaths. At least four million Chinese had also been killed. The suffering of those who lost their homes and families is incalculable and cannot be shown on any chart or graph.

In Japan itself all now wondered what the Americans would be like. The Japanese truly adopted a "never look back" philosophy; rather than rationalizing their defeat, newspapers filled their columns with advice on how to get along with the Anglo-Saxons. Some women, perhaps victims of wartime propaganda, nonetheless husbanded poison capsules especially issued by the government. Or perhaps they anticipated the sort of treatment Japan would have given a conquered nation under the Samurai code. All Japan trembled, wondering what the Americans would be like.

General MacArthur was later to be criticized for not trying the emperor as a war criminal. But he did not do so for very practical reasons: he came to realize that he would probably face a civil insurrection at the least if Hirohito were put before a tribunal. Indeed he told the American leadership as much when they complained of his decision. Perhaps knowledge of Japanese government "folkways" motivated him as well. The military had not informed the emperor in 1931 when they invaded Manchuria, and a small army clique had tried to invoke the doctrine of *gekokujo* to overturn the surrender decision before it was broadcast to the Japanese nation. Hirohito, for all of his theoretical power, was no more than a bystander to the conflict; he was trained to reign, not rule. He could not prevent war in China, which was begun without his knowledge, or war against America, which he regarded as the greatest tragedy of his life.

For many years the subsequent American occupation of the home islands was generically known to the Japanese as "the period in which we had visitors." Only recently have the Japanese come to grapple with the true history of the war and their subsequent defeat. Even with the physical and economic ruin caused by the fighting, the Japanese in a sense long refused to acknowledge the war's bitter legacy.

This can be better understood when one examines the aftermath of the conflict and the continued suffering the Japanese endured at the hands of their American conquerors. General MacArthur in one respect did a poor job of attempting to ready Japan for self-rule during his tenure as occupation commander. Giving little thought to the immediate welfare of those under his jurisdiction, he set about attempting to reform the government in what he thought was the correct manner.

The most obvious example of his neglect, from a Japanese standpoint, was the diet that was mandated for the general populace. The meager few ounces of rice and one or two potatoes per week on which they were expected to live were simply insufficient to sustain life. The Japanese were forced to turn to the thriving black market, which expanded tremendously in occupied Japan, to secure their daily bread. For some, it may well have consisted largely of Spam and Hershey bars if there was an American base or PX nearby. Still the Japanese were grateful to MacArthur. At the very least, he was better than having Soviet troops on Japanese soil. Indeed there were plans to erect a huge statue of MacArthur in Tokyo Bay just after he was relieved of command in 1951. After MacArthur testified in Washington at the hearings concerning his removal that the Japanese were childlike and longing for American guidance, these plans were quietly shelved.

During the occupation and afterward American and Japanese culture mingled as never before. But it was the conflicts in Korea and then Vietnam that primed the economic pump in Japan, leading to the staggering growth and development of the Japanese economy that is so in evidence today.

Although the Greater East Asian Co-Prosperity Sphere could never be realized through overt, aggressive means, which stretched the Japanese military beyond their limits, it is arguable that what the Japanese could not achieve through war they have more than managed through peaceful means. And while the Americans did indeed crush all of their foes in 1945, standing unrivaled in economic and military strength, they have seen their *relative* position in the world diminish. Few seem to realize that the Japanese ''economic miracle'' is predicated on peace; in a war, the Japanese economy would suffer very severe reverses, particularly if Japan's supply of imported oil were interrupted. As in 1941, almost all of its raw resources today are imported, and anything like an effective naval blockade would quickly decimate the Japanese economic infrastructure.

But let no one doubt the zeal of the Japanese leadership and their people to think in policy planning in terms of years and decades rather than weeks or months. The Japanese people and their leaders have indeed followed the advice given in Hirohito's surrender rescript: *''Keep pace with the progress of the world.''*

Suggestions for Further Reading

The standard work on Japan's surrender is still Robert Butow's *Japan's Decision to Surrender* (Stanford, CA: Stanford University Press, 1954), from which the authors have derived a considerable amount of factual information. Some primary source material of considerable importance is contained in the Pacific War Research Society's *Japan's Longest Day* (New York: Ballantine Books, 1972); the quote by Premier Suzuki to General Anami, "If we don't act now . . ." is found in this volume. Thomas Coffey's *Imperial Tragedy: Japan in World War Two—The First Days and the Last* (New York: The World Publishing Company, 1970) also contains some interesting material on the subject. See also *The Day Man Lost* (New York: Kodansha, 1981) by the Pacific War Research Society and Leon V. Sigal, *Fighting to a Finish: The Politics of War Termination in the United States and Japan, 1945* (Ithaca, NY: Cornell University Press, 1988), which approaches the surrender from the standpoint of a political scientist who analyzes the processes involved. Important eyewitness material may be gleaned from Michihiko Hachiya, *Hiroshima Diary* (Chapel Hill: University of North Carolina Press, 1955). The actual mechanics of the formal surrender are recorded in Toshikazu Kase, *Journey to the Missouri* (New Haven, CT: Yale University Press, 1950). Those portions of the text recounting the surrender in John Toland, *The Rising Sun: The Decline and Fall of the Japanese Empire, 1936–1945* (New York: Bantam Books, 1970) are reliable and have supplied interesting detail to this narrative. The official British history concerning Japanese surrender is Woodburn S. Kirby et al., *The War against Japan* (London: Her Majesty's Stationary Office, 1969). For an Australian reaction to MacArthur's decision regarding POWs still held at the time of surrender by the Japanese, see Hank Nelson " 'The Nips are Going for the Parker [pen]': The Prisoners Face Freedom," *War and Society 3* (September 1985): 127–43.

References

Primary Sources

Austin, Victor, ed., *To Kokoda and Beyond: The Story of the 39th Battalion*. Melbourne: Melbourne University Press, 1988.

Correspondents of *Time, Life, & Fortune* magazines, *December 7: The First Thirty Hours*. New York: Knopf, 1942.

Dyess, Edwin, *The Dyess Story*. New York: Putnam, 1944.

Fuchida, Mitsuo and Masatake Okumiya, *Midway: The Battle that Doomed Japan*. Annapolis, MD: Naval Institute Press, 1955.

Gay, George H., *Sole Survivor*. Naples, FL: Naples Graphics Services, 1979.

Grew, Raymond, *Turbulent Era*. 2 vols. Boston: Houghton Mifflin, 1952.

———. *Ten Years in Japan*. New York: Simon & Schuster, 1944.

Groves, Leslie, *Now It Can Be Told*. New York: Harper & Row, 1962.

Kase, Toshikazu, *Journey to the Missouri*. New Haven, CT: Yale University Press, 1950.

Kirby, Woodburn S., et al., *The War against Japan*. 5 vols. London: Her Majesty's Stationary Office, 1957–69.

Layton, Edwin T, *And I Was There: Pearl Harbor and Midway—Breaking the Secrets*. New York: Morrow, 1985.

Manchester, William, *Goodbye Darkness: A Memoir of the Pacific War*. Boston: Little, Brown, 1979.

Morley, James, ed., *Japan's Road to the Pacific War*. 5 vols. New York: Columbia University Press, 1976–1985.

Nagatsuka, Ryuji, *I Was a Kamikaze*. London: Schuman, 1972.

O'Kane, Richard, *Clear the Bridge! The War Patrols of the U.S.S. Tang*. Novato, CA: Presidio Press, 1989.

Orita, Zenji, *I-Boat Captain*. Canoga Park, CA: Major Books, 1976.

Pacific War Research Society, *The Day Man Lost*. New York: Kodansha, 1981.

———. *Japan's Longest Day*. New York: Ballantine Books, 1972.

Phinney, Peter, *The Barbarians: A Soldier's New Guinea Diary*. St. Lucia, Australia: University of Queensland Press, 1989.

Sakamaki, Kazuo, *I Attacked Pearl Harbor*. New York: Associated Press, 1949.

Trefousse, Hans L., ed., *Pearl Harbor: The Continuing Controversy*. Malabar, FL: Krieger, 1982.

————, ed., *What Happened at Pearl Harbor? Documents Pertaining to the Japanese Attack of December 7, 1941, and Its Background.* New York: Twayne, 1958.

United States Commission on Wartime Relocation and Internment of Civilians, *Personal Justice Denied.* Washington, DC: Government Printing Office, 1982.

United States Congress, *Pearl Harbor Attack: Hearings before the Joint Committee on the Investigation of the Pearl Harbor Attack.* 39 vols. Washington, DC: Government Printing Office, 1946.

Yamamoto, Tsunetomo, *The Book of the Samurai.* New York: Kodansha, nd.

Secondary Sources

Agawa, Hiroyuki, *The Reluctant Admiral: Yamamoto and the Imperial Navy.* New York: Kodansha, 1979.

Asia Society, *The Encyclopedia of Asian History.* 4 vols. New York: Charles Scribner's Sons, 1988.

Bagnasco, Erminio, *Submarines of World War Two.* Annapolis, MD: Naval Institute Press, 1977.

Barbey, Daniel, *MacArthur's Amphibious Navy: Seventh Amphibious Force Operations, 1943–1945.* Annapolis, MD: Naval Institute Press, 1969.

Barker, A.J., *Suicide Weapon.* New York: Ballantine Books, 1971.

Barnhart, Michael, *Japan Prepares for Total War: The Search for Economic Security, 1919–1941.* Ithaca, NY: Cornell University Press, 1987.

Bartley, Whitman, *Iwo Jima.* Washington, DC: Government Printing Office, 1948.

Bell, Roger J., *Unequal Allies: Australian-American Relations and the Pacific War.* Melbourne: Melbourne University Press, 1977.

Belote, James H. and William M. Belote, *Typhoon of Steel: The Battle for Okinawa.* New York: Harper & Row, 1969.

Benedict, Ruth, *The Chrysanthemum and the Sword.* Boston: Little, Brown, 1946.

Blair, Clay, *Silent Victory.* New York: Lippincott, 1975.

Burns, James M., Russell Gugler, and John Stevens, *Okinawa: The Last Battle.* Washington, DC: Department of the Army, 1948.

Butow, Robert J., *Japan's Decision to Surrender.* Stanford, CA: Stanford University Press, 1954.

Bradley, John H., *The Second World War: Asia and the Pacific.* Wayne, NJ: Avery, 1984.

Brougher, William E., *South to Bataan, North to Mukden.* Athens: University of Georgia Press, 1971.

Buell, Thomas, *The Quiet Warrior: A Biography of Admiral Raymond A. Spruance.* Boston: Little, Brown, 1974.

Burns, Richard D. and Edward Bennett, eds., *Diplomats in Crisis: United States-Chinese-Japanese Relations, 1919–1941.* Santa Barbara, CA: ABC-Clio Press, 1974.

Butow, Robert, *Tojo and the Coming of the War.* Stanford, CA: Stanford University Press, 1961.

Byrd, Martha, *Chennault: Giving Wings to the Tiger.* Tuscaloosa: University of Alabama Press, 1987.

Caidin, Martin, *A Torch to the Enemy: The Fire Raid on Tokyo*. New York: Ballantine, 1960.

Chong-Tung, Lee, *Counterinsurgency in Manchuria: The Japanese Experience, 1931–1940*. Santa Monica, CA: Rand Corporation, 1967.

Clark, Ronald W., *The Birth of the Bomb*. New York: Horizon Press, 1961.

Coffey, Thomas, *Imperial Tragedy: Japan in World War Two—The First Days and the Last*. New York: World Publishing Company, 1970.

Coggins, Jack, *The Campaign for Guadalcanal*. Garden City, New York: Doubleday, 1972.

Corbett, Scott P., *Quiet Passages: The Exchanges of Civilians between the United States and Japan during the Second World War*. Kent, OH: Kent State University Press, 1987.

Crowl, Philip, *Campaign in the Marianas*. Washington, DC: Army Historical Office, 1960.

David, Thomas, *The Battle of the Java Sea*. New York: Stein & Day, 1969.

Dower, John, *War without Mercy: Race and Power in the Pacific War*. New York: Pantheon Books, 1986.

Duus, Masayo, *Tokyo Rose: Orphan of the Pacific*. New York: Kodansha, 1978.

Edoin, Hoito, *The Night Tokyo Burned: The Incendiary Campaign against Japan, March–August 1945*. New York: St. Martin's Press, 1987.

Enright, Joseph, *Shinano!* New York: St. Martin's Press, 1987.

Falk, Stanley, *Decision at Leyte*. New York: Norton, 1966.

Feis, Herbert, *The Road to Pearl Harbor*. Princeton, NJ: Princeton University Press, 1950.

Feist, Joe M., "Bats Away." *American Heritage 33* (April–May 1982): 93–95.

Feldt, Eric, *The Coastwatchers*. New York: Oxford University Press, 1978.

Fermi, Laura, *Illustrious Immigrants: The Intellectual Migration from Europe, 1930–1940*. Chicago: University of Chicago Press, 1968.

Field, James A., *The Japanese at Leyte Gulf; The Sho Operation*. Princeton, NJ: Princeton University Press, 1947.

Francillon, Rene J., *Japanese Aircraft of the Pacific War*. New York: Funk & Wagnalls, 1970.

Garfield, Brian, *The Thousand Mile War: World War II in Alaska and the Aleutians*. Garden City, NY: Doubleday, 1969.

Glines, Carroll, *The Doolittle Raid*. New York: Orion Books, 1988.

Goulden, Joseph C., *Korea: The Untold Story of the War*. New York: McGraw-Hill, 1982.

Gow, Ian, *Okinawa 1945: Gateway to Japan*. New York: Barnes & Noble, 1988.

Gowing, Margaret, *Britain and Atomic Energy, 1939–1945*. London: St. Martin's Press, 1964.

Grady, Gallant T. *The Friendly Dead*. Garden City, NY: Doubleday, 1964.

Grodzins, Morton, *Americans Betrayed*. Chicago: University of Chicago Press, 1949.

Guillain, Robert, *I Saw Tokyo Burning*. New York: Doubleday, 1981.

Hachiya, Michihiko, *Hiroshima Diary*. Chapel Hill: University of North Carolina Press, 1955.

Haggie, Paul, *Britannia at Bay: The Defense of the British Empire against Japan, 1931–1941*. New York: Oxford University Press, 1981.

Hammel, Eric, *Guadalcanal: The Carrier Battles*. New York: Crown Publishers, 1987.

Hammel, Eric and John Lane, *Seventy-Six Hours: The Invasion of Tarawa*. New York: Tower Books, 1980.

Hane, Kikiso, *Modern Japan: A Historical Survey*. Boulder, CO: Westview Press, 1986.

Hashimoto, Mochitsura, *Sunk! The Story of the Japanese Submarine Fleet, 1941– 1945*. New York: Holt, 1954.

Hata, Ikuhiko and Yasuho Izawa, *Japanese Naval Aces and Fighter Units in World War Two*. Annapolis, MD: Naval Institute Press, 1989.

Havens, Thomas, *Valley of Darkness: The Japanese People and World War Two*. New York: Norton, 1978.

Herzberg, James R., *A Broken Bond: American Economic Policies toward Japan, 1931–1941*. New York: Garland, 1988.

Hess, Gary R., *America Encounters India, 1941–1947*. Baltimore: Johns Hopkins University Press, 1971.

Hirokoshi, Jrio, *Eagles of Mitsubishi: The Story of the Zero Fighter*. Seattle: University of Washington Press, 1981.

Hoehling, A.A., *The Week before Pearl Harbor*. New York: Norton, 1963.

Hoyt, Edwin. *The Battle of Leyte Gulf*. New York: Weybright and Talley, 1972.

———. *To the Marianas*. New York: Van Nostrand, 1980.

Ienega, Saburo, *The Pacific War, 1931–1945*. New York: Pantheon Books, 1978.

Inoguchi, Rikihei, Tadashi Nakajima, and Roger Pineau, *The Divine Wind*. Annapolis, MD: Naval Institute Press, 1959.

Iriye, Akira, *The Origins of the Second World War in Asia and the Pacific*. London: Longman, 1987.

Iseley, Peter and Philip Crowl, *The U.S. Marines and Amphibious War: Its Theory and its Practice in the Pacific*. Princeton, NJ: Princeton University Press, 1951.

James, D. Clayton, *The Years of MacArthur*. 3 vols. Boston: Houghton Mifflin, 1970–85.

Jones, F.C., *Japan's New Order: Its Rise and Fall, 1937–45*. London: Oxford University Press, 1954.

Karnow, Stanley, *In Our Image: America's Empire in the Philippines*. New York: Ballantine, 1990.

Kerr, E. Bartlett, *Surrender and Survival: The Experience of American POWs in the Pacific, 1941–1945*. New York: William Morrow, 1985.

Knox, Donald, *Death March: The Survivors of Bataan*. New York: Harcourt Brace Jovanovich, 1981.

Kozumplik, Peter W., "The Chinese Civil War." West Point Military History Series, *The Arab-Israeli Wars, the Chinese Civil War and the Korean War*. Wayne, NJ: Avery, 1987.

Ladd, James, *Assault from the Sea: The Craft, the Landings, the Men*. New York: Hippocrene Books, 1976.

Lebra, Joyce V., ed., *Japan's Greater East Asia Co-Prosperity Sphere in World War Two: Selected Readings and Documents*. New York: Oxford University Press, 1975.

Leckie, Robert, *The Battle for Iwo Jima*. New York: Random House, 1967.

Lewin, Ronald, *The American Magic: Codes, Ciphers and the Defeat of Japan.* New York: Farrar Straus Giroux, 1982.

Lind, Andrew, *Hawaii's Japanese: An Experiment in Democracy.* Princeton, NJ: Princeton University Press, 1946.

Liu, F.F. *A Military History of Modern China, 1924–1949.* Princeton, NJ: Princeton University Press, 1956.

Lord, Walter, *Lonely Vigil: Coastwatchers of the Solomons.* New York: Viking Press, 1977.

Lorelli, John, *The Battle of the Komandorski Islands.* Annapolis, MD: Naval Institute Press, 1984.

Lowe, Peter, *Great Britain and the Origins of the Pacific War.* Oxford: Clarendon Press, 1977.

Lundstrom, John B., *The First South Pacific Campaign: Pacific Fleet Strategy, December 1941—June 1942.* Annapolis, MD: Naval Institute Press, 1976.

———. *The First Team: Pacific Naval Air Combat from Pearl Harbor to Midway.* Annapolis, MD: Naval Institute Press, 1984.

McCarthy, Dudley, *South-West Pacific Area—First Year, Kokoda to Wau.* Canberra: Australian War Memorial, 1956.

Mcintyre, Donald, *Leyte Gulf: Armada in the Pacific.* New York: Ballantine, 1970.

McKinnon, Donald, "Battalion Surgeon on Iwo Jima," *Marine Corps Gazette 66* (February 1982): 28–37.

Maga, Timothy, *Defending Paradise.* New York: Garland, 1987.

Manchester, William, *Goodbye Darkness: A Memoir of the Pacific War.* New York: Dell, 1979.

Merrill, James M, *Target Tokyo: The Halsey-Doolittle Raid.* Chicago: Rand McNally, 1964.

Meyer, Dillon S., *Uprooted Americans.* Tucson: University of Arizona Press, 1971.

Mikesh, Robert C., *Japan's World War II Balloon Bomb Attacks on North America.* Washington, DC: Smithsonian Institution Press, 1973.

Miller, Samuel, *Victory in Papua.* Washington, DC: Army Historical Office, 1957.

Miller, Thomas, *The Cactus Air Force.* New York: Harper & Row, 1969.

Millot, Bernard, *The Battle of the Coral Sea.* Annapolis, MD: Naval Institute Press, 1974.

Morison, Samuel Eliot, *History of United States Naval Operations in World War Two.* 15 vols. Boston: Little, Brown, 1947–62.

Morris-Suzuki, Tessa, *Showa: An Inside History of Hirohito's Japan.* New York: Schocken Books, 1985.

Naito, Nahuso, *Thunder Gods.* New York: Kodansha, 1989.

Nelson, Hank, " 'The Nips Are Going for the Parker [pen]': The Prisoners Face Freedom." *War and Society III* (September 1985): 127–143.

Neu, Charles E., *The Troubled Encounter: The United States and Japan.* Malibar, Florida: Krieger, 1981.

Newcomb, Richard, *Iwo Jima.* New York: Holt, Rinehart and Winston, 1965.

Pelz, Stephen E., *Race to Pearl Harbor: The Failure of the Second London Naval Conference and the Onset of World War Two.* Cambridge, MA: Harvard University Press, 1974.

Prange, Gordon W., *December 7, 1941: The Day the Japanese Attacked Pearl Harbor.* New York: McGraw-Hill, 1988.

———. *Miracle at Midway.* New York: McGraw-Hill, 1982.

———. *Pearl Harbor: The Verdict of History.* New York: McGraw-Hill, 1986.

Reischauer, Edwin, *The Japanese.* Cambridge, MA: Harvard University Press, 1981.

Rhodes, Richard, *The Making of the Atomic Bomb.* New York: Simon & Schuster, 1986.

Sbrega, John J., *Anglo-American Relations and Colonialism in East Asia, 1941–1945.* New York: Garland, 1983.

Seagrave, Sterling, *The Soong Dynasty.* New York: Harper & Row, 1985.

Selden, Mark and Kyoko Selden, eds., *The Atomic Bomb: Voices from Hiroshima and Nagasaki.* Armonk, NY: M.E. Sharpe, 1989.

Sheridan, James, *China in Disintegration: The Republican Era in Chinese History, 1912–1949.* New York: The Free Press, 1975.

Sherwin, Martin. *A World Destroyed: The Atomic Bomb and the Grand Alliance.* New York: Knopf, 1975.

Sigal, Leon V., *Fighting to a Finish: The Politics of War Termination in the United States and Japan, 1945.* Ithaca, NY: Cornell University Press, 1988.

Sims, Edward, *The Greatest Aces.* New York: Harper & Row, 1967.

Slim, William, *Defeat into Victory.* London: Widenfield & Nicholson, 1960.

Smith, Stanley, *The Battle of Savo.* New York: Macfadden-Bartell, 1962.

Smith, William W., *Midway: Turning Point of the Pacific.* New York: Crowell, 1966.

Stefan, John, *Hawaii under the Rising Sun: Japan's Plans for Conquest after Pearl Harbor.* Honolulu: University of Hawaii Press, 1984.

Stewart, Adrian, *The Battle of Leyte Gulf.* New York: Charles Scribner's Sons, 1979.

Szasz, Ferenc M., *The Day the Sun Rose Twice.* Albuquerque: University of New Mexico Press, 1984.

Thorne, Christopher, *Allies of a Kind: The U.S., Britain and the War against Japan, 1941–1945.* New York: Oxford University Press, 1978.

Toland, John, *The Rising Sun: The Decline and Fall of the Japanese Empire, 1936–1945.* New York: Bantam Books, 1970.

Tolley, Kemp, *Cruise of the Lanikai: Incitement to War.* Annapolis, MD: Naval Institute Press, 1973.

Tuchman, Barbara, *Stilwell and the American Experience in China, 1911–1945.* New York: Macmillan, 1970.

United States Navy, *Iwo Jima, February–March 1945 and SOWESPAC Activity.* San Francisco: Pacific Fleet, 1945.

———. *The Japanese Story of the Battle of Midway.* Washington, DC: Government Printing Office, 1947.

Utley, Jonathan G., *Going to War with Japan, 1937–1941.* Knoxville: University of Tennessee Press, 1985.

Van Osten, F.C., *The Battle of Java Sea.* Annapolis, MD: Naval Institute Press, 1976.

Walton, Frank E., *Once They Were Eagles: The Men of the Black Sheep Squadron.* Lexington: University of Kentucky Press, 1986.

Webber, Bert, *Retaliation: Japanese Attacks and Allied Countermeasures on the Pacific Coast in World War II*. Corvallis: Oregon State University Press, 1975.

Weglyn, Michi, *Years of Infamy*. New York: William Morrow, 1976.

Wheeler, Richard, *Iwo*. Philadelphia: Lippincott and Crowell, 1980.

Wilcox, Robert K., *Japan's Secret War: Japan's Race against Time to Build Its Own Atomic Bomb*. New York: William Morrow, 1985.

Williams, Peter and David Wallace, *Unit 731: Japan's Secret Biological Warfare in World War Two*. New York: Macmillan, 1989.

Willmott, H.P., *The Barrier and the Javelin: Japanese and Allied Pacific Strategies, February to June 1942*. Annapolis, MD: Naval Institute Press, 1983.

———. *Empires in the Balance: Japanese and Allied Pacific Strategies to April 1942*. Annapolis, MD: Naval Institute Press, 1982.

Wohlsetter, Roberta, *Pearl Harbor: Warning and Decision*. Stanford, CA: Stanford University Press, 1962.

Woodward, C. Vann, *The Battle for Leyte Gulf*. New York: Macmillan, 1947.

Newspapers

These are of value not only for the war years but for January of 1989, following the death of Hirohito. This is particularly true for the *Asahi Shimbun*.

Asahi Shimbun
Baltimore Sun
London Times
Mainichi Shimbun
New York Times
Nichi Nichi
Nippon Times
Tokyo Times and Advertiser

Index

William A. Renzi received his Ph.D. from the University of Maryland in 1968, where he studied with the late Gordon W. Prange. Professor Renzi was a member of the history faculty of the University of Wisconsin, Milwaukee; his primary research interests were the diplomatic and military history of the two world wars. Among his other works are *In the Shadow of the Sword: Italy's Neutrality and Entrance into the Great War, 1914–1915*. Professor Renzi died in December 1990.

Mark Roehrs received his Masters Degree in History from the University of Wisconsin, Milwaukee, and is currently completing Ph.D. studies at Louisiana State University. His studies focus primarily on the military and diplomatic relations of the United States in the middle decades of the twentieth century.